Student's Companion

Modern Pharmaceutical Analytical Techniques

Rxpert SERIES
Student's Companion

Modern Pharmaceutical Analytical Techniques

Pawan Tiwari
Professor
Shambhunath Institute of Pharmacy, Prayagraj, UP.

Ashish Dixit
Director & Professor
Spectrum Hi Pharmacy, Sultanpur, UP.

Vivekanand K. Chatap
Associate Professor
H. R. Patel Institute of Pharmaceutical Education and Research,
Shirpur, Dist. Dhule, MH.

Neha V. Bhilare
Associate Professor
Arvind Gavali College of Pharmacy, Satara, MH.

Neelesh Malviya
Professor & Principal
Smriti College of Pharmaceutical Education, Indore, MP.

PharmaMed Press
An imprint of BSP Books Pvt. Ltd.
4-4-309/316, Giriraj Lane,
Sultan Bazar, Hyderabad - 500 095.

Modern Pharmaceutical Analytical Techniques
***by* Dr. Pawan Tiwari, Dr. Vivekanand K. Chatap, Dr. Neha V. Bhilare, Dr. Ashish Dixit and Dr. Neelesh Malviya**

***Published by*:**

PharmaMed Press
An imprint of BSP Books Pvt. Ltd.
4-4-309/316, Giriraj Lane, Sultan Bazar, Hyderabad - 500 095.
Phone: 040-23445688; Fax: 91+40-23445611
E-mail: info@pharmamedpress.net
www.bspbooks.net/www.pharmamedpress.net

ISBN: 978-93-48734-81-5 (Hardback)

Preface

The book **Modern Pharmaceutical Analytical Techniques** of instrumental method of analysis is designed to introduce the recent developments and changes of various analytical techniques, their underlying principles, instrumentation, Advantages/Disadvantages and applications. The book comprehensively deals with the application of instrumental methods in qualitative and quantitative analysis of drugs. This book is very precisely designed to impart a fundamental knowledge on the principles and instrumentation of spectroscopic and chromatographic techniques. It is also emphasizing on theoretical as well as practical knowledge on modern analytical instruments which are used for drug testing. It includes precise diagrams and flow sheets for better understanding of various analytical techniques. It covers XVII units with detailed concepts of different analytical techniques like UV visible spectroscopy, chromatography, electrophoresis, Radioimmunoassay (RIA), ELISA, X-ray Crystallography, Infra-red Spectroscopy, Fluorimetry, Flame photometry, Atomic absorption spectroscopy, Nepheloturbidometry, NMR Spectroscopy and Mass Spectroscopy. Every units also comprises of multiple-choice questions, short type and long type questions along with their answers which is beneficial for revision purpose.

This book is highly useful for all undergraduate and postgraduate students of pharmacy, Biotechnology, chemical engineering, Biochemistry, Microbiology and chemistry. It is useful for a person engaged in teaching and academic research.

We must thank our family members for their constant encouragement and support without which this book would not have been possible

-Authors

Acknowledgement

If this work is able to provide even slightest help, to the students of pharmacy in understanding and using the subjects like Pharmaceutical Analysis, the authors shall find themselves highly satisfied. We would like to thank the management for the timely encouragement given to us, we are thankful to to **Dr. Dhirendra Kumar** President Utthan, **Dr. K. K. Tewari** Secretary, Utthan Shambhunath group of institution, Prayagraj (UP) for their valuable support, motivation and constant encouragement without which this book would have not taken its infant step. Authors are thankful to **Dr. Manoj Kumar Mishra** Director, Shambhunath institute of Pharmacy Prayagraj (UP) for forewords this book. We gratefully acknowledge to our colleagues and faculty members for their direct and indirect support provided by them. We also extend our acknowledgement to our family members for their constant support, motivation and freedom to write this book.

Authors are thankful to **Dr. Anju Goyal** Professor Head (Department of Pharmaceutcal Chemistry) Bhupal Nobles college of Pharmacy Udaipur (Rajasthan) for implanting the idea and constant encouragement to write this book. I would like to extend my deep sense of gratitude and a sincere and special thanks to **Dr. Neelesh Malviya** Professor and Principal Smriti college of Pharmaceutical Education Indore (M.P.) and **Dr. Gajanand Engla** Professor, School of Pharmacy, DAVV Indore (M.P.) from the bottom of my heart for their constructive moral support, encouraging guidelines, affectionate & friendly behaviour, finding the quick solution of the complications emerged during the work. Our sincere thanks to Publisher Director Mr. Anil Shah & Production Manager Mr. Naresh Davergave BSP Book Pvt., Ltd. (PharmaMed Press) and his staff for taking all the efforts to convert a hand-written script into a beautiful book like this. Our sincere thanks to all our well-wisher's family members and friends for their support and inspiration.

Authors

Contents

Chapter 4A

Atomic Absorption Spectroscopy

Chapter 5

Nuclear Magnetic Resonance

Chapter 6

Mass Spectroscopy

Chapter 7

Chromatography

Chapter 13

High Performance Liquid Chromatography

Chapter 14

Affinity Chromatography

Chapter 15

Electrophoresis

Chapter 16

Radio Immuno Assay (RIA)

Chapter 19

Potentiometry

Chapter 20

Thermal Techniques

Chapter 21

High Performance Thin Layer Chromatography (HPTLC)

CHAPTER 1 UV VISIBLE SPECTROSCOPY

1.1 INTRODUCTION

The term spectroscopy is derived from the word's spectrum, which implies a curve of distinct colours caused by wavelength differences, and skopin, which means examination or evaluation. Spectroscopy is thus the discipline of science concerned with the analysis or examination of spectrum.

The term "absorption spectroscopy" refers to spectroscopic methods that assess how much radiation interacts with a material and is absorbed as a function of frequency or wavelength. The sample takes in photons, or energy, from the emitting field. The absorption spectrum is the variation in absorption intensity as a function of frequency. Throughout the electromagnetic spectrum, absorption spectroscopy is used. When the molecule, atom, or ion in the sample changes from one energy state to another and the change in rotational, vibrational, and/or electronic energies is detected, electromagnetic radiation (EMR) is absorbed or emitted.

1.2 THEORY

The wavelength range of UV radiation is 200 nm- 400 nm. There are mainly two types of UV region.

1. 200 nm-400 nm that is called near ultraviolet region.
2. Below 200 nm that is called far ultraviolet region.
3. Visible light has a wavelength between 400 and 800 nm.

In the UV and visible spectrum, wavelength is measured in nanometres or angstroms. Wavenumber is used to express absorption (cm^{-1}).

The transfer of an electron or electrons within a molecule from one electronic energy level to another produces absorption spectra. The reversible kinds of transition give rise to ultraviolet emission spectra. The UV portion of the EMR spectrum is required for radiation to cause electronic excitation.

The energy of the radiation in this area is high enough to cause the outer valence electrons to undergo an electronic transition.

If a substance preferentially absorbs light in the visible spectrum, it seems to be coloured.

The primary purpose of absorbed energy is to elevate the molecule from its ground state (E_0) to a more highly excited state (E_1). The distinction is explained by:

$$\Delta E = E_1 - E_0 = h_v = h_c/\lambda$$

ΔE depends upon how tightly the electrons are bound in the bonds and accordingly, absorption will occur in UV or visible range, for example; if the electrons of a molecule are tightly bound as in compounds containing sigma bonds (e.g. saturated compounds) no light of region will be absorbed. The light of UV region will only be absorbed and hence compound appears colorless. If the electrons of molecule are loosely bound as in unsaturated compound, such absorption may occur in visible region and substance will appear as colored.

Energy absorbed in the ultraviolet region produces change in the electronic energy of the molecule that is resulting from transitions of valance electrons in the molecule. There are three types of electrons in organic molecules.

(a) σ (sigma) electrons: In saturated systems like alkane, a) σ (sigma) electrons are present. They don't exhibit UV absorption since their activation requires a significant amount of energy. In the vacuum UV area, their absorption band may be seen. Consequently, substances containing σ- bonds do not absorb in the range of near UV. For instance, saturated hydrocarbons can be utilised as solvents since they are transparent in the vicinity of the UV spectrum.

(b) **π (pie) electrons:** they are found in multiple bonds. They are generally mobile electrons. Since π–bonds are weak bonds, the energy produced by UV radiation can excite π–electrons to higher energy levels.

(c) ***n* (non-bonding) electrons:** valance electrons which do not participate in chemical bonding in molecule are called as non-bonding electrons or n-electrons. These are located principally in atomic orbital of N, O, S and halogens (X) as a lone pair of electrons. They can be excited by UV radiation.

Electronic Transition

The σ, π, and n electrons are present in molecule and can be excited from the ground state to excited state by the absorption of UV radiation. The various transitions are $n \rightarrow \pi^*$, $\pi \rightarrow \pi^*$, $n \rightarrow \sigma^*$, & $\sigma \rightarrow \sigma^*$.

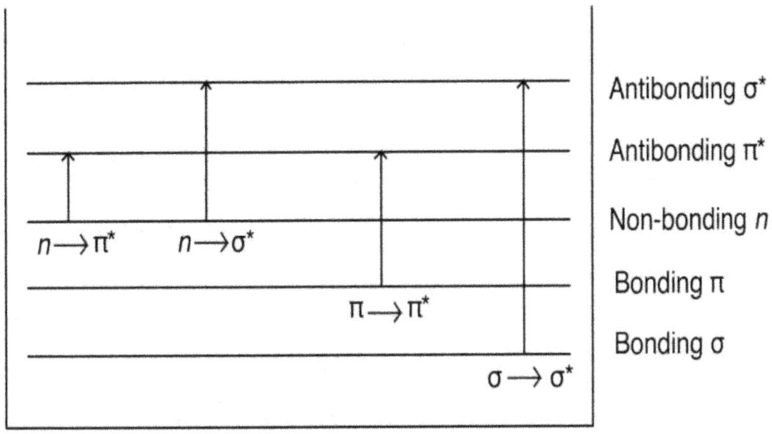

Figure 1.1: Shows the energy requirements for different electronic transitions.

The energy requirement order for excitation for different transitions is as follows. $n \rightarrow \pi^* < \pi \rightarrow \pi^* < n \rightarrow \sigma^* < \sigma \rightarrow \sigma^*$ $n \rightarrow \pi^*$ transition requires lowest energy while $\sigma \rightarrow \sigma^*$ requires highest amount of energy.

(1) **$n \rightarrow \pi^*$ transition:** $n \rightarrow \pi^*$ transition requires lowest energy due to longer wavelength. So, they are forbidden and corresponding bands are characterized by low molar absorptivity. $\varepsilon_{max} < 100$. It is also known as R- band. They are further characterized by hypochromic shift or blue shift observed with an increase in solvent polarity.

(2) **$\pi \rightarrow \pi^*$ transition:** It is due to the promotion of an electron from a bonding π orbital to an anti-bonding π * orbital. Energy requirement is between
$n \rightarrow \pi^*$ and $n \rightarrow \sigma^*$. But the extended conjugation and alkyl substituents shift the λ_{max} towards longer wavelength (Bathochromic shift). It is also called K band.

(3) **$n \rightarrow \sigma^*$ transition:** Saturated compounds with lone pair of electrons undergo $n \rightarrow \sigma^*$ transition in addition to $\sigma \rightarrow \sigma^*$ transition. Corresponding absorption bands appear at longer wavelengths in near UV region.

(4) **$\sigma \rightarrow \sigma^*$ transition:** These transitions can occur in such compounds in which all the electrons are involved in single bonds and there is no lone pair of electrons.

Energy required for $\sigma \rightarrow \sigma^*$ transition is very large so the absorption band occurs in the far UV region. So, this transition can't normally be observed.

1.3 PRINCIPLE (LAMBERT BEER LAW)

This principle states that when a light passes through absorbing medium at right angle to the plane of surface or the medium or the solution, the rate of decrease in the intensity of the transmitted light decreases exponentially as the thickness of the medium increases arithmetically.

Accordingly, Lambert's law can be stated as follows:

"When a beam of light is allowed to pass through a transparent medium, the rate of decrease of intensity with the thickness of medium is directly proportional to the intensity of light."

Mathematically, the Lambert's law may be expressed as follows.

$$-dI / dt \propto I$$

$$-dI / dt = KI \qquad \ldots(1)$$

Where,

I = intensity of incident light

t = thickness of the medium

K = proportionality constant

By integration of equation (1), and Putting $I = I_0$ when $t = 0$, $I_0/I_t = kt$ or $I_t = I_0\, e^{-kt}$

Where,

I_0 = intensity of incident light

I_t = intensity of transmitted light

k = constant which depends upon wavelength and absorbing medium used.

By changing the above equation from natural log.

We get, $I_t = I_0\, e^{-Kt}$ ...(2)

Where

$K = k/2.303$

So, $I_t = I_0\, e^{-0.4343kt}$

$I_t = I_0 10^{-Kt}$ ...(3)

Beer's law may be stated as follows:

"Intensity of incident light decreases exponentially as the concentration of absorbing medium increases arithmetically".

The above sentence is very similar to Lambert's law. So, $I_t = I_0\, e^{-k'c}$

$I_t = I_0\ 10^{-0.4343\ k'c}$

$I_t = I_0\ 10^{K'c}$ ...(4)

Where

k' and K' = proportionality constants

c = concentration by combining equation (3) and (4), we get,

$I_t = I_0\ 10^{-act}$

$I_0/I_t = 10^{act}$

Where

K and K' = a or εc = concentration

t or b = thickness of the medium $\log I_0 / I_t = \varepsilon bc$ ...(5)

Where ε = absorptivity, a constant dependent upon the λ of the incident radiation and the nature of absorbing material. The value of ε will depend upon the method of expression of concentration.

The ratio I_0/I_t is termed as transmittance T, and the ratio $\log I_0/I_t$ is termed as absorbance A. formerly, absorbance was termed as optical density D or extinction coefficient E. the ratio I_0/I_t is termed as opacity. Thus,

$$A = \log I_0/I_t \quad ...(6)$$

From equation (5) and (6),

$$A = \varepsilon bc \quad ...(7)$$

Thus, absorbance is the product of absorptivity, optical path length and the concentration of the solution.

The term $E^{1\%}_{1cm}$ or A refers to the to the absorbance of 1 cm layer of the solution whose concentration 1 % at a specified λ. According to equation (7), $A = \log I_0/I_t$. Transmittance T is a ratio of intensity of transmitted light to that of the incident light.

$$T = I_0/I_t$$

The more general equation can be written as follows:

$$\mathbf{A = \log I_0/I_t = \log 1/T = -\log T = abc = \varepsilon bc}$$

1.3.1 Deviation of Beer-Lambert Law

Beer-Lambert's law proves a direct correlation between the absorbance (A) of a molecule to the concentration (c) and the path length (b) of the sample as has been observed in the article for the Derivation of Beer Lambert Law. This relationship is a linear for the most part. However, under certain circumstances the Beer Lambert relationship breaks down and gives a non-linear relationship. These deviations from the Beer Lambert law can be classified into three categories:

1. Real Deviations– These are fundamental deviations due to the limitations of the law itself.
2. Chemical Deviations– These are deviations observed due to specific chemical species of the sample which is being analyzed.
3. Instrument Deviations– These are deviations which occur due to how the absorbance measurements are made.

1.3.2 Real Limitation and Deviation of Beer-Lambert Law

Beer law and Lambert law is capable of describing absorption behavior of solutions containing relatively low amounts of solutes dissolved in it (<10mM). When the concentration of the analyte in the solution is high (>10mM), the analyte begins to behave differently due to interactions with the solvent and other solute molecules and at times even due to hydrogen bonding interactions.

1.3.2.1 At high concentrations, solute molecules can cause different charge distribution on their neighboring species in the solution. Since UV-visible absorption is an electronic phenomenon, high concentrations would possibly result in a shift in the absorption wavelength of the analyte. At times, even electrolyte concentrations (such as those present in buffers) play an important role in altering the charge distributions and affecting UV-visible absorbance. Some large ions or molecules show deviations even at very low concentrations. For e.g. methylene blue absorptivity at 436 nm fails to observe Beer Lambert law even at concentrations as low as 10μM.

1.3.2.2 High analyte concentrations can also possibly alter the refractive index (η) of the solution which in turn could affect the absorbance obtained. If the addition of solute causes a significant change in the refractive index of the solution a correction to the Beer Lambert formula can be placed as:

$$A = \varepsilon bc\,(\eta^2 + 2)^2$$

1.3.3 Chemical Deviations and Limitations to Beer-Lambert Law

Chemical deviations happen as a result of analyte molecule connection, dissociation, and contact with the solvent, which results in a product with various absorption properties. For instance, the transition of phenol red from its acidic form (yellow) to its basic form involves a resonance transformation (red). The electron distribution of a molecule's bonds varies with the pH of the solvent in which it is dissolved as a result of this resonance. Since UV-visible spectroscopy is an electron-related phenomena, the pH of the solvent affects how the sample's absorption spectrum varies.

1.3.4 Instrumental Deviations and Limitations to Beer-Lambert Law

A. Due to Polychromatic Radiation (Also the reason why absorbance measurements are taken at the wavelength of maximum absorbance λ_{max})

When a monochromatic radiation source is present, Beer-Lambert law is carefully adhered to. To generate a monochromatic beam from a polychromatic source of radiation with a continuous distribution of wavelengths, however, a filter or grating unit (monochromators) is typically used.

When the molar absorptivities at both wavelengths are equal (i.e. ε' = ε""), Beer-Lambert rule is used to create a straight line to represent the connection between absorbance and concentration. However, the deviations from linearity also rise as the gap between ε' and ε" increases.

Beer-Lambert law is seldom violated if the spectrometer's band of wavelength is chosen in a way that the analyte's molar absorptivities are almost constant. However, the analyte's absorbance will deviate from Beer-Lambert law if a band is selected so that the analyte's molar absorptivity at these wavelengths changes significantly. When the wavelength being examined is at its maximum, it is found that variations in absorbance over wavelengths are at their lowest. This is why measurements of absorption are made at certain wavelengths.

B. Due to Presence of Stray Radiation

Radiation from the device that is beyond the chosen nominal wavelength range is referred to as stray radiation or dispersed radiation. The wavelength of stray radiation typically differs much from the chosen wavelength band. It is well known that the radiation that emerges from a monochromator frequently contains very small amounts of dispersed or stray radiation. Usually, the surfaces of lenses, mirrors, gratings, filters, and windows reflect and scatter this radiation. Similar to the deviation brought on by polychromatic radiation, the Beer-Lambert equation deviates if the analyte absorbs at the wavelength of the stray radiation.

C. Due to Mismatched Cells or Cuvettes

It stands to reason that the Beer-Lambert equation would deviate if the cells containing the analyte and the blank solutions had different path lengths or different optical properties. In such cases when a plot of absorbance versus concentration is made, the curve will have an intercept k and the equation will be defined as: $A = \varepsilon bc + k$

In today's instrument this problem is generally not observed, however if it is present, appropriate linear regression to quantify this deviation must be made.

1.4 INSTRUMENTATION

Instruments for measuring the absorption of U.V. or visible radiation are made up of the following components;

1. Sources (UV and visible)
2. Filter or monochromator
3. Sample containers or sample cells
4. Detector

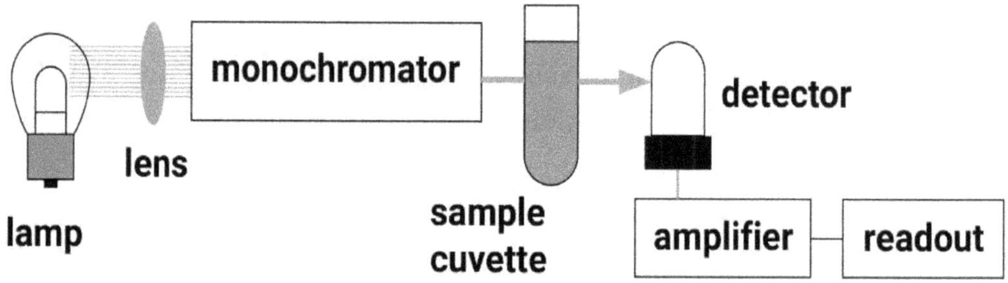

Figure 1.2: Line diagram of UV Spectrophotometer.

Radiation source

It is crucial that the radiation source's power does not fluctuate drastically along the spectrum of its wavelengths. A continuous UV spectrum is produced when deuterium or hydrogen is electrically excited at low pressure. The process that causes this requires the production of an excited molecular species, which splits into two atomic species and an ultraviolet photon. Lamps made of deuterium and hydrogen both produces radiation between 160 and 375 nm. These lamps must have quartz cuvettes and windows since glass absorbs light with wavelengths less than 350 nm.

The characteristics of Ideal source of radiation:

1. It should be stable and should not allow fluctuation.
2. It should emit light of continuous spectrum of high and uniform intensity over the entire wave length region in which it is used.
3. It should provide incident light of sufficient intensity for the transmitted energy to be detected at the end of optic path.
4. It should not show fatigue on continuous use.

Various UV radiation sources are as follows: -

a. Deuterium lamp
b. Hydrogen lamp
c. Tungsten lamp
d. Xenon discharge lamp
e. Mercury arc lamp

Various Visible radiation sources are as follows: -

a. Tungsten lamp

b. Mercury vapour lamp

- **Tungsten lamp**
    - ➢ Its construction is similar to a house hold lamp.
    - ➢ The bulb contains a filament of Tungsten fixed in evacuated conditions and then filled with inert gas.
    - ➢ The filament can be heated up to 3000k, beyond this temperature the Tungsten starts sublimating.
    - ➢ It is used when polychromatic light is required. To prevent this with inert gas some amount of halogen is introduced (Preferably Iodine).
    - ➢ Sublimated form of Tungsten reacts with iodine to form Tungsten-iodine complex. Which migrates back to the hot filament where it gets decompose and Tungsten get deposited. □ Demerit- it emits the major portion of its radiation energy in near IR region of spectrum.
- **Hydrogen lamp**
    - ➢ In hydrogen discharge lamp pair of electrodes is enclosed in a glass tube (provided with silica or quartz window for UV radiation to pass through) filled with hydrogen gas.
    - ➢ When current is passed through these electrodes maintained at high voltage, discharge of electrons occurs which excites the hydrogen molecule which in turn causes emission of UV radiation in near UV region.
    - ➢ They are stable and robust.
- **Xenon discharge lamp**
    - ➢ It possesses two tungsten electrode separated by some distance.
    - ➢ These are enclosed in a glass tube with quartz or fused silica and xenon gas is filled under pressure.

- ➢ An intense arc is formed between electrodes by applying high voltage. This is good source of continuous plus additional intense radiation. Its intensity is higher than The hydrogen discharge lamp.
- ➢ Demerit- the lamp since operates at high voltage becomes very hot during operation and hence needs thermal insulation.

- **Mercury Arc lamp**

- ➢ In mercury arc lamp, mercury is filled under high pressure and excitation of mercury atoms is done by electric discharge.
- ➢ Demerit-not suitable for continuous spectral studies because it does not give continuous radiation.

- **Filters or monochromators**

All monochromators contain the following component parts;

- ➢ An entrance slit
- ➢ A collimating lens
- ➢ Dispersing device (a prism or a grating)
- ➢ A focusing lens
- ➢ An exit slit

- **Collimating lens**

The radiation emitted by the source is collimated (made parallel) by lens, mirrors and slits.

- ➢ Material used for the lenses must be transparent to the radiation being used.
- ➢ Ordinary silicate glass transmits between 350 to 3000 nm and is suitable for visible and IR region.
- ➢ Quartz or fused silica is used as a material for lenses to work below 300 nm.

- **Mirrors**
  - ➢ These are used to reflect, focus or collimate light beams in spectrophotometer.
  - ➢ To minimize the light loss, mirrors are aluminized on their front surfaces.
- **Slits**
  - ➢ Slit is important device in resolving polychromatic radiation into monochromatic radiation.
  - ➢ To achieve this, entrance slit and exit slit is used.
  - ➢ The width of slit plays an important role in resolution of polychromatic radiation.
- **Monochromators**

  It is a device used to isolate the radiation of the desired wavelength from the continuous spectra. Following types of monochromatic devices are used.

  1. Filters
  2. Prisms
  3. Gratings
- **Filters**

  Selection of filters is usually done on a compromise between peak transmittance and band pass width; the former should be as high as possible and later as narrow as possible.
- **Sample containers or sample cells**

  A variety of sample cells available for UV region. The choice of sample cell is based on:-

  (a) The path length, shape, size

  (b) The transmission characteristics at the desired wavelength

  (c) The relative expense

The sample-holding cell needs to be transparent to the wavelength range being measured.

For UV spectroscopy, quartz or fused silica cuvettes are necessary. For usage between 350 and 2000 nm, cuvettes can be made from silicate glasses. In most cases, a cell is 1 cm thick. Cells might be cylindrical with flat ends or rectangular in form.

- **Detectors**

In order to detect radiation, three types of photosensitive devices are:-

(a) Photovoltaic cells or barrier-layer cell

(b) Phototubes or photo emissive tubes

(c) Photomultiplier tubes

a. A barrier layer or photronic cell is another name for a **photovoltaic cell**. One electrode is a metallic base plate made of iron or aluminium that makes up the device. A tiny coating of a semiconductor metal, such as selenium, is placed on its surface. Then, a very thin coating of silver or gold is applied to the surface of the selenium, serving as a second collection tube.

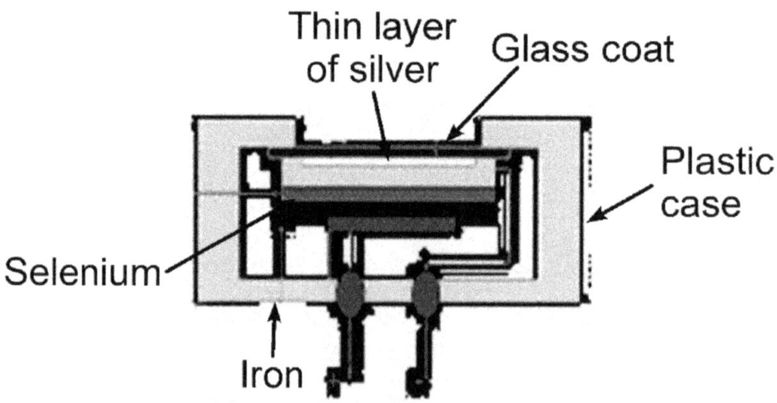

Figure 1.3: Photovoltaic Cell.

When radiation strikes the surface of selenium, electrons are produced at the selenium-silver interface, and the silver absorbs them. Between the silver surface and the cell's foundation, this accumulation at the silver surface generates an electric voltage differential.

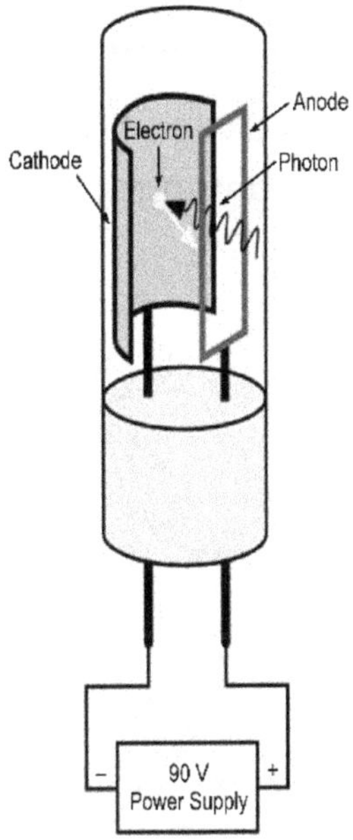

Figure 1.4: Phototubes.

b. Photo emissive cells are another name for **phototubes**. A glass bulb that has been emptied makes up a phototube. It contains a light-sensitive cathode. Silver oxide and potassium oxide are two light-sensitive materials that are applied to the inner surface of the cathode. Photoelectrons are released when radiation strikes a cathode. By using an anode, they are gathered. These are then sent back through an external circuit. This procedure also amplifies the current and records it.

c. One popular detector in UV spectroscopy is the photomultiplier tube. It is made up of an anode, many dynos, which emit multiple electrons for each photon of radiation that strikes them, a photo emissive cathode, which emits electrons when impacted by photons of radiation.

When a photon of radiation enters the tube and hits the cathode, many electrons are released. The first dynode is where these electrons are accelerated (which is 90V more positive than the cathode). For every electron that strikes the initial dynode, numerous more electrons are released. These electrons are subsequently accelerated in the direction of the second dynode, creating more electrons that are accelerated in the direction of the third dynode and so on. The anode is where the electrons are eventually gathered. By this time, each original photon has produced 106-107 electrons. The resulting current is amplified and measured.

Photomultipliers are very sensitive to UV and visible radiation. They have fast response times. Intense light damages photomultipliers; they are limited to measuring low power radiation.

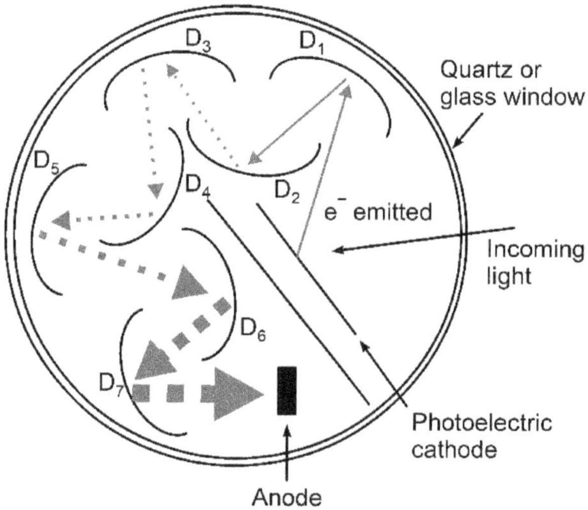

Figure 1.5: The photomultiplier tube.

1.5 TYPES OF UV SPECTROPHOTOMETER

A. UV Spectrophotometer Single Beam System

The source emits UV light in a single beam system. The radiation beam is gathered and focused on the inlet slit using a convex lens. The inlet slit lets source light through while blocking stray radiation. The monochromator is where the light is separated into its constituent wavelengths as it reaches it. The exit light is placed such that it may let through the necessary wavelength of light. All other wavelengths of radiation are suppressed. The detector gauges the radiation's strength as it receives the chosen radiation through the sample cell. By comparing the intensity of radiation before and after it passes through the sample, it is possible to measure how much radiation is absorbed by the sample at the particular wavelength used. The output of the detector is usually recorded on graph paper.

One problem with the single beam system is that it measures the total amount of light reaching the detector, rather than the percentage absorbed.

Another issue is that the detector's reaction considerably changes depending on the wavelength of radiation it is exposed to. By adopting a twofold beam system, the instrument variation issue may be significantly solved.

B. UV Spectrophotometer Double Beam UV System

The basic layout of a double beam ultraviolet spectrophotometer is shown in figure 1.6.

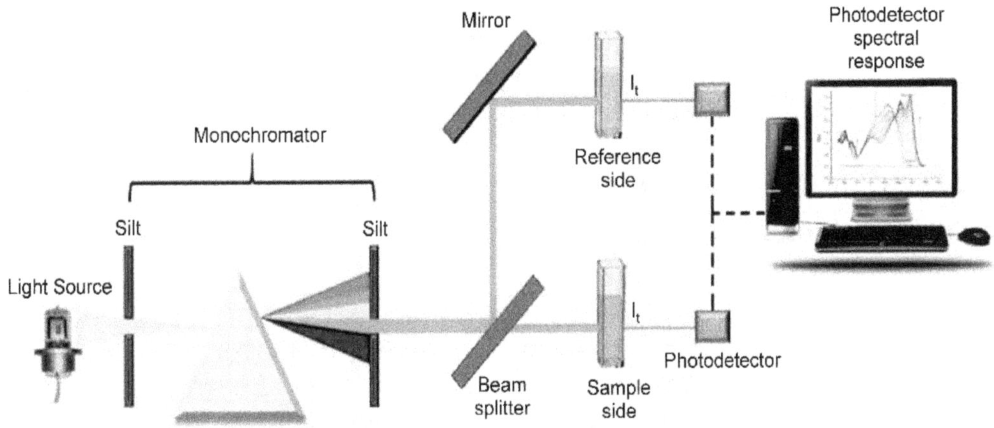

Figure 1.6: Double Beam UV Spectrophotometer.

A. The radiation from the source is allowed to pass via mirror system to the monochromator unit. The function of the monochromator is to allow a narrow range of wavelength to pass through an exit slit.

B. The radiation coming out of the monochromator through the exit slit is received by the rotating sector which divides the beam into two beams, one passing through the reference and the other through the sample cell.

C. After passing through the sample and references cells, the light beams are focused onto the detector.

D. The output of the detector is connected to phase sensitive amplifier which responds to any change in transmission through sample and reference.

E. The phase sensitive amplifier transmits the signals to the recorder which is followed by the movement of the pen on chart. The chart drive is coupled to the prism and thus the absorbance or transmittance of the sample is recorded as a function of wavelength.

1.6 ADVANTAGE OF DOUBLE BEAM SPECTROPHOTOMETER

The double beam instruments provide the following benefits while being more complicated and expensive:

- It is necessary to continually replace the blank with the sample or to zero adjust at each wave length as in the single beam units.
- The ratio of the powers of the sample and reference beams is constantly obtained and used. Any error due to variation in the intensity of the source and fluctuation in the detector is minimized.
- Because of the previous two factors, the double beam spectrophotometer lends itself to Rapid scanning over a wide wavelength region and to the use of a recorder or digital read out.

1.7 EFFECTS IN UV TRANSITIONS

Different transitions between the bonding and anti-bonding electronic states when light energy is absorbed in UV-Visible Spectroscopy.

When a sample is exposed to light energy that matches the energy difference between possible electronic transitions within the molecule, a fraction of the light energy would be absorbed by the molecule and the electrons would be promoted to the higher energy state orbital. A spectrometer records the degree of absorption by a sample at different wavelengths and the resulting plot of absorbance (A) versus wavelength (λ) is known as a spectrum. The wavelength at which the sample absorbs the maximum amount of light is known as λ_{max}. For example, shown below is the spectrum of isoprene. Isoprene is colorless as it does not absorb light in the visible spectrum, and has a λ_{max} of 222nm.

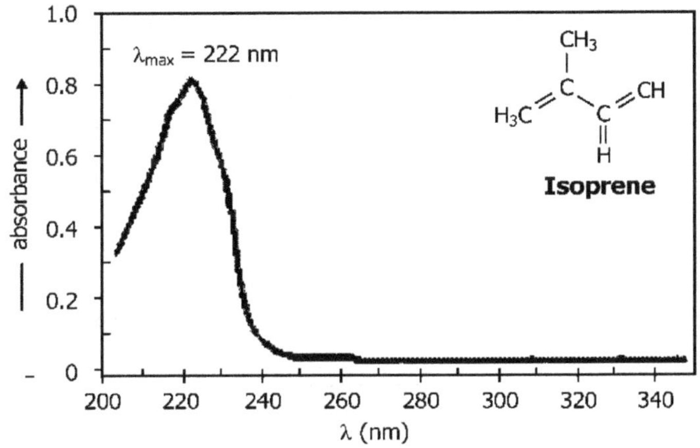

Figure 1.7: UV-visible spectrum of isoprene showing maximum absorption at 222 nm.

1.8 CHROMOPHORE

Due to the electron arrangement in the functional group, certain chemical groups or entities are prone to absorb light. These groups are referred to as chromophores. The table below, for instance, lists frequently occurring chromophores along with their estimated absorbances.

Chromophore	Example	Excitation	λ_{max} (nm)	Solvent
C = C	Ethene	$\pi \rightarrow \pi^*$	171	Hexanes
C = O	Ethanal	$\pi \rightarrow \pi^*$ $n \rightarrow \pi^*$	180 290	Hexane
N = O	Nitro methane	$\pi \rightarrow \pi^*$ $n \rightarrow \pi^*$	200 275	Hexane

1.8.1 Effect of Conjugation

Conjugation of π-electrons affects the energy levels of the π-electrons. Four molecular orbitals are created when two double bonds are conjugated by their electrons (i.e. two bonding and two anti-bonding). See the illustration below the lowest unoccupied molecular orbital (LUMO) is at a lower energy level as a result, and the highest occupied molecular orbital (HOMO) is at a higher energy state. Therefore, less energy would be needed to excite the electrons from the HOMO to the LUMO in order to excite this system. This decrease in energy levels causes the wavelength at which conjugated molecules are absorbed to grow.

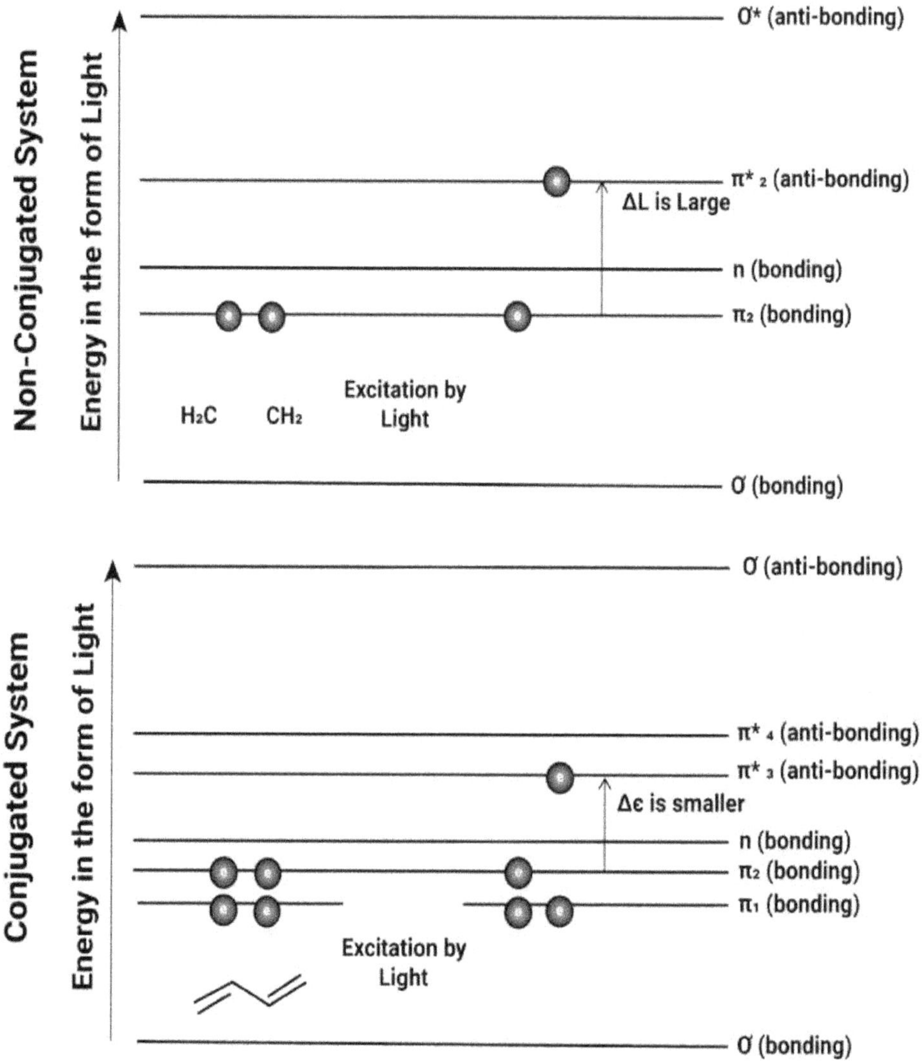

Figure 1.8: Diagram shows how a non-conjugated system would require more energy for absorption as compared to conjugated system.

The vibrational energy levels produced by vibrational changes within the system are located between the various electronic energy levels. It should be kept in mind that UV-visible light can also stimulate some chemical vibrational frequencies. This phenomenon causes the UV-Visible spectra to produce a smooth curve-shaped peak for absorption rather than a single sharp peak, as will be seen in various cases.

1.9 PHARMACEUTICAL APPLICATIONS

1) Detection of Impurities

UV absorption spectroscopy is one of the best methods for determination of impurities in organic molecules. Additional peaks can be observed due to impurities in the sample and it can be compared with that of standard raw material. By also measuring the absorbance at specific wavelength, the impurities can be detected. Benzene appears as a common impurity in cyclohexane. Its presence can be easily detected by its absorption at 255 nm.

2) Structure elucidation of organic compounds

UV spectroscopy is useful in the structure elucidation of organic molecules, the presence or absence of unsaturation, the presence of hetero atoms. From the location of peaks and combination of peaks, it can be concluded that whether the compound is saturated or unsaturated, hetero atoms are present or not etc.

3) Quantitative analysis

UV absorption spectroscopy can be used for the quantitative determination of compounds that absorb UV radiation. This determination is based on Beer's law which is as follows.

$$A = \log I_0/I_t = \log 1/T = -\log T = abc = \varepsilon bc$$

Where ε is extinction co-efficient, c is concentration, and b is the length of the cell that is used in UV spectrophotometer. Other methods for quantitative analysis are as follows.

a. calibration curve method

b. simultaneous multicomponent method

c. difference spectrophotometric method

d. derivative spectrophotometric method

4) Qualitative Analysis

UV absorption spectroscopy can characterize those types of compounds which absorbs UV radiation. Identification is done by comparing the absorption spectrum with the spectra of known compounds.

UV absorption spectroscopy is generally used for characterizing aromatic compounds and aromatic olefins.

5) Dissociation Constants of Acids and Bases

$$PH = PKa + \log [A^-]/[HA]$$

From the above equation, the PKa value can be calculated if the ratio of $[A^-]/[HA]$ is known at a particular PH. and the ratio of $[A^-]/[HA]$ can be determined spectrophotometrically from the graph plotted between absorbance and wavelength at different PH values.

6) Chemical kinetics

Kinetics of reaction can also be studied using UV spectroscopy. The UV radiation is passed through the reaction cell and the absorbance changes can be observed.

7) Quantitative analysis of pharmaceutical substances

Many drugs are either in the form of raw material or in the form of formulation. They can be assayed by making a suitable solution of the drug in a solvent and measuring the absorbance at specific wavelength. *Diazepam tablet can be analyzed by 0.5% H_2SO_4 in methanol at the wavelength 284 nm.

8) Molecular weight determination

Molecular weights of compounds can be measured spectrophoto-metrically by preparing the suitable derivatives of these compounds.

For example, if we want to determine the molecular weight of amine then it is converted in to amine picrate. Then known concentration of amine picrate is dissolved in a litre of solution and its optical density is measured at λ_{max} 380 nm. After this the concentration of the solution in gm moles per litre can be calculated by using the following formula.

$$C = \frac{\log l_0/l_1}{\varepsilon_{max} \times 1}$$

"**c**" can be calculated using above equation, the weight "**w**" of amine picrate is known. From "**c**" and "**w**", molecular weight of amine picrate can be calculated. And the molecular weight of picrate can be calculated using the molecular weight of amine picrate.

9) As HPLC detector

A UV/V is spectrophotometer may be used as a detector for HPLC. The presence of an analyte gives a response which can be assumed to be proportional to the concentration. For more accurate results, the instrument's response to the analyte in the unknown should be compared with the response to a standard; as in the case of calibration curve.

1.10 WOODWARD-FIESER RULES FOR CALCULATING ABSORPTION MAXIMA

Form the study of the ultraviolet absorption spectra of a large number of compounds, Woodward gave certain rules for correcting λ_{max} with molecular structure. Since then these rules have been modified by Scott and Fisher because of more experimental data. The modified rules known as Woodward-Fisher rules can be used to calculate the position of λ_{max} for a given structure by relating the position of λ_{max} with the position and degree of substitution of chromophore.

A. Woodward: Fieser rules for calculating λmax in conjugated dienes, trienes and polyenes

1. Homoannular diene: It is a cyclic diene having conjugated double bond in the same ring. Example are-

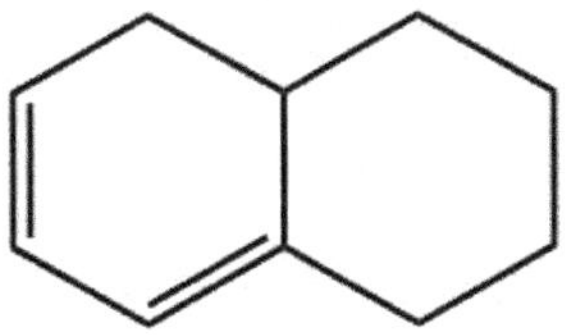

2. **Heteroannular diene:** It is a cyclic diene in which double bonds in conjugation are present in different rings. Example are-

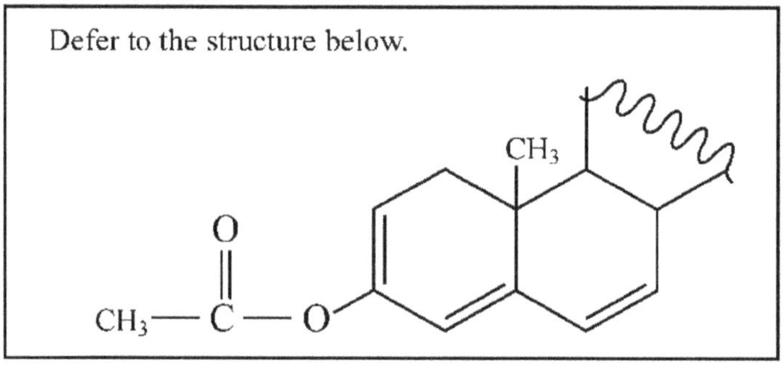

I. **Endocyclic double bond.** It is a double bond present in a ring as shown in example

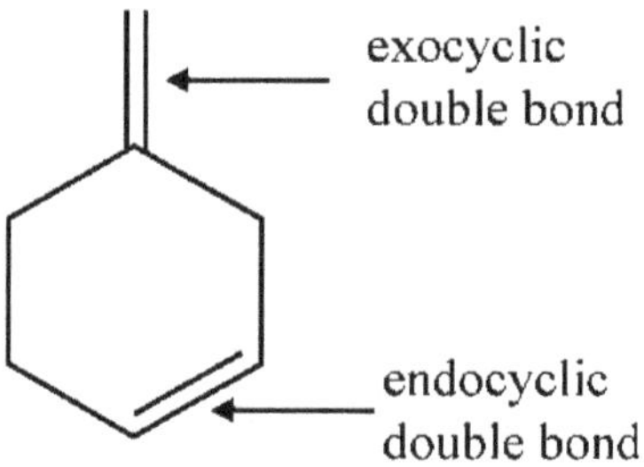

II. **Exocyclic double bond.** It is a double bond in which one of the doubly bonded atoms is a part of a ring system as shown in example

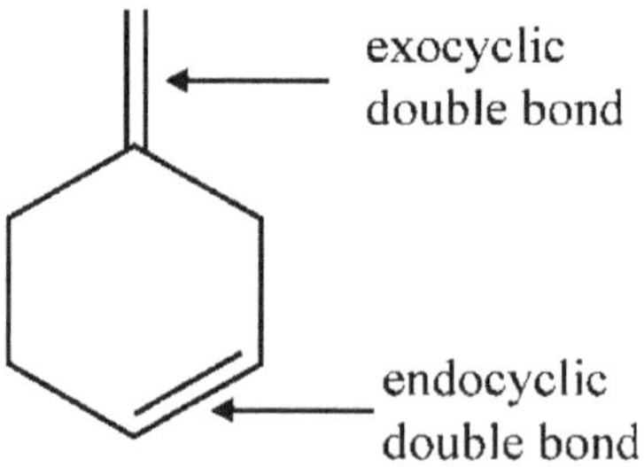

Woodward-Fieser rules conjugated dienes, trienes and polyenes

According to these rules, each type of diene or triene system is having a certain fixed value at which absorption takes place. This makes the basic value or parent value. The values of certain alkyl substituents or ring residue, double bond extending conjugation and polar groups such as chloride, bromide and –OR are added to the basic value to obtain λMAX for a particular compound.

Table 1.1: Parent values and increments for different substituents/groups.

1	**Parent Values**	Acyclic conjugated diene and heteroannular conjugated diene	215 nm
		Homuncular Conjugated diene	253 nm
		Acyclic triene	245 nm
2	**Increments**	Each alkyl substituent or ring residue	5 nm
		Exocyclic double bond	5 nm
		Double bond extending conjugation	30 nm
3	**Auxochromes**	-OR	6 nm
		-SR	30 nm
		-Cl,-Br	5 nm
		NR2	60 nm
		$-OCOCH_3$	0 nm

B. Woodward-fieser rules for α, β-unsaturated carbonyl compounds

Woodward fieser rules for calculating λ_{max} for α, β-unsaturated carbonyl compounds modified by Scott which is shown in tabulated form.

Table 1.2: Parent values and increments for different substituents/groups.

1.	Parent Values	α, β-unsaturated acyclic or six membered ring lactones	215 nm		
		α, β-unsaturated aldehyde	207 nm		
2.	Increments	Each alkyl substituent or ring residue	At α position 10 nm	At β position 12 nm	At ϒ and higher position 18 nm

Table 1.2 contd....

		Exocyclic double bond	5 nm		
		Double bond extending conjugation	30 nm		
		Homoannular conjugated diene	39 nm		
3.	Auxochromes		At α position	At β position	At Υ position
		-OH	35	30	50
		-OR	35	30	17
		-SR	-	85	-
		-Cl	15	12	-
		-Br	25	30	-
		NR_2	-	95	-
		$-OCOCH_3$	6	6	6

In these compounds, the actual spectra obtained are affected considerably by the nature of the solvent employed. Hence a solvent correction is applied to the calculated value to get the value for that particular solvent.

CHAPTER 2

INFRA-RED SPECTROSCOPY

2.1 INTRODUCTION

The infrared absorption spectroscopy examines the unique absorption spectra produced by molecules that absorb infrared energy. From the red end of the visible spectrum to the microwave portion of the electromagnetic spectrum (0.8 to 200μ), there lies the infra-red section of the electromagnetic spectrum. For analytical purposes, the range between 4000 and 400 cm^{-1} is the most helpful. From the perspectives of both application and instrumentation, this region is frequently referred to as the fundamental region. The limitations of the near infrared, medium infrared, and far infrared regions of the infrared spectrum are shown here.

Region	Wavelength (k) Range μ	Wave number (υ) range cm^{-1}
Near IR	0.78-2.5	12800-4000
Middle IR	2.5-50	4000-200
Far IR	16-200	625-10
Infra-red	2.5-16	4000-625

We know that wave number is related to wavelength by the expression:

$$\lambda = \frac{C}{\upsilon} = \frac{\text{Velocity of Light}}{\text{Frequency}} \text{cm/sec}$$

Further, energy of quantum E corresponding to radiation of frequency μ is given by,

$$E = h\,\upsilon$$

$$\text{so } \upsilon = \frac{c}{\lambda}$$

$$E = \frac{hC}{\lambda}$$

Final Equation

In the above equation both h and c are constant. Thus, the energy of radiation is directly proportional to the wave number and inversely proportional to the wavelength.

As the IR radiation is of longer wavelength, it is associated with much lower energy than visible and UV radiation.

When exposed to IR radiation, a compound revealed distinct bands of selective absorption. This is due to the fact that molecules of matter vibrate at various rates after absorbing IR radiation, creating densely packed absorption bands that are known as the IR absorption spectrum. The distinctive functional groups and bonds that are present in a material cause the different bands visible in the IR spectrum. So, a chemical substance's IR spectrum is utilised to identify it and is thought of as a fingerprint. The number, where unit is cm^{-1}, can be used to concisely represent band positions in an IR spectrum. Wave number on the abscissa and transmittance (T) or absorbance (A) on the ordinate are two ways to indicate band intensities.

2.2 THE ORIGIN OF IR SPECTRA

Electron, vibrational, and rotational levels of a molecule are altered by UV-visible electromagnetic radiation. Infrared radiation impacts the vibrational and rotational energy levels connected to a molecule but cannot cause electrical changes since it is a lesser energy. The 2.5– 15 υ range from a broad spectrum of IR radiation has enough energy to alter the rotational and vibrational energies of a molecule. The only rotational transition that may occur is in the upper area of the IR (over 25~0). It should be emphasised that the resultant spectrum is characterised as a vibrational-rotational spectrum since changes in vibrational levels also imply changes in rotational levels.

2.2.1 Fingerprint Region

The vibrational modes in an IR spectrum are entirely and heavily dependent on the remainder of the molecule. The frequency of C–C stretching, for example, is heavily influenced by what else is linked to the carbon atoms. It's worth noting that this specific area of the spectrum is highly filled with bands. As we know, no two 'fingerprints' can be identical in humans; similarly, no two chemicals can have the same 'fingerprint area'. As a result, each molecule generates a distinct spectrum that provides a distinguishing attribute of the same.

2.3 THEORY

The basic principle of infrared spectroscopy is based on molecular vibrations, which are further constituted of a molecule's stretching and bending vibrations. As a result, a good understanding of the many modes of vibrations often observed in diverse molecules with a range of functional moieties, the rules regulating them, and the mathematical derivations connected to them would be required.

A. Molecular Vibration

A molecule should not be seen as a hard assembly of atoms. Rather, it may be thought of as a flexible system made up of balls of variable masses that represent the atoms of a molecule and springs of varying strengths that represent the chemical bonds of a molecule.

The vibrations for molecules are of *two* types, namely:

(a) Stretching, and

(b) Bending (or deformation).

(a) Stretching: Stretching is a result of vibration, in which the distance between the two atoms changes but the atoms stay along the same bond axis.

(b) Bending (or Deformation): Vibration results in bending, which shifts the atom's location with relation to the initial bond axis. As a result, a bond's different stretching and bending vibrations often occur at specific quantized frequencies. Thus, energy is absorbed when infrared light of the same frequency is incident on the molecule, and the overall result may be seen by an increase in the vibration's amplitude. The absorbed energy is sometimes released as heat as the molecule transitions from the excited state to the ground state.

A schematic representation of the many stretching and bending vibrations that can exist within a molecule is provided in Figure. There are *two* types of Bending (or deformation) Modes, namely:

(i) Below the plane of paper and perpendicular to it designated by (+) sign, and (ii) Above the plane of paper and perpendicular to it represented by (–) sign.

❖ Stretching Vibrations

In this particular instance, the atoms move invariably along the bond that joins them *e.g.*,

C—H; C = O; O—H; N—H.

The stretching vibrations may be further sub-divided into *two* categories, namely:

Symmetrical Stretching: In this case, the two hydrogen atoms either move towards or away from the central carbon atom in unison, thereby either altering the interatomic distance or causing no change in valence angle (Figure 1).

Asymmetrical Stretching: In this instance, one hydrogen atom approaches the carbon atom while the other moves away from the carbon atom (Figure 1).

❖ Bending (or Deformation) Vibrations

In the event when a three-atom system forms part of a larger molecule, it is quite possible to have bending (or deformation) vibrations which essentially involve oscillation of the atoms, or group as a whole and is perpendicular to its chemical bond (Figure 2). Such bending vibrations can take place either in-plane or out-of-plane.

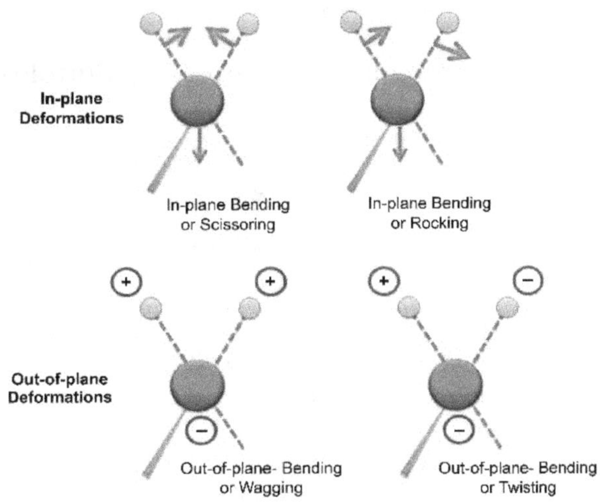

Bending Vibrations

- **In-Plane Bending Vibrations:** These are *two* types:
  1. **Scissoring or Symmetrical Bending:** In this case, the two atoms connected to a central atom either move toward or away from each other with certain deformation of the valence angle.
  2. **Rocking:** In this case, the structural unit swings back and forth in the plane of the molecule.

- **Out-of Plane Bending Vibrations**

  These are also of *two* kinds, namely:
  1. **Wagging:** In this case the structural unit swings back and forth out of the plane of the molecule.
  2. **Twisting:** In this case the structural unit rotates about the bond that joins it to the rest of the molecule.

- **Explanations of Bending and Stretching Vibrations**

The bending (or deformation) vibrations generally require less energy and take place at longer-wavelength than the corresponding stretching vibrations.

In contrast, the stretching vibrations are observed to occur with respect to their corresponding bond strengths.

Examples: The typical examples of triple-bond, double-bond and single-bond are given below:

S. No.	Type of Bond	Example	Force Constant (dyne/cm)	Absorption At	
				Wave length (μ)	Frequency (cm^{-1})
1	Triple Bond	C≡C, C≡N	15×10^5	4.4-5.0	2300-2000
2	Double Bond	C=O, C=C, C=NH	10×10^5	5.3-6.7	1900-1500
3	Single Bond	C-C, C-OH, C-N	5×10^5	7.7-12.5	1300-800

Whenever a very small proton like: C—H; O—H; or N—H is involved in a single bond, the stretching vibrations normally take place at much higher frequency *i.e.*, 3700-2630 cm– 1 (or 2.7-3.8 μ). It is, however, interesting to note that O—H bond absorbs at 2.8 μ (or 3570 cm–1), whereas O—D bond absorbs at 3.8 μ (or 2630 cm–1). In this specific case, the strengths of the two bonds are more or less the same, but the mass of one atom is almost doubled.

2.4 CALCULATION OF VIBRATIONAL FREQUENCIES

The vibrational frequency may be calculated with fairly remarkable accuracy by the help of Hooke's Law and is expressed as

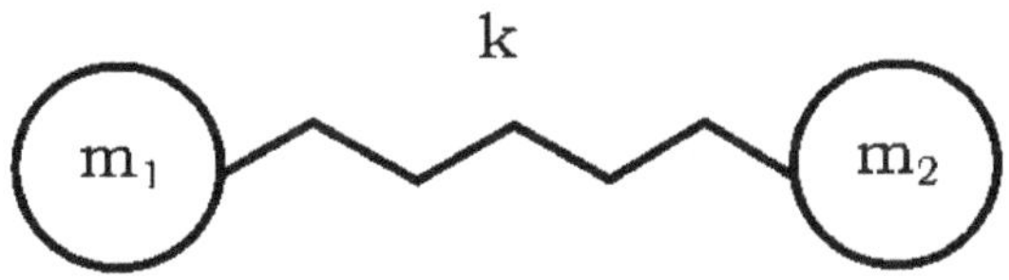

$$\bar{\upsilon} = \frac{1}{2x}\sqrt{\frac{k}{\mu}} \qquad \mu = \frac{m_1.m_2}{m_1 + m_2}$$

$\bar{\upsilon}$ = frequency μ = reduced mass

where, υ=Frequency, k = Force constant of the bond, and $m1$ and $m2$ = Masses of two atoms.

The quantity $m_1m_2/\ (m_1 + m_2)$ is often expressed as μ, the reduced mass of the system. The force constant for a bond varies slightly from one compound to another. However, it can be calculated.

Example- C-O bond in methanol, it has f = 5 × 10^5 dyne per centimeter and p=6.85. It shows wave number of 1110 cm^{-1}. In spectrum a strong band for methanol is observed around wave number 1034 cm. It is thus seen that if force constant is known, approximate frequency of band can be calculated.

For vibrational mode to occur on striking Infrared radiation, it is essential that there is a change in dipole moment during vibration. In diatomic molecules if there is no change in dipole, no vibration is seen in infrared region. Polyatomic molecules having no dipole moment of their own may be made to undergo vibrational rotational transition.

The vibrational energy of a chemical bond is calculated and given by following formula

Where

υ = number of vibrational levels as 0,1,2 h = Plank's Constant

υ = vibrational frequency of the bond the energy difference between two vibrational levels by-

$$\Delta E_{Vib} = h\upsilon$$

In this ΔE_{Vib} is the difference between lowest vibrational level and higher vibrational level.

2.4.1 Polyatomic Vibrational Spectra

As the atoms and bonds of polyatomic molecules are not securely coupled together, they oscillate from their resting position to higher vibrational levels, producing fundamental and overtone bands.

The degree of freedom in a molecule is correlated with the number of basic bands. The total number of coordinates required to locate every atom in a molecule in space equals the number of degrees of freedom. Each atom has three degrees of freedom, or three perpendicular coordinates (X, Y, and Z) that represent the atom's location. N atoms make up a polyatomic molecule, which has 3 N degrees of freedom. While three coordinates are needed to describe the rotating motion, three coordinates represent the transitional motion. While linear 3N-5 vibrational modes are referred to as normal or fundamental vibrational modes, nonlinear molecules with N atoms are considered to have 3N-6 vibrational degree of freedom. In addition to the basic modes, overtones, or non-fundamental vibrations, also exist.

2.4.2 Factors Influencing Vibrational Frequencies

There are a number of factors that influence the precise frequency of a molecular vibration, namely:

(A) Coupled vibrations

(B) Fermi resonance

(C) Electronic effects

(D) Hydrogen bonding

A. Coupled Vibrations

An isolated C-H bond has only one stretching vibrational frequency whereas methylene group shows two stretching vibrations, symmetrical and asymmetrical.

This is because of mechanical coupling or interaction between C-H stretching vibrations in the CH_2 group. Asymmetric vibrations occur at higher frequencies or wave numbers than symmetric stretching vibrations. These are known as coupled vibrations because these vibrations occur at different frequencies than that required for an isolated C-H stretching. A strong vibrational coupling is present in carboxylic acid anhydrides in which symmetrical and asymmetrical stretching vibrations appear in the region 1720–1825 cm^{-1}. The interaction is very effective probably because of the partial double bond character in the carbonyl oxygen bonds due to resonance which also keeps the system planar for effective coupling. • Asymmetrical stretching band in acyclic anhydride is more intense whereas symmetrical stretching band is more intense in cyclic anhydrides.

B. Requirements for Coupled Vibrations

For interaction to occur, the vibrations must be of same symmetry species. There must be a common atom between the groups for strong coupling between stretching vibrations. For coupling of bending vibrations, a common bond is necessary. Interaction is greatest when coupled groups absorb, individually, near the same frequency. Coupling is negligible when groups are separated by one or more carbon atoms and the vibrations are mutually perpendicular.

C. Fermi Resonance

It is a vibration of large amplitude produced by a relatively small vibration. Coupling of two fundamental vibration modes produces two new modes of vibration, with frequencies higher and lower than that observed in absence of interaction. Interaction can also take place between fundamental vibrations and overtones or combination tone vibrations and such interactions are known as Fermi Resonance. If the two different vibrational levels are belonging to the same species, have nearly the same energy. A mutual perturbation of energy may occur. Shifting of one towards lower and other towards higher frequency occur that is a substantial increase in the intensity of the respective bands occurs. In this, a molecule transfers its energy from fundamental vibrational level to overtone or combination tone level and back. Resonance pushes the two levels apart and mixes their character, consequently each level has partly fundamental and partly overtone or combination tone character.

For example- symmetrical stretching vibration of CO_2 in Raman spectrum shows band at 1337 cm^{-1}.

The two bending vibrations are equivalent and absorb at the same frequency of 667.3 cm^{-1}. The First overtone of this is $2 \times 667.3 = 1334.6$ cm^{-1}.

Fermi resonance occurs- There is mixing of 1337 $cm^{-1}$and 1334.6 cm^{-1} to give two bands at 1285.5 $cm^{-1}$and at 1388.3 cm^{-1} with intensity ratio 1: 0.9 respectively.

Asymmetric stretching Symmetric stretching

Hydrogen bonding

It occurs in any system containing a proton donor group (X-H) and a proton acceptor if the s-orbital of the proton can effectively overlap the P or π orbital of the acceptor group. The stronger the hydrogen bond, the longer the O-H bond, the lower the vibration frequency and broader and more intense will be the absorption band. The N-H stretching frequencies of amines are also affected by hydrogen bonding as that of the hydroxyl group but frequency shifts for amines are lesser than that for hydroxyl compounds. Because nitrogen is less electronegative than oxygen so the hydrogen bonding in amines is weaker than that in hydroxy compounds.

Intermolecular hydrogen bonds give rise to broad bands, while intramolecular hydrogen bonds give sharp and well-defined bands. The inter and intramolecular hydrogen bonding can be distinguished by dilution. Intramolecular hydrogen bonding remains unaffected on dilution and as a result the absorption band also remains unaffected where as in intermolecular, bonds are broken on dilution and as a result there is a decrease in the bonded O-H absorption.

The strength of hydrogen bonding is also affected by:

- Ring strain
- Molecular geometry
- Relative acidity and basicity of the proton donor and acceptor groups

Electronic Effect:

This changes in the absorption frequencies for a particular group take place when the substituents in the neighbourhood of that particular group are changed. It includes

- Inductive Effect
- Mesomeric Effect
- Field Effect

Inductive Effect:

The introduction of alkyl group causes +I effect which results in the lengthening or the weakening of the bond. Hence the force constant is lowered and wave number of absorptions decreases. Let us compare the wave numbers of v(C=O) absorptions for the following compounds: Formaldehyde (HCHO) 1750 cm^{-1}., Acetaldehyde (CH_3CHO) 1745 cm^{-1}., Acetone (CH_3COCH_3) 1715 cm^{-1}.

Introduction of an electronegative atom or group causes–I effect which results in the bond order to increase. Hence the force constant increases and the wave number of absorptions rises.

Mesomeric Effect:

It causes lengthening or the weakening of a bond leading in the lowering of absorption frequency. As nitrogen atom is less electronegative than oxygen atom, the electron pair on nitrogen atom in amide is more labile and participates more in conjugation. Due to this greater degree of conjugation, the C=O absorption frequency is much less in amides as compared to that in esters.

Field Effect:

In ortho substituted compounds, the lone pair of electrons on two atoms influences each other through space interactions and changes the vibrational frequencies of both the groups. This effect is called field effect. **Example-** Ortho halo acetophenone.

2.5 INSTRUMENTATION

The infrared spectrophotometers are based on either single monochromation or double monochromation:

(a) Single-Monochromator Infrared Spectrophotometer, and

(b) Double-Monochromator Infrared Spectrophotometer.

The optical diagrams, components used and their modes of operation shall be discussed briefly in this context under different heads.

2.5.1 Single Monochromator Infrared Spectrophotometers

The important features of an infrared spectrophotometer are as follows:

(i) Infrared sources,
(ii) Monochromators
(iii) Sample cells and Sampling of substances
(iv) Detectors

Infrared Sources:

In common with other types of absorption spectrophotometers, infrared instruments require a source of radiant energy which provides a means for isolating narrow frequency bands. The most common infrared sources are electrically heated rods of the following types:

A. Sintered mixtures of the oxides of Zirconium (Zr), Yttrium (Y), Erbium (Er) etc., also known as 'Nernst Glower'. It consists of a hollow rod which is about 2 mm in diameter and 30 mm in length. Nernst glower is non-conducting at room temperature and must be heated by external means. Glower is generally heated to a temperature between 1000 to 1800°C. It emits maximum radiation at about 7100 cm^{-1}.

B. Silicon Carbide 'Globar'- It is a rod of sintered silicon carbide which is about 50 mm in length and 4 mm in diameter. When it is heated to a temperature between 1300 to 1700°C, it strongly emits radiations in the IR region. It emits maximum radiation at about 5200 cm^{-1}.

(a) Various ceramic or clay materials:

It is quite evident that the infrared output from all these different sources invariably varies in intensity over a definite frequency range; therefore, a compensating variable slit is usually programmed to operate in unison with the scanning over the individual frequencies.

Monochromators:

Three types of substances are normally employed as monochromators, namely:

1. **Metal Halide Prisms:** Any prism used as a dispersive element must be constructed of material like various metal halide prisms, such as: Potassium bromide (12-25 μm), Lithium fluoride (0.2-6 μm) and Cesium bromide (15-38 μm) have been used earlier, but they have become more or less obsolescent now a day.

2. **NaCl Prism (2-15 µm):** Sodium chloride prism are of use for the whole of the region from 4000-650 cm^{-1}. First, it offers low resolution at 4000-2500 cm^{-1}, and secondly, because of its hygroscopic nature the optics has got to be protected at 20 °C above the ambient temperature.

Gratings: In general, gratings are commonly employed in the design of the instruments and offer better resolution at higher frequency than the prisms. They offer much better resolution at low frequency, *viz.*, typical rulings are 240 lines per nm for the 4000-1500 cm^{-1} region and 120 lines per nm for the 1500-650 cm^{-1} region.

Sample cells and sampling of Substances

As infrared spectroscopy has been applied for the characterization of solid, liquid and gas samples so sampling procedure of different phases should be like that the sample prepared must be transparent to IR radiation.

In IR Spectroscopy the sample cells are usually constructed using rock salt. They have a size of 0.1 to 1 mm much narrower than one used in Ultraviolet- Visible region.

Sampling of substances can be done using some techniques which are as follows:

- **Pressed Pellet Technique:** This is also known as disk method. This technique is most commonly used for qualitative work. In this a small amount of; finely ground solid sample (dried) is intimately mixed with about 100 times its weight of powdered potassium bromide using pestle and mortar. This mixture is pressed under a high pressure in an infrared tablet press to form a small pellet or tablet. The resulting pellet is transparent to infrared radiation.

  This technique has some advantages over Nujol technique. Firstly, it removes the problem of absorption bands which appear in infrared spectrum compounds with Nujol. The other advantage of pellet technique is that the properly preserved KBr pellets can be used again for the analysis of compounds. The disadvantage of this technique is that the high pressure can generate the polymorphic changes absorption spectrum of inorganic compounds.

- **Mull Technique:** This technique is also known as Nujol technique. In this, the solid technique sample is mixed with mineral oil liquid paraffin to form the paste. This paste is then sand witched between two salts plates and then used for spectral measurement.

  Although Nujol is transparent in most part of infrared region but it has some specific absorption maxima like 2915, 1376 cm^{-1}. The main disadvantage of this technique is that there are similar absorptions of both Nujol and compounds. This technique is mostly used for qualitative work in pharmaceutical industries.

- **Solid Film Technique:** If a solid is polymer resins & amorphous solids, the sample is dissolved in any reasonable volatile solvent & this solution is poured on a rock salt plate (NaCl or KBr) & solvent is evaporated by gentle heating. If solid is non-crystalline, a thin homogenous film is deposited on the plate which can be mounted and scanned directly.

Sometimes polymers can be "hot pressed" onto plates.

Merit and Demerit: This method is useful for rapid qualitative analysis but becomes useless for carrying out quantitative analysis.

- **Sampling of Liquid**

Liquid sample cells can be sandwiched using liquid sample cells of highly purified alkali halides, normally NaCl. Other salts such as KBr and CaF2 can also be used. Aqueous solvents cannot be used because they cannot dissolve alkali halides. Organic solvents like chloroform can be used. The sample thickness should be selected so that the transmittance lies between 15-20%. For most liquids, the sample cell thickness is 0.01- 0.05 mm. Some salt plates are highly soluble in water, so the sample and washing reagents must be anhydrous.

- **Sampling of Gases**

The sample cell is made up of NaCl, KBr etc. and it is similar to the liquid sample cell. A sample cell with a long path length (5–10 cm) is needed because the gases show relatively weak absorbance.

- **Detectors**

There are ions all three different types of detectors that are used in the infrared region:

A. Thermocouples (or Thermopiles): The principle of a thermocouple is that if two dissimilar metal wires are joined head to tail, then a difference in temperature between head and tail causes a current to flow in the wires. In the infrared spectrophotometer this current shall be directly proportional to the intensity of radiation falling on the thermocouple. Hence, the thermocouples are invariably employed in the infrared region, and to help in the complete absorption of 'available energy' the 'hot' junction or receiver is normally blackened.

B. Golay Detector: This is another type of detector in IR spectroscopy. In this specific instance the absorption of infrared radiation affords expansion of an inert gas in a cell- chamber. One wall of the cell-chamber is provided with a flexible mirror and the resulting distortion alters the intensity of illumination falling on a photocell from a reflected beam of light. Thus, the current from the photocell is directly proportional to the incident radiation.

C. Bolometers: These are based on the principle that makes use of the increase in resistance of a metal with increase in temperature. For instance, when the two platinum foils are appropriately incorporated into a Wheatstone bridge, and radiation is allowed to fall on the foil, a change in the resistance is observed ultimately. This causes an out-of- balance current that is directly proportional to the incidental radiation. Just like the thermocouples, they are used in the infrared region.

2.6 APPLICATIONS OF IR SPECTROSCOPY

In addition to research, infrared spectroscopy is frequently employed in industry. For measurement, quality control, and dynamic measurement, it is an easy and dependable procedure. Additionally, it is used in forensic investigations for both civil and criminal cases.

The following are some of the main uses for IR spectroscopy:

1. Identification of Functional Group and Structure Elucidation

Group frequency region and fingerprint region are subdivided into the whole IR area. Group frequency ranges from 4000 to 1500 cm-1, whereas the finger print region ranges from 1500 to 400 cm^{-1}.

The peaks belonging to various functional groups may be seen in the group frequency area. It is possible to identify the functional group based on the related peaks.

Each connection connecting the atoms in the molecule requires a separate IR area, which is why distinctive peaks may be seen. The finger print region of the molecule is the name given to this area of the IR spectrum. It may be identified by distinctive peaks.

Identification of Substances

To determine if a specific sample of an organic compound is identical to another or not, IR spectroscopy is utilised. This is due to the fact that there are several absorption bands visible in the IR spectra of organic molecules, and it is highly unlikely that any two substances would yield spectra that are similar to one another. Therefore, if the IR spectra of two compounds are the same, then they are samples of the same material.

IR spectra of two enantiomeric compound are identical. So, IR spectroscopy fails to distinguish between enantiomers.

For example, an IR spectrum of benzaldehyde is observed as follows.

C-H stretching of aromatic ring -	3080 cm^{-1}
C-H stretching of aldehyde -	2860 cm^{-1} and 2775 cm^{-1}
C=O stretching of an aromatic aldehyde-	1700 cm^{-1}
C=C stretching of an aromatic ring -	1595 cm^{-1}
C-H bending -	745 cm^{-1} and 685 cm^{-1}

No other compound then benzaldehyde produces same IR spectra as shown above.

2. Studying the Progress of the Reaction

Examining a little sample of the reaction mixture that is periodically removed from the mixture allows one to monitor the progress of a chemical reaction. It is noticed how quickly a reactant group's distinctive absorption band vanishes and/or how quickly a product group's characteristic absorption band emerges as a result of product formation.

3. Detection of Impurities

IR spectrum of the test sample to be determined is compared with the standard compound. If any additional peaks are observed in the IR spectrum, then it is due to impurities present in the compound.

4. Quantitative Analysis

Both the substance's pure form and its mixture with two or more other compounds can be used to calculate its amount. This involves selecting the distinctive peak that corresponds to the drug ingredient and comparing the log I0/It of the peaks in the standard and test samples. This method of estimating the substance's amount is known as the base line method.

CHAPTER 3 SPECTRO FLUORIMETRY

3.1 INTRODUCTION

When molecules relax from electronic excited states, photon emission processes called fluorescence and phosphorescence take place. Transitions between the electronic and vibrational states of polyatomic fluorescent molecules take place during these photonic processes (fluorophores). The main component of fluorescence spectroscopy is fluorophores. Molecules' fluorophores are the elements that give them this property. Tyrosine, Tryptophan, Fluorescein, and other molecules with aromatic rings are the most common fluorophores. A material emitting light without being heated is said to be luminescent, making it a kind of cold body radiation. Chemical interactions, electrical energy, subatomic vibrations, or stress on a crystal are all potential causes. Two conditions must be met for luminescence:

The luminescent material must have a semiconductor structure with a nonzero band gap. [Metals do not provide luminescence if they have no band gap].

The energy must be imparted to this material before luminescence can take place.

3.2 TYPES OF LUMINESCENCE

A. By Mechanism:

i. Fluorescence

ii. Phosphorescence

B. By Excitation Source:

i. Chemiluminescence

ii. Cathodoluminescence

iii. Electroluminescence

iv. Photoluminescence

A photon source is used to excite sample molecules in the sensitive optical emission method known as fluorescence spectroscopy. By measuring the intensity of such emission, it is possible to identify the molecules that relax through radiant emission.

3.3 PRINCIPLE OF FLUORESCENCE SPECTROSCOPY

Measurements of the excitation wavelength are made in UV-visible spectroscopy. The emission wavelength is measured here, though.

The electrons in an atom enter the singlet excited state when exposed to radiation with an excitation wavelength. Then, by the emission of light with a certain wavelength, they transition from the singlet excited state to the singlet ground state. For analysis, the emitted radiation is measured.

The vibrational level structures in the ground and excited electronic states, respectively, are reflected in the fluorescence excitation and emission spectra.

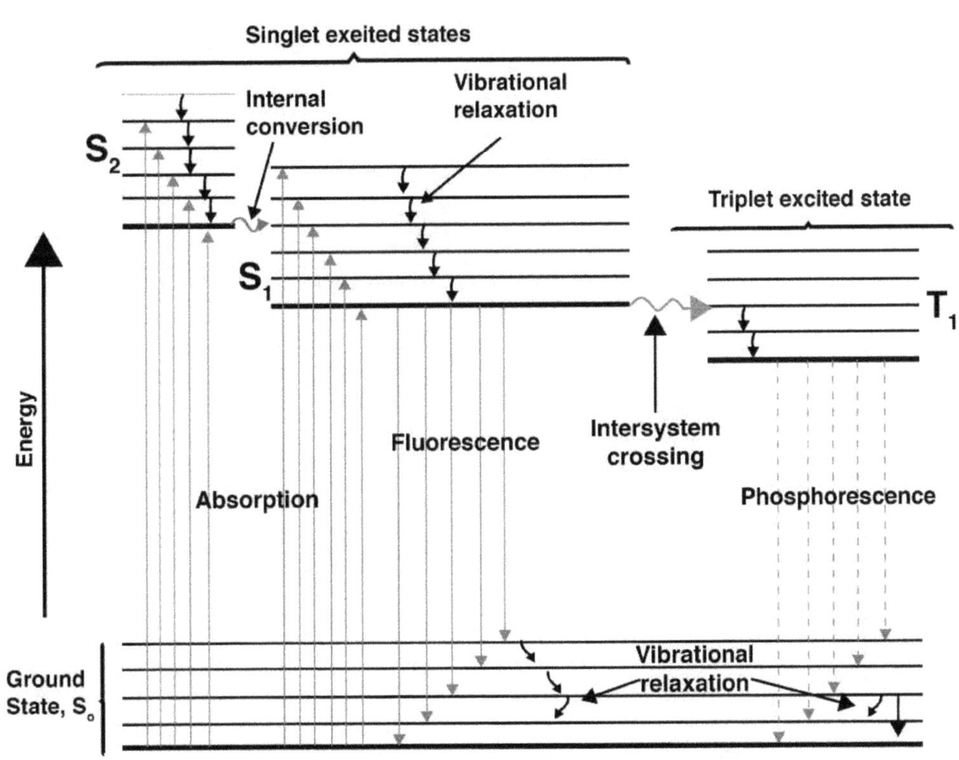

Figure 3.1: Jablonski Diagram.

3.4 INSTRUMENTATION

The fluorescence spectroscopy instrumentation is similar to UV-Visible spectroscopy. It has the following:

1. **Light source:** Xenon arc lamp, mercury vapor lamp and tungsten lamp
2. **Monochromators:** These help to separate light bands.
3. **Sample cells:** The sample cell is mostly quadrilateral. It is made of glass.
4. **Detectors:** This is a photomultiplier tube which helps to detect radiation with low intensity.

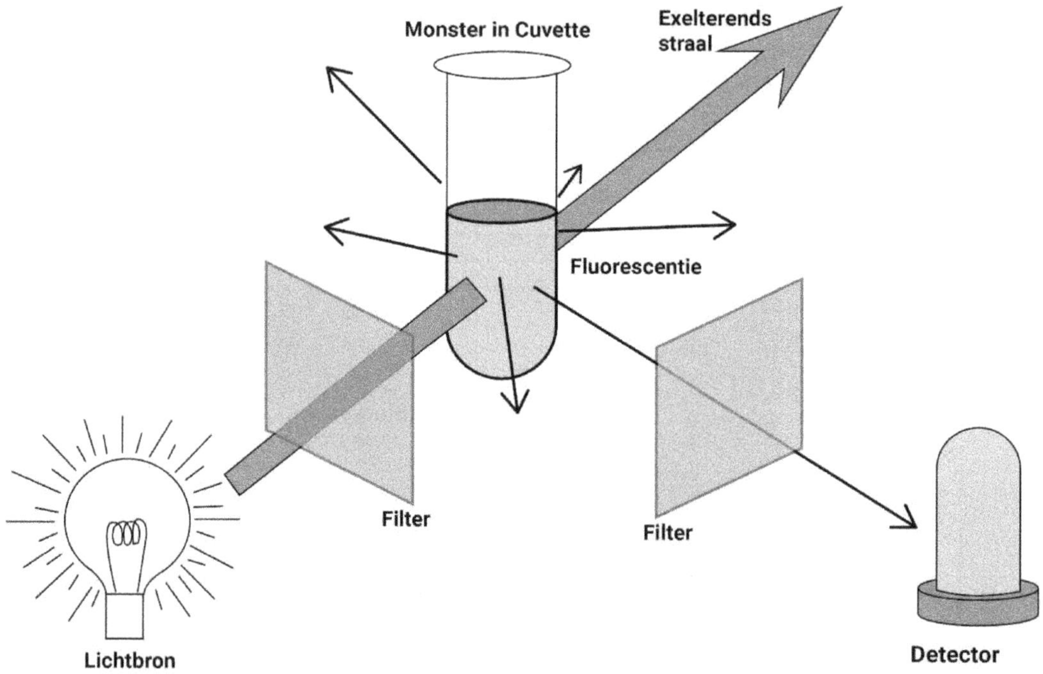

Figure 3.2: Fluorometric Instrumentation.

Fluorometric instrumentation is of two types like filter fluorometer and spectrofluorometer. Among them, spectrofluorometer is advanced with high sensitivity and efficiency. But both of them have similar instrumentation as below:

Light Source: The source should provide stable radiation with sufficient intensity over an entire range.

Xenon Lamp: This is widely used in spectrofluorometers. Here light is produced by passing electricity through ionized Xenon gas under high pressure. It provides a bright light with intense radiation over a wide range. Hence, most compounds can be analyzed.

Mercury Vapor Lamp: Here mercury vapor is subjected to a high pressure of 8 atmospheres. It gives intense radiation over 350nm. At low pressures, this vapor also provides one more radiation at 254nm. But, this is preferred in inexpensive filter type fluorimeters.

Tungsten lamp: This lamp has radiation with low intensity. It is used when the excitation radiation is in the visible region.

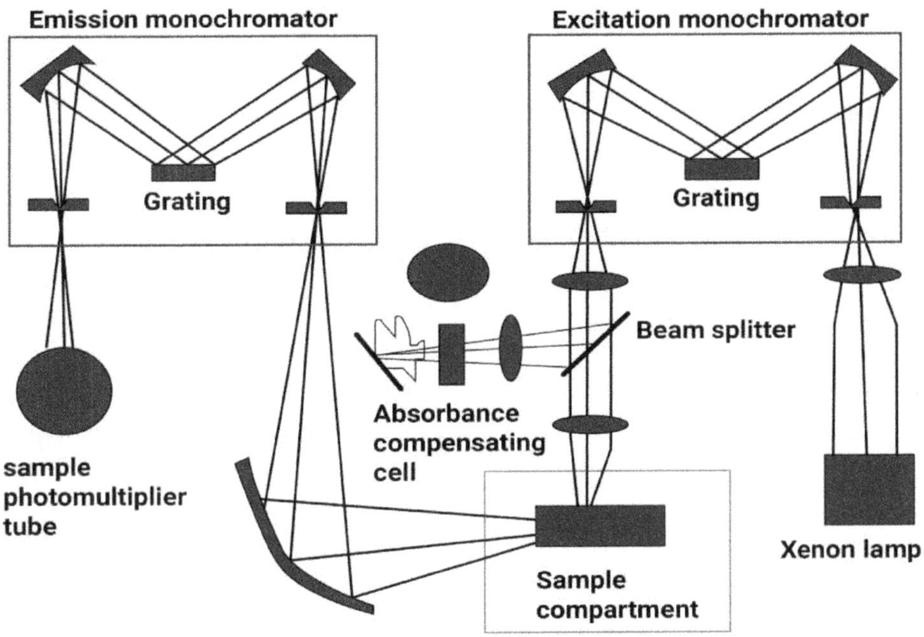

Figure 3.3: Schematic Diagram of a Spectrofluorometer.

Filters and monochromators: The light source produce polychromatic light. So, filters or monochromators are needed to convert them into monochromatic light. The filters have less resolution capacity and hence the light radiation has a band pass of ±30nm. Consequently, they are inexpensive and used in filter fluorometers. Whereas, the monochromators have a very high-resolution capacity with a band pass of just ±0.1nm. But, they are expensive and hence in spectrofluorometers.

Sample cells: The fluorometer cuvettes are small tube-like structures used to hold the sample for analysis. They are made of color corrected fused glass. All the sides of the cell have polished surfaces. The path length of the sample holder is 10mm.

Detectors: Photo-multiplier tubes are employed as detectors. These are efficient and accurate for radiations with low intensity.

3.5 FACTORS AFFECTING FLUORESCENCE

Conjugation

Molecule must have unsaturation i.e. it must have π electrons so that UV/vis radiation can be absorbed. If there is no absorption of radiation, there will not be fluorescence.

Rigidity of structures

Rigid structures will produce more fluorescence, while flexible structure will produce less fluorescence.

Nature of substituent groups

Electron donating groups like amino, hydroxyl groups enhance fluorescence activity. Electron withdrawing groups like Nitro, carboxylic group reduce fluorescence. Groups like SO_3H or on NH_4^+ have no effect on fluorescence intensity.

Effect of temperature

When the temperature rises, molecules collide more often and the intensity of the fluorescence decreases, while when the temperature drops, molecules collide less frequently and the intensity of the fluorescence increases.

Viscosity

When viscosity is raised, molecule collisions are reduced, enhancing fluorescence intensity, but when viscosity is lowered, molecule collisions are increased, decreasing fluorescence intensity.

Oxygen

There are two ways that oxygen reduces the fluorescence intensity: converts fluorescent materials into non-fluorescent ones by oxidation. Its paramagnetic characteristics cause fluorescence to be quenched.

Effect of pH

A. **Aniline:** Neutral or alkaline medium shows visible fluorescence while acidic conditions give fluorescence in UV region only.

B. Phenols: Acidic conditions do not give fluorescence while alkaline conditions give good fluorescence.

3.6 EFFECT OF CONCENTRATION ON FLUORESCENCE INTENSITY

Fluorescence intensity = Q x I_a

Where,

Q = Fluorescence efficiency

I_a = Intensity of absorbed light Since emission is proportional to absorption, I_a has to be known

Where,

I_o = Intensity of incident light and

I_t = Intensity of incident light

It is known that, $I_t = I_0e$ -act [from beer lamberts law] $I_a = I_0$ [1-e -act] $I_a = I_0$ x act

Fluorescence intensity = Q × I_a F = QI_0 act

In this equation, Q = Constant for a particular substance I_a = Constant for an instrumental = Molecular extinction coefficient t = path length, c = concentration of substances

So, Fluorescence intensity is directly proportional to the substances.

3.7 ADVANTAGES OF FLUORESCENCE SPECTROSCOPY

Sensitivity: Fluorimetry is a highly efficient spectroscopic with its ability to measure samples of small quantity. Sample concentrations as low as µg and ng/ml can be determined by using this technique.

Precision: The accuracy of the result is also high in this fluorimetry spectroscopy. A margin of up to 1% is achievable.

Specificity: UV Vis spectroscopy relies on just the excitation wavelength of the substance. In fluorescence spectroscopy both excitation and emission wavelengths are characteristic. If two compounds could have the same excitation wavelength, they would differ in emission wavelength. Hence, the specificity for a compound is enhanced.

A wide range of compounds: This method is used to analyze many compounds. Even those compounds which do not have fluorescent property can be made by chemical conversion.

3.8 DISADVANTAGES OF FLUORIMETRY

In spite of many benefits of this method, some limitations exist. These are related to fluorescent intensity.

(i) pH changes and the presence of oxygen can affect fluorescent intensity.

(ii) When a sample is subjected to UV absorption, it can undergo chemical changes due to the high energy of radiation.

(iii) Not all substances can be converted to be fluorescent. So, not all compound can be analyzed by this method. iv. Presence of heavy metals and electronegative halides can change the fluorescent intensity.

3.9 APPLICATIONS OF FLUORIMETRY

3.9.1 Applications in Inorganic Chemistry

1. Determination of Ruthenium

It is determined in the presence of platinum metal. Palladium forms a precipitate with the reagent which can be removed by centrifuging. Iron should be absent as it forms a complex that quenches the fluorescence. Any other element of the platinum group can be present to the extent of at least 30mμ.mL^{-1}, without interfering the determination of ruthenium in the range of 0.3 - 2.0mμ.mL^{-1}.

2. Determination of boron in steel

It is determined by means of complex formed with benzoin. The boron present in the acid solution of the sample is first converted in to boric acid, which is then separated from the other constituents by co-distillation with methyl alcohol. The resulting distillate containing boric acid is neutralised by NaOH and methyl alcohol is evaporated off.

3.9.2 Application in Organic Chemistry

1. Assay of thiamine:

Assayed by blue fluorescence of its oxidation product, thiochrome. The sample such as meat, cereals etc. is first treated with acid and extract is treated with enzyme phosphatase. The latter causes hydrolysis of phosphate esters of thiamine which are present in the food materials. An oxidising agent such as $K_4Fe\ [CN]_6$ is added to the first, while equal amount of NaOH and isobutyl alcohol are added to the both the aliquots. After shaking aqueous layer is removed and alcoholic layer is examined in a fluorimeter.

2. Estimation of quinine sulphate by fluorimetry

For the construction of calibration curve: In to a series of 10 ml volumetric flasks transfer 1ml, 2ml, 3ml, 4ml and 5ml of standard solution of quinine sulphate [1μg/ml] and dilute to mark with 0.1N sulphuric acid. Select the proper excitation and emission filters [365nm and 459 nm]. Measure the fluorescence with a fluorometer.

For the analysis of tablets: weigh 20 tablets and reduce to a fine powder. Weigh accurately a quantity of the tablet powder equivalent to 100mg of quinine sulphate and mix with 75ml of 0.1 N sulphuric acid in a 100 ml volumetric flask. Mix the contents thoroughly to dissolve the drug and adjust the volume to 100 ml with 0.1N sulphuric acid and filter the contents.

3.9.3 Special Fluoremetric Applications

1. Investigation of Chemical Structures and Processes

- Fluoremetric methods have successfully been applied in the investigation of hydrogen bonding, cis trans isomerism polymerization, tautomerism and rates of reactions etc.

- The free radicals can best be detected with a spectrograph so that the whole spectrum of a short-lived component may be photographed at the same time.
- Steric hindrance in diphenyl can be studied by constraining the two-phenyl group to move out of a single plane, by substituting CH3 groups adjacent to the centre bond [ortho substitution]. The molecule behaves like two benzene-insulated chromophores.

2. Chemical Analysis

This type analysis may be quantitative as well as qualitative.

- Detection of impurity – solvents used for spectrofluorometry must be free of absorbing impurities. Thus, cyclohexane must be purified until it shows no trace of benzene bands at 2600 A^0.
- If absorbing impurities are present in the vitamin, they can be removed either by chemical method or utilizing the change of shape of absorbing band in the presence of an impurity.

3. Accurate Determination of Glucose

In biological processes, glucose is regarded as a crucial part of animal and plant carbohydrates. Additionally, blood glucose levels are a sign of other human health issues. The presence of aberrant glucose levels offers important insight into a variety of illnesses, including diabetes and hypoglycemia. Fluorophotometry was frequently utilised since it was easy to use and had a high sensitivity.

CHAPTER 4

FLAME EMISSION SPECTROSCOPY

4.1 INTRODUCTION

Bowling Barnes, David Richardson, John Berry, and Robert Hood developed an instrument to gauge a solution's low sodium and potassium contents in the 1980s. This device is known as a flame photometer. The measurement of the intensity of the light that is emitted when a metal is added to the flame is the basis of the flame photometer's working principle. The color's wavelength provides information about the element, and the flame's colour provides information about the concentration of the element in the sample.

One of the subfields of atomic absorption spectroscopy is flame photometry. It is additionally referred to as flame emission spectroscopy. It is currently a necessary tool in the discipline of analytical chemistry. Flame photometer can be used to determine the concentration of certain metal ions like sodium, potassium, lithium, calcium and cesium etc. In flame photometer spectra the metal ions are used in the form of atoms. The International Union of Pure and Applied Chemistry (IUPAC) Committee on Spectroscopic Nomenclature has named this technique as flame atomic emission spectrometry (FAES).

4.2 PRINCIPLE OF FLAME PHOTOMETER

When placed in the flame, the compounds of the Group II alkali and alkaline earth metals separate into atoms. Some of these atoms experience increased degrees of excitement.

However, at higher altitudes, these atoms are not stable.

As a result, when these atoms return to their ground state, they release radiation. Typically, the visible portion of the spectrum is where these radiations are located. Alkali and alkaline earth metals each have a distinctive wavelength.

Element	Emitted wavelength	Flame colour
Sodium	589 nm	Yellow
Potassium	766 nm	Violet
Barium	554 nm	Lime green
Calcium	622 nm	Orange
Lithium	670 nm	Red

For certain concentration ranges, the intensity of the emission is directly proportional to the number of atoms returning to the ground state. And the light emitted is in turn proportional to the concentration of the sample.

4.3 INSTRUMENTATION

A simple flame photometer consists of the following basic components:

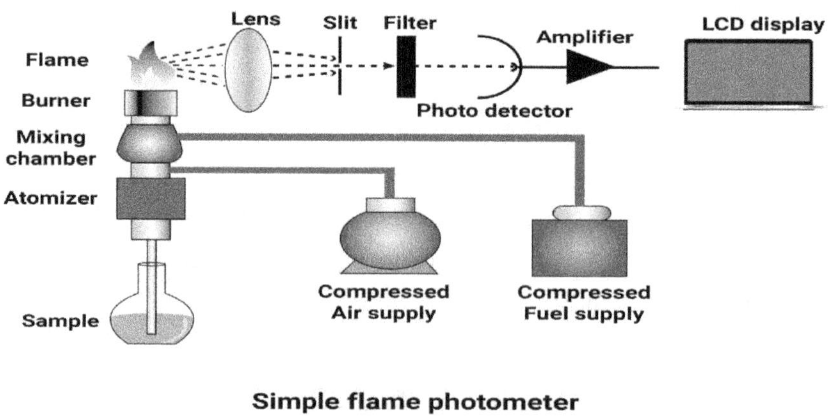

Figure 4.1: Simple Flame Photometer.

The radiation from a hollow cathode lamp is produced to fall on the sample of the analyte inhaled into the flame in a conventional flame atomic absorption spectrophotometric measurement, where a portion of it is absorbed. A monochromator then spreads out the transmitted light before being transferred to the detector. The detector output is appropriately processed, and a suitable readout device displays it. These single channel instruments can only conduct measurements in one channel at a single wavelength. These days, there are also dual- channel equipment that allow for simultaneous observations at two distinct wavelengths. For the purpose, they have two separate monochromators. Thus, these can be used for the simultaneous determination of two elements; one can be the analyte to be determined and the other may be a reference element.

4.3.1 Fuel Gas, Pressure Regulator and Flow Meters

In order to supply suitable thermal energy through flame, fuel gas is burnt in burner. A structural diagram of flame is shown in figure 2. The unburnt fuel gas emerging from region A, mixes with air/oxygen at outlet of burner comes into pre- heating region B. Gases emerging from this mainly consist of CO, H_2, CO_2 and hydrocarbon. On burning, a steady temperature is provided throughout the outer mantle of flame.

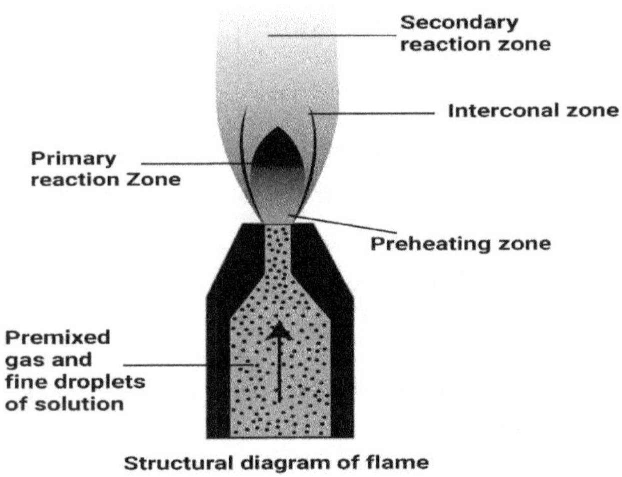

Figure 4.2: Structural Diagram of Flame.

4.3.2 Atomisers

A representative amount of the analyte must be placed in the optical path and transformed into free neutral ground state atoms using an atomizer. The most popular means of atomization in atomic absorption spectrophotometry are flames and furnaces that produce temperatures between 1500 and 3000 °C. Flame atomizers and electrothermal atomizers are two popular types of atomizers that are used to produce atomic species in the vapour phase.

4.3.2.1 Flame Atomizer

4.3.2.2 Electro thermal atomisers or Non-flame Atomizer

1. Flame Atomizers

Flame used shall produce temperature in excess of 2000k. This requirement can only be met by burning the fuel gas in oxidant gas which is usually air, nitrous oxide or oxygen or oxygen diluted with either N_2 or argon.

Fuel	Oxidant	Temperature
Acetylene	Air	2400-2700
Acetylene	Oxygen	3300-3400
Acetylene	Nitrous oxide	2900-3100
Hydrogen	Air	2300-2400

Flame atomizers are primarily utilised with liquid or dissolved samples. A pneumatic nebulizer aspirates the sample solution, turning it into an aerosol that is then injected into a spray chamber where it is mixed with the flame gases and controlled such that only the smallest aerosol particles (< 10 µm) penetrate the flame.

A burner head that produces a flame that is only a few millimetres deep and typically 5 to 10 cm long is located on top of the spray chamber.

The flame's gas flow rate may be changed to provide the largest concentration of free atoms when the radiation beam passes through it at its longest axis.

The burner height may also be changed to direct the radiation beam through the area of the flame with the densest atom cloud formation, producing the highest sensitivity.

Disadvantage of Flame Atomization Technique

Only 5-15% of the nebulised sample reaches the flame. A minimum sample volume of 0.5-1.0 ml is needed to give a reliable reading. Sample which are viscous require dilution with a solvent.

4.3.3 Nebuliser

Nebulizer is a device used for sample introduction into the flame. The process is called nebulisation and consists of thermal vapourisation and dissociation of aerosol particles at high temperatures producing small particle size with high residence time.

A number of nebulisation methods are available. A few are listed below:

- Pneumatic nebulisation
- Ultrasonic nebulisation
- Electro thermal vapourisation
- Hydride generation (used for certain elements only)

Pneumatic Nebulisation

It is the most commonly employed nebulisation method in flame photometers. Pneumatic nebuliser is the most commonly used nebuliser for introducing aqueous/liquid samples. In this the sample solution is fed or aspirated into the nebuliser which converts liquid into a fine mist, or aerosol which is then fed into the flame. A common type of pneumatic nebuliser is called concentric pneumatic nebuliser, as shown in Figure 3.

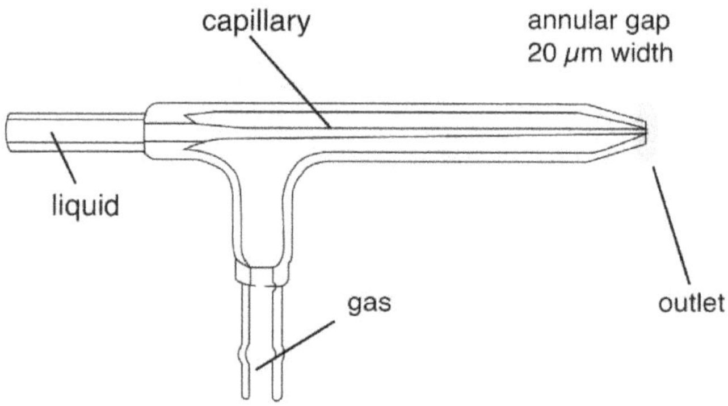

Figure 4.3: Pneumatic nebuliser.

The concentric pneumatic nebuliser consists of a fine capillary surrounded by concentric tube with a small orifice near one end of the capillary. The capillary is dipped into a solution of the analyte while the outer tube is connected to a high-pressure gas supply. The analyte is sucked into the capillary by the high- pressure gas stream flowing around the tip of the capillary using the Bernoulli effect. The process is called aspiration. The high velocity gas breaks up the liquid into various sized fine drop lets. The other types of the pneumatic nebulisers also work on the same principle.

4.3.4 Atomiser Burners

The sample is introduced in the form of a fine spray at a controlled rate into the flame of a burner with the help of nebuliser. In the burner, the analyte undergoes a number of processes as mentioned earlier. Two types of atomisation burners have been used in flame photometry which are given below and explained in the following paragraphs.

(a) Pre-mix or Lundegarh Burner

(b) Total consumption Burner

(a) Premix or Lundegarh Burner

Prior to leaving the burner ports and entering the primary-combustion or inner zone of the flame, fuel and oxidant are fully mixed inside the premix burner's burner housing. In this kind of burner, the analyte solution is inhaled from the sample container into the mixing chamber, where the fuel gas is also added, using a nebulizer. Baffles in the mixing chamber halt the bigger drips, which are then drained out. The mixing chamber smoothest out pressure and density variations of the aerosol brought on by atomization, and the mixture of aerosol, fuel gas, and oxidant burns to produce a steady, noiseless flame. Prior to leaving the burner ports and entering the primary-combustion or inner zone of the flame, fuel and oxidant are fully mixed inside the premix burner's burner housing. In this kind of burner, the analyte solution is inhaled from the sample container into the mixing chamber, where the fuel gas is also added, using a nebulizer. Baffles in the mixing chamber halt the bigger drips, which are then drained out. The mixing chamber smoothest out pressure and density variations of the aerosol brought on by atomization, and the mixture of aerosol, fuel gas, and oxidant burns to produce a steady, noiseless flame. The smaller droplets' solvent partially evaporates first in the mixing chamber, then in the burner's conduit, and finally in the flame. Only liquid droplets of a specific size can enter the burner and burn fully. As a result, the premix burner's efficiency is poor and only 5% of the sample really makes it to the burner. The addition of an impact bead just after the nebulizer has increased the burner's efficiency. The impact bead has the effect of breaking up large droplets as they come out from the nebuliser, thereby increasing the number of smaller droplets and the efficiency of nebulisation. The schematic diagram of a premix burner is given in Figure 4

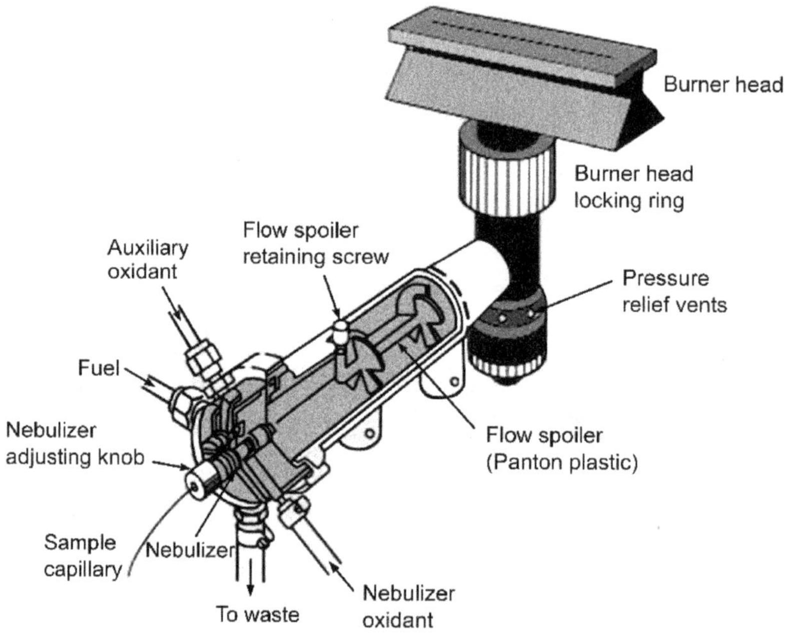

Figure 4.4: Premix Burner.

Depending on whether they contain one large hole, several small holes, or a slot as the outlet port(s) for the gas mixture, premix burners are referred to as Bunsen, Méker, or slot burners, respectively. Premix burners typically produce a flame that is roughly laminar, and they are frequently used in conjunction with a separate device for nebulizing the sample. The slot burner typically stops the flame from flashing back into the burner housing inadvertently.

Premix burners have the advantage of being quieter to use and producing a much cleaner analytical signal than total consumption burners.

However, it also has certain drawbacks, such as the fact that most of the sample solution drains away, which reduces the sensitivity of determining a particular analyte.

(b) Total Consumption Burner

Nebulizer and burner functions are combined in a total consumption burner. The sample is introduced into the flame in this type of burner even if it contains suspended particles or big solvent droplets due to the suction caused by the compressed oxidant streaming past the inner capillary; hence the term "complete consumption burner." Here, the fuel and oxidant exit from different ports and mix above the burner orifices as a result of their turbulent motion. Such a burner produces a turbulent flame.

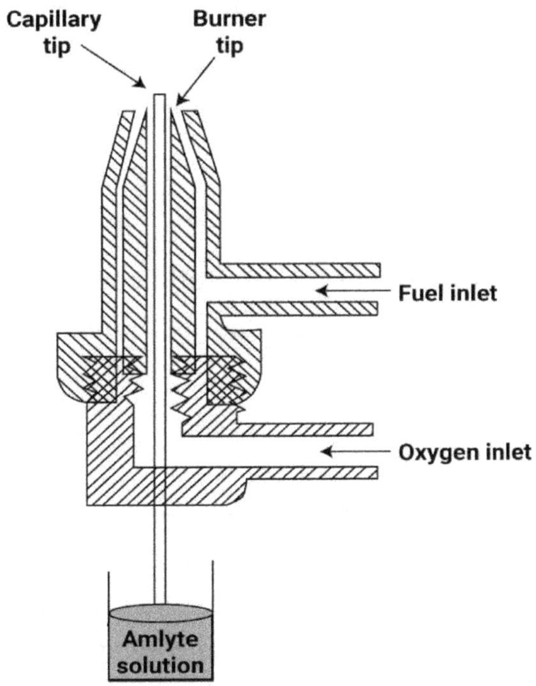

Figure 4.5: Total Consumption Burner.

The total consumption burner has the following advantages.

There are no material losses due to spray condensation; all of the material enters the flame. Due to this, the emission from a premix flame (with indirect atomization) is greater for a given concentration of analyte in solution.

Aspiration does not result in sample fractionation. This prevents errors brought on by non-volatile component loss.

Petroleum, for example, can be aspirated directly into the flame photometry without risk of an explosion.

However, the total consumption burner suffers from the following disadvantages:

- During aspiration, droplets of widely varying sizes are produced. The flame typically blows through many of the bigger droplets without fully evaporating or pyrolyzing the solute.
- The flame is more effectively cooled by a heavier liquid load.
- The aspiration rate of the solvent can alter if salts left over after solvent evaporation become embedded in the burner tip.
- The burners produce a lot of noise, both physically and electronically, which makes it difficult to reproduce analytical data.
- Due to the aforementioned factors, the total consumption burner is rarely utilised aside from in the case of exploding flames, such as hydrogen with other oxidants.

4.3.5 Mirrors

Radiation from flames is released into space in all directions. Signal loss occurs as a result of the loss of much radiation. Mirror placed behind burner to reflect radiation back to monochromator's entry slit. Concave in design, the mirror provides maximum solid coverage away from the flame. The front of the mirror has a reflecting surface. The best mirrors are those with a front surface.

4.3.6 Slits

Before and after the dispersion elements, entrance and exit are utilised. Most of the radiation from the environment is blocked by the entrance slit, leaving just the radiation from the flame and its reflected reflection to enter the optical system. Only a specific wavelength range is permitted to pass through the exit slit, which is situated after the monochromator and before the detector. Such interfering lines must not pass through the slit and into the detector.

4.3.7 Monochromators

Simple flame photometers employ prisms as their monochromators, whereas more expensive devices use grating monochromators.

Although quartz's dispersive power is smaller than that of glass', it is nevertheless the material that is most frequently employed to create prisms. This is because the entire region of quartz is transparent. The grating monochromator uses a grating, which is basically a series of parallel straight lines carved onto a plane surface.

4.3.8 Filter

In flame photometry, it's important to keep an eye on both the element's radiation's wavelength and intensity. Therefore, a monochromator or filter should be utilised. A simple flame photometer typically comprises a filter wheel with several filters for Ca, Li, Na, or K. The right filter is chosen when a particular element needs to be studied.

4.3.9 Detectors

Most of the light that the elements emit is in the visible spectrum. Therefore, traditional detectors such as photovoltaic or barrier layer cells as well as photomultiplier tubes can be employed. A maximum signal is provided by them for weak emission lines.

4.3.10 Read Out Device or Recorder

The photo current produced by detectors is often amplified and fed to light spot moving coil galvanometer. The sensitivity of this is adjusted through coarse and fine knobs, which adjust sensitivity ranging from 0.007 to 0.004μ/mm scale divisions.

4.4 FLAME PHOTOMETER PROCEDURE

- Fresh distilled water is used to prepare both the sample solution and the standard stock solution.

- The air and gas are adjusted to calibrate the photometer's flame. The flame is then given time to stabilise for around five minutes.
- The device is now turned on, and the filter chamber's lids are opened so that the proper colour filters can be inserted.
- Spraying distilled water into the flame resets the galvanometer's readings to zero.
- Spraying the most concentrated standard working solution into the flame changes the sensitivity. The galvanometer's full-scale deflection is now recorded.
- Distilled water is once more sprayed into the flame to maintain a steady galvanometer measurement. Following that, the galvano meter is reset to zero.
- Now, three times each of the normal working solutions are sprayed into the flame, and the galvanometer values are noted. The device needs to be thoroughly cleaned after each spray.
- After spraying the sample solution onto the flame three times, the galvanometer readings are recorded. The device needs to be thoroughly cleaned after each spray.
- Determine the galvanometer reading's mean.
- To determine the element's concentration in the sample, plot the concentration graph against the galvanometer value.

Air, oxygen, or nitrous oxide makes up the majority of the oxidants in a flame photometer. The temperature of the flame depends on the ratio of fuel and oxidant. The processes occurring during flame photometer analysis are summarized below:

Desolvation: Desolvation involves drying a sample in a solution. The metal particles in the solvent are dehydrated by the flame and thus solvent is evaporated.

Vaporization: The metal particles in the sample are also dehydrated. This also led to the evaporation of the solvent.

Atomization: Atomization is the separation of all atoms in a chemical substance.

The metal ions in the sample are reduced to metal atoms by the flame.

Excitation: The electrostatic force of attraction between the electrons and nucleus of the atom helps them to absorb a particular amount of energy. The atoms then jump to the higher energy state when excited.

Emission: Since the higher energy state is unstable the atoms jump back to the ground state or low energy state to gain stability. This jumping of atoms emits radiation with characteristic wavelength. The radiation is measured by the photo detector.

4.5 SCHEIBE-LOMAKIN EQUATION

Scheibe-Lomakin equation describes intensity of light emitted with the help of following formula:

$$I = k \times c^n$$

Where:

I = Intensity of emitted light

c = Concentration of the element

k = Proportionality constant

At the linear part of the calibration curve $n \sim 1$, then $I = k \times c$. In other words, the intensity of emitted light is directly related to the concentration of the sample.

4.6 APPLICATIONS OF FLAME PHOTOMETER

1. Flame photometers can be used for both qualitative and quantitative elemental analysis. The radiations that the flame photometer emits are

unique to each metal. Therefore, we may use a flame photometer to determine whether a given sample contains a particular element.

2. Certain group II elements are essential for the health of the soil. By using a flame test, we may find out which alkali and alkaline earth metals are present in a soil sample. After that, the soil can be fertilised with a certain fertiliser.
3. The body's Na+ and K+ ion concentrations are crucial for carrying out many metabolic processes. Blood serum samples can be diluted and aspirated into the flame to determine their concentrations.
4. Flame photometry can be used to analyse soft drinks, fruit juices, and alcoholic beverages to find out how much of certain metals and elements are present in them.

4.7 ADVANTAGES OF FLAME PHOTOMETER

1. The method of analysis is very simple and economical.
2. It is quick, convenient, selective and sensitive analysis.
3. It is both and qualitative and quantitative in nature.
4. Even very low concentrations (parts per million/ppm to parts per billion/ ppb range) of metals in the sample can be determined.
5. This method compensates for any unexpected interfering material present in the sample solution.
6. This method can be used to estimate elements which are rarely analysed.

4.8 DISADVANTAGES OF FLAME PHOTOMETER

In spite of many advantages, this analysis technique has quite a few disadvantages:

A. The accurate concentration of the metal ion in the solution cannot be measured.

B. It cannot directly detect and determine the presence of inert gases.

C. This method does not reveal the molecular composition of the metal present in the sample, even if it measures the overall amount of metal contained in the sample.

D. You can only use liquid samples. Additionally, in some situations, sample preparation takes time.

E. Flame photometry cannot be utilised to determine each and every metal particle directly. This technique cannot be used to analyse some metal atoms. Due to their non-radiative nature, elements like carbon, hydrogen, and halides cannot be detected.

CHAPTER 4A ATOMIC ABSORPTION SPECTROSCOPY

4.9 INTRODUCTION

Atomic Absorption Spectroscopy is a popular technique for detecting metals and metalloids in samples.

- It is extremely dependable and simple to use.
- It can analyse over 62 elements and determine the concentration of metals in a sample. The first atomic absorption spectrometer was built by CSIRO scientist Alan Walsh in 1954.Shown in the picture Alan Walsh (Left), with a spectrometer.

4.10 PRINCIPLE

The technique works on the basis that free atoms (gas) produced in an atomizer can absorb radiation at a specific frequency. The absorption of ground state atoms in gaseous states is quantified by atomic absorption spectroscopy. Atoms absorb ultraviolet or visible light and undergo transitions to higher levels of electronic energy. The amount of absorption determines the analyte concentration. After calibrating the instrument with known concentration standards, concentration measurements are typically determined from a working curve. Atomic absorption is a popular method for detecting metals and metalloids in environmental samples.

4.11 INSTRUMENTATION

A typical atomic absorption spectrophotometer consists of the following components.

A. Radiation source

B. Atom reservoir

C. Monochromator

D. Detector

E. Readout device

A block diagram showing the basic components of an atomic absorption spectrophotometer is given in Figure 1

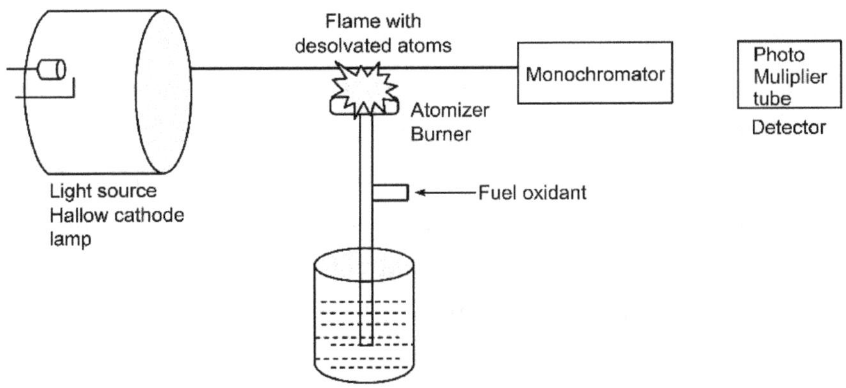

Figure 4A.1: Atomic Absorption Spectrophotometer.

In a typical flame atomic absorption spectrophotometric determination, radiation from a hollow cathode lamp is directed at an analyte sample aspirated into the flame, where a portion of it is absorbed. A monochromator disperses the transmitted radiation before it is sent to the detector. The detector output is appropriately processed and displayed by a suitable readout device. These single channel instruments can only perform measurements in one channel at a single wavelength. Dual-channel instruments that allow simultaneous measurements at two different wavelengths are now available. For this purpose, two independent monochromators are used. Thus, these can be used to determine two elements at the same time; one can be the analyte to be determined and the other can be a reference element.

A. Radiation Sources

All atomic absorption spectrophotometers that are for sale make use of a radiation source that emits the desired element's distinctive spectra. The radiation source's ability to generate radiation with consistency and intensity is a crucial requirement. Line sources and continuum sources are the two main types of sources used. Initially, continuous sources were used, and a high- resolution monochromator was used to separate the principal radiation needed. These, however, did not offer a high enough sensitivity and had low radiant densities. Currently, the first type's hollow cathode lamp (HCL) has seen the most usage.

Hollow Cathode Lamp

The metal that needs to be analysed serves as the cathode, which is the form of a hollow cylinder. The anode is a filament of tungsten. They are contained in a tube that contains an inert gas, such as neon or argon. The inert gas ionises and forms plasma when there is a high voltage applied across the anode and cathode. Atoms are sputtered off as a result of these ions being propelled towards the cathode. Collisions between the ions and metal atoms cause excitation. When they reach the ground state, they release photons with a particular wavelength.

A. Atomisers

A representative amount of the analyte must be placed in the optical path and transformed into free neutral ground state atoms using an atomizer. The most popular means of atomization in atomic absorption spectrophotometry are flames and furnaces that produce temperatures between 1500 and 3000°C. Flame atomizers and electro thermal atomizers are two popular types of atomizers that are used to produce atomic species in the vapour phase.

1. Flame Atomizer
2. Electrothermal Atomisers or Non-flame Atomizer

1. Flame Atomizers

The flame utilised must create temperatures more than 2000 K. Only by burning the fuel gas in an oxidant gas-typically air, nitrous oxide, oxygen, or oxygen mixed with either argon or N_2-can this requirement be satisfied.

Fuel	Oxidant	Temperature
Acetylene	Air	2400-2700
Acetylene	Oxygen	3300-3400
Acetylene	Nitrous oxide	2900-3100
Hydrogen	Air	2300-2400

Flame atomizers are primarily utilised with liquid or dissolved samples. A pneumatic nebulizer aspirates the sample solution, turning it into an aerosol that is then injected into a spray chamber where it is mixed with the flame gases and controlled so that only the smallest aerosol droplets (< 10 µm) reach the flame. A burner head that produces a flame that is only a few millimetres deep and typically 5 to 10 cm long is located on top of the spray chamber. The flame's gas flow rate can be changed to provide the largest concentration of free atoms as the radiation beam passes through it at its longest axis. The burner height can also be changed to direct the radiation beam through the area of the flame with the densest atom cloud formation, producing the best sensitivity.

Disadvantage of Flame Atomization Technique

Only 5–15% of the sample that is nebulized makes it to the flame. For an accurate measurement, a minimum sample volume of 0.5 –1.0 ml is required. Viscous samples need to be diluted with a solvent.

2. Electro thermal Atomisers or Non-Flame Atomizer

In this category carbon atomiser is used but it is rarely used in atomic absorption spectroscopy.

B. Nebuliser

A nebulizer is a device used to introduce samples into the flame. The process is called nebulisation and consists of thermal vapourisation and dissociation of aerosol particles at high temperatures producing small particle size with high residence time.

A number of nebulisation methods are available. A few are listed below:

- Pneumatic Nebulisation
- Ultrasonic Nebulisation
- Electro Thermal Vapourisation
- Hydride Generation (used for certain elements only)

- **Pneumatic Nebulisation**

It is the nebulization technique that flame photometers use the most frequently. For introducing aqueous or liquid samples, pneumatic nebulizers are most frequently utilised.

This process involves feeding or aspirating the sample solution into the nebulizer, which turns the liquid into an aerosol or fine mist that is then introduced into the flame. The term "concentric pneumatic nebulizer" refers to a popular variety of pneumatic inhaler as depicted in Figure 2.

The fine capillary and concentric tube surrounding the concentric tube with a small opening close to one end of the capillary make up the concentric pneumatic nebulizer. While the outer tube is attached to a high-pressure gas source, the capillary is submerged in an analyte solution. The high-pressure gas stream flowing around the capillary's tip uses the Bernoulli effect to draw the analyte into the tube. The action is referred to as aspiration. The liquid is divided into fine droplets of varying sizes by the high-velocity gas.

The same basic idea underlies the operation of the different varieties of pneumatic nebulizers.

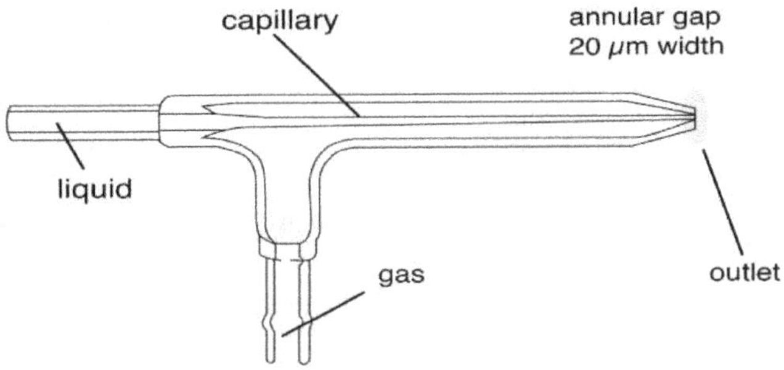

Figure 4A.2 : Pneumatic Nebulizer

C. Monochromators

Simple flame photometers employ prisms as their monochromators, whereas more expensive devices use grating monochromators.

Although quartz's dispersive power is smaller than that of glass', it is nevertheless the material that is most frequently employed to create prisms. This is because the entire region of quartz is transparent. The grating monochromator makes use of a grating, which is essentially a collection of parallel straight lines that have been carved out of a flat surface.

D. Detectors

Most of the light that the elements emit is in the visible spectrum. Therefore, standard detectors like photovoltaic or barrier layer cells as well as photomultiplier tubes can be employed. In the latter, a maximum signal is provided for weak emission lines.

E. Read out device or recorder

The photo current generated by detectors is often amplified and fed to light spot moving coil galvanometer. The sensitivity of this is adjusted through coarse and fine knobs, which adjust sensitivity ranging from 0.007 to 0.004 μ/mm scale divisions.

4.12 WORKING OF AAS

- The atoms of the solid are converted to gaseous state in the atomiser.
- The hollow cathode lamp emits radiation of a specific wavelength onto the gaseous atoms in the atomiser.
- The monochromator directs specific wavelengths into the detector.

- The detector measures the amount of light absorbed; and
- The concentration of atoms in the sample is proportional to the absorbance.

4.13 APPLICATION OF ATOMIC ABSORPTION SPECTROSCOPY

- Atomic absorption spectroscopy is one of the most widely used techniques for determining metal concentrations in solution at trace levels. Its popularity over flame emission is due to its relative freedom from inter-element interferences and relative insensitivity to changes in flame temperature.
- Flame photometry is typically used only for routine determination of alkali and alkaline earth metals.
- Frequently used for metal analysis in environmental samples (air, water, and soil), as well as biological fluids and t issues.

CHAPTER 5 NUCLEAR MAGNETIC RESONANCE

5.1 INTRODUCTION

End of 1945 saw the first experimental detection of nuclear magnetic resonance (NMR), almost simultaneously with work groups led by Edward Purcell of Harvard University and Felix Bloch of Stanford University. In the same edition of the Physical Review in January 1946, the first NMR spectra were initially made public. The 1952 Nobel Prize in Physics was shared by Bloch and Purcell for their work on nuclear magnetic resonance spectroscopy.

For organic chemists, nuclear magnetic resonance (NMR) spectroscopy is a vital analytical tool. The NMR has substantially enhanced the research being done in the organic lab. In addition to revealing the molecular structure, it can also reveal the sample's composition and purity. One of the NMR techniques that organic chemists utilize the most frequently is proton (1H) NMR. It is possible to elucidate the structure of a molecule by observing how the protons in it respond to the chemical environment around them.

A spectroscopic method for observing the local magnetic fields surrounding atomic nuclei is nuclear magnetic resonance spectroscopy, also referred to as magnetic resonance spectroscopy (MRS) or NMR spectroscopy.

It is a method of spectroscopy that relies on the nuclei of atoms' ability to absorb electromagnetic radiation in the radio frequency range of 4 to 900 MHz.

NMR has emerged as the standard method for figuring out the structure of organic substances over the past 50 years.

It is the only spectroscopic technique for which a thorough examination and interpretation of the entire spectrum is often anticipated.

5.2 DEFINITION OF NMR

Nuclear magnetic resonance is defined as a condition when the frequency of the rotating magnetic field becomes equal to the frequency of the processing nucleus. If ratio frequency energy and a, magnetic field are simultaneously applied to the nucleus, a condition as given by the equation $v = \gamma H_0/2\pi$ is met.

The system at this condition is said to be in resonance [v – frequency of radiation associated with transition from one state to the other; γ = proportionality constant and H_0 = magnetic field]'.

5.3 PRINCIPLE OF NMR

5.3.1 The Spinning Molecules

Because it carries both electric charge and mechanical spin, the nucleus of a hydrogen atom (proton) functions as a single spinning bar magnet. A magnetic field is generated by any charged body, including the nucleus of hydrogen.

5.3.2 Magnetic and Non-Magnetic Nuclei

All atomic nuclei include nucleonic particles, particularly protons, the positively charged particle, and neutrons, which are neutral. As a result, the nucleus is positively charged. Nuclear particles, like electrons, spin on their own axis. This circulation produces a magnetic dipole along the spin axis.

The spinning charge's angular momentum can be expressed in terms of spin quantum number. Individual protons have spin quantum numbers of +1/2 and -1/2 alone. The total spin quantum number (I) is a nucleus property that depends on the number of nucleons and the symmetry of the charge distribution.

Several atomic nuclei have angular momentum, or spin. A charged spinning particle creates a magnetic dipole along its spin axis, hence an isolated nucleus devoid of electrons may be thought of as a miniature bar magnet. The value of nuclear angular momentum (P) is given by the quantum mechanics expression:

$$p = h2\pi\sqrt{\{I(I+1)\}}$$
$$= h\sqrt{\{I(I+1)\}}$$

Where

h = Plank's constant;

h=h/2π = Modified Plank's Constant and

I = Spin Quantum Number

The nuclear magnetic resonance principle is based on the spins of atomic nuclei. Magnetic measurements are affected by the spin of an unpaired electron, whereas nuclear magnetic resonance is affected by the spin of protons and neutrons. Because both of these nucleons contain intrinsic angular momenta or spins, they function as elementary magnets. Nuclear magnetism was discovered in the hyperfine structure of spectral lines. When a nucleus with a certain magnetic moment is put in a magnetic field, we may see the phenomena of space quantization, with a slightly different energy level for each allowable direction.

5.4 THEORY OF NMR

Since the hydrogen nucleus or protons may be thought of as a rotating positively charged unit, it will produce a weak magnetic field along its axis of rotation (HO) (as shown in figure). Now, if a magnetic field H0 is applied to this nucleus, it will naturally line up either parallelly or antiparallelly to the field's direction. Due to its lesser energy, the A will be more stable.

The energy difference AE between two states will be absorbed or emitted as the nucleus flips from one orientation to the other. This is called as the precessional motion.

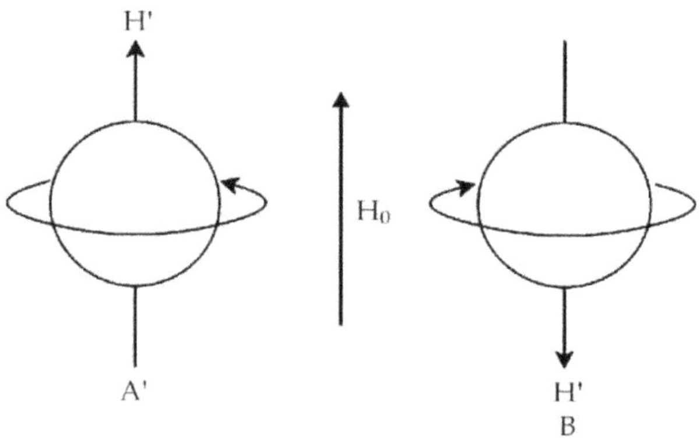

Figure 5.1: Spinning Nuclei.

$$AE = hv$$

Where

v = a radiation frequency and

h = Planck's constant

If correct frequency is applied to the sample containing hydrogen nuclei and sample is placed in the external field HQ, then low energy nuclei A will absorb AE = hv, and flips to B. Thus, on flipping back down, they remit hv as a radiation signal which is picked up by the instrument.

The nucleus' precessional frequency is directly related to the intensity of the external field as well as the type of the nuclear magnet.

In other words, if both radio frequency and magnetic field are simultaneously applied to the nucleus, transition from lower to higher level will occur when equation (1) will be equal to

$$\Delta E = \partial hH/2\pi \quad ...(1)$$

$$\Delta E = hv \quad ...(2)$$

Or $v = \delta H/2\pi$ ...(3)

δ = Gyromagnetic ratio, a constant characteristic of a particular nucleus.

Where

ΔE = energy difference between two spin states,

h = Planck's constant,

v = frequency of resonance absorption,

H = strength of applied magnetic field at nucleus.

The system at this condition is said to be in resonance and hence the name nuclear magnetic resonance. The observed value of H is therefore a function of molecular environment of proton affording the signal.

5.4.1 Energy Transition

When a proton is held in an external magnetic field, it will process and can assume one of two orientations with regard to the external field's axis: aligned (parallel) or opposed (Antiparallel).

5.4.1.1 When a proton is precessing in the aligned orientation, it can absorb energy and shift into the opposing orientation by losing energy, and vice versa.

5.4.1.2 The low energy nuclei may absorb this energy and shift to a higher energy state if we subject the precessing nuclei to a beam of radio frequency (energy of the proper frequency).

5.4.1.3 The precessing proton will absorb energy from the radiofrequency source, if the precessing frequency is same as the frequency of radio frequency beam. When this occurs the nucleus and the radio frequency beam are said to be in resonance, hence the termed as "Nuclear Magnetic resonance"

1. Relaxation Process:

The term "relaxation processes" refers to several radiation-free transitions that allow a nucleus in an upper spin state to move back to a lower spin state.

Generally, there are two types of relaxation processes:

(a) **Spin-spin Relaxation:** It is impacted by the mutual spin exchange of two processing nuclei that are near to one another.

(b) **Spin Lattice Relaxation** (lattice term refers to frame work of molecules containing the precessing nuclei):

This process keeps an excess of nuclei in a lower state, which is the critical basic condition for the observation of nuclear resonance phenomenon.

Broad lines are seen for short-lived excited stales and sharp resonance lines are seen for longer excitation stales in an NMR spectroscopy. The width of a spectral line is affected by both spin- spin relaxation and spin lattice relaxation processes.

2. Condition of Resonance Signals:

The atoms like O^{16} and C^{12} which have even number of protons and neutrons have no magnetic moment and hence refuse to give resonance signals. While atoms such as P^{21}, F^{19}, which have odd number of protons and even numbers of neutrons, if any, generate nuclear magnetic moments and "hence give resonance signals.

3. Units of NMR:

The nuclear magnetic resonance values are expressed in any of three ways:

(a) δ-the reference compound be quoted (δ denotes that chemical shift is independent of oscillator frequency).

(b) Cps-the reference compound must be quoted and the oscillator frequency given.

(c) τ-TMS (tetra methyl silane) or DSS (2, 2 dimethyl-2 silapentane-5 sulphonate) is assumed independent of both oscillator frequency and reference compound.

5.5 NUCLEAR MAGNETIC RESONANCE SPECTROMETERS

The basic elements of a typical N.M.R. spectrometer consist of the main parts;

1. A magnet with strong, stable homogeneous field. The field must be constant over the area of the sample.
2. A radio frequency oscillator (transmitter) connected to coil which transmits energy to the sample in a direction perpendicular to the magnetic field.
3. A sample container, usually a glass tube spun by an air driven turbine to average the magnetic field over the sample dimensions.

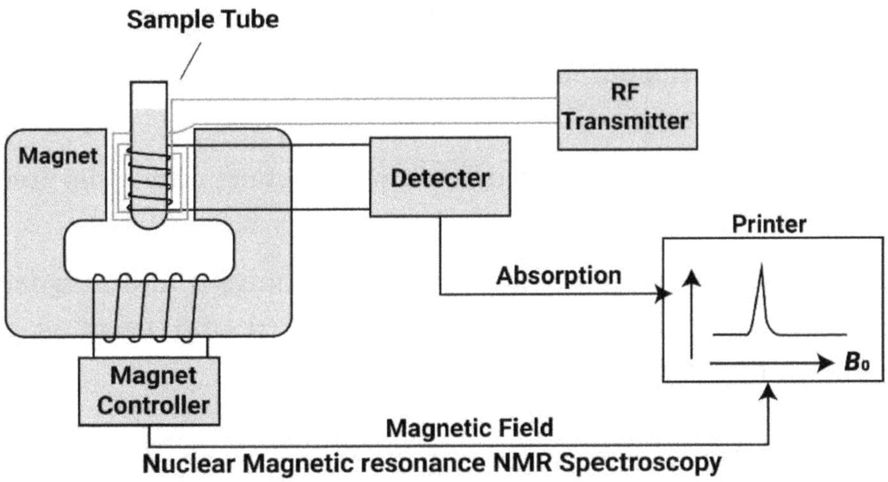

Figure 5.2: Instrumentation of NMR Spectrometer.

4. A radio frequency receiver connected to a coil encircling the sample. The two coils are perpendicular to each other and to the magnetic field.
5. A read-out system. The other supporting parts are- consisting of an amplifier, recorder and additional components for increasing sensitivity, accuracy or convenience.

6. A sweep generator which supplies a variable d-c current to a secondary magnet so that the total applied magnetic field can be varied (swept) over a limited range.

5.5.1 Experimental Technique

A diluted solution is often analysed. In most cases, the substance to be investigated is combined with a solvent, such as CCl_4 or tetramethyl silane, and the diluted solution is put into a tube.

Next the sample under study is placed in the magnetic field and subjected to Rf field of oscillator then at particular combinations of the oscillator frequency and field strength, the rf. energy is absorbed by certain nuclei and an rf. signal is picked up by the detector.

Two ways have been employed in NMR experiments for getting the desired particular combinations:

1. In one way, the magnetic field remains constant and radio frequency is varied.
2. In second, the radio frequency remains unchanged and magnetic field is varied till resonance conditions are obtained and there is detectable absorption by the nucleus.

5.5.2 Instrument

The block diagram for a sample NMR spectrometer is shown in Figure 3. In block diagram, the blocks labelled N and S represent the poles of the large HO magnet, which is generally an electromagnet operated through a stabilized power supply. A field of up-to 1400 gauss and a pole of about 1.75-1.8 inch is necessary for high resolution spectra.

The frequency and field strength are related to each other by Larmor condition.

$$v = \gamma H_0 / 2\pi$$

[This equation represents the condition of resonance.] Where HO = magnetic field, v = is the frequency of radiation associate with transition from one state to another. It is generally known as Larmor frequency, γ = proportionality constant or gyromagnetic ratio.

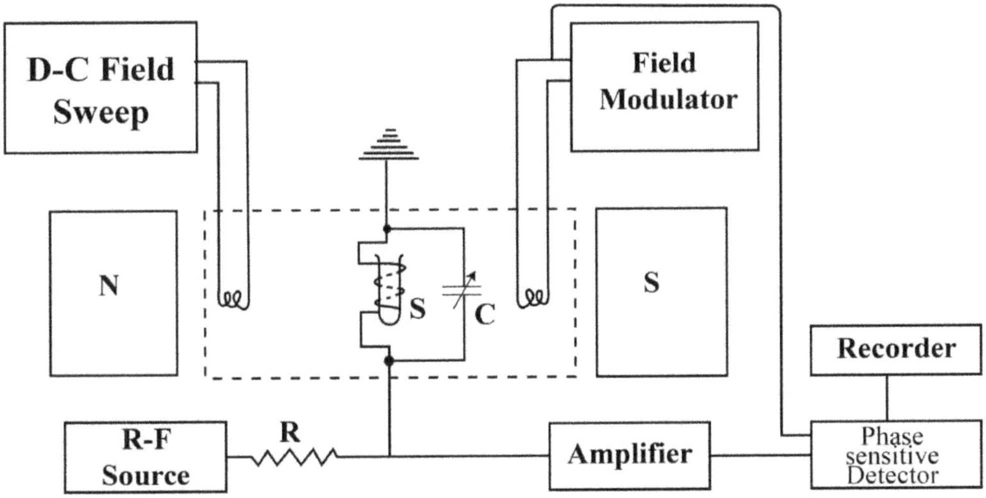

Figure 5.3: Block diagram of NMR Spectrometer.

5.6 CHEMICAL SHIFT

The chemical shift is the most significant molecular property obtained by NMR. The chemical shift is described as a measurement of the nuclei's resonance frequency in a certain chemical environment.

The magnitude of the chemical shift is proportional to the applied field strength and is induced by the circulation of electrons around the protons.

The chemical shift parameter 6 is defined by following equation.

$$\delta = (Hr - Hs)/Hr \times 10^6 \text{ ppm}$$

Where Hr and Hs are field strengths corresponding to resonance for a particular nucleus in the sample (Hs) and reference (Hr).

But as spectra are usually calibrated in cycles per second (cps), the equation can be written as:

$$\delta = \Delta v \times 10^6/\text{Oscillator frequency (cps)}$$

Where Δv = Difference in absorption frequencies of the sample and the reference in cps; Oscillator frequency is the characteristic of the instrument: For a 60 MHz instrument, the oscillator frequency is 60×10^6 cps.

The factor 10^6 has been included for convenience.

5.6.1 Units

The units of 5, is expressed as parts per million (ppm). The tetra methyl silane (TMS) is generally taken as acceptable standard (because of low boiling point 27°C).

If the compound has a symmetrical structure, each proton is identical to all others and is found in an identical electronic environment which gives a very high shielding. As a result, TMS gives a single sharp resonance line.

Chemical shift is also designated by τ where $\tau = 10 - \delta$. The standard $(CH_3)_4Si$ protons appear between 0 on 5 scale and 10 on τ scale.

5.6.2 Measurement of Chemical Shift

In reality, measuring chemical shift provides information about the different sorts of magnetic surroundings. In simple molecules, the chemical shift is quite characteristic and may be utilized for analysis and characterization.

5.6.3 Causes of Chemical Shift

In NMR bands are observed at different chemical shift δ or τ values. This difference may arise due to secondary magnetic field associated with molecule. These secondary fields arise due to the applied field H_0.

The effect of secondary fields may affect the chemical shift in one of the following ways:

i. When the secondary fields formed by circulating electrons oppose the applied field at a certain nucleus in a molecule, it indicates that the effective field experienced by the nucleus is smaller than the applied field.

This is referred to as positive shielding.

ii. If the circulating electron's secondary field strengthens the applied field, the position of resonance shifts down field. This is referred to as negative shielding.

There are two types of shielding effect which modify the resonance peaks in an NMR spectrum, these are-

1. **Local shielding:** The field experienced by a nucleus may be modified by fields due to induced circulation of electrons localised on that nucleus. This is called as local shielding.
2. **Low range shielding:** In an aromatic compound the secondary fields setup by the induced circulation of π electrons often influence the fields experienced by nuclei not directly associated with the π electrons.

- ➢ Due to this, additional shielding and deshielding effects may be included within the molecule.
- ➢ Long range shielding effects are more pronounced in unsaturated groups than saturated groups.

5.6.4 Shielding and Deshielding Effects

The electronic charge around hydrogen nuclei in a molecule protects the nucleus from the impact of the applied field.

➢ As a result, a larger external field is required to overcome the shielding effect and bring the protons to resonance.

➢ Clearly, the higher the electron density surrounding the proton, the stronger the generated secondary magnetic field (local diamagnetic effect) that opposes the applied field, and so, a higher external magnetic field would cause proton adsorption. The amount of shielding indicated by the shielding parameter α. When absorption happens, the proton's field H is given as

$$H = H_0(1-\alpha)$$

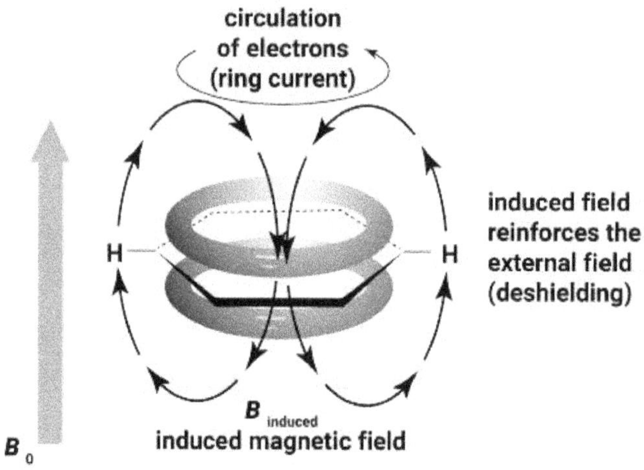

Figure 5.4: Shielding and De-shielding effects.

Where H_0 is the applied field strength clearly, the field belt by the proton does not correspond to the applied field.

➢ Greater the value of α, greater will be the value of applied field strength which has to applied to get effective field required for absorption and vice versa

So, $$V = \frac{YH}{2\pi}$$

Then $$V = \frac{YH0(1-\alpha)}{2\pi}$$

➢ From this relation, it is clear that the protons with different electronic environment or with different shielding parameter can be brought into resonance in two ways:

i. The strength of external field is kept steady and the radiofrequency is constantly varied.

ii. The radio frequency is kept steady and the strength of the applied field is constantly

5.6.5 Factors Affecting Chemical Shift

In fact, the chemical shift parameter δ is a function of electron density around the nucleus as the electrons are directly involved in the diamagnetic shielding which acts to attenuate the applied magnetic field.

Hence following factors are responsible for influencing its value:

1. **Electronegativity Effects:** A proton is said to be deshielded if it is attached to the electronegative atom or group. Greater is the electronegativity of the atom, greater is the deshielding caused to the proton. Larger is the deshielding of a proton, larger is the chemical shift value (δ). The chemical shift values of CH_4, CH_3F, CH_3Cl, CH_3Br and CH_3I protons are 0.33, 4.26, 3.05, 2.68 and 2.16 respectively. Since 'F' is the most electronegative atom and hence the chemical shift of CH_3F protons is very high, whereas the Iodine being least electronegative among the halogens, show the lower value of chemical shift.

   As the number of electronegative atoms or groups attached to a particular carbon containing the proton increases, the chemical shift value also increases because of the increasing deshielding of the concerned of proton. The chemical shift values CH_4, CH_3Cl, CH_2Cl_2, $CHCl_3$ protons are 0.33, 3.05, 5.28 and 7.23 respectively.

   With increasing distance, the inductive effect lessens. As a result, as the distance between the proton and the electronegative atom increases, the deshielding effect lessens, and the further protons from the electronegative atom exhibit a lower value of chemical shift than the near protons. The chemical shift values of methyl protons in CH_3Cl and CH_3CH_2Cl are 3.05 and 1.48 respectively.

2. **Steric Effects or Vander-waals Deshielding:** Some protons in overcrowded molecules may occupy sterically hindered positions, resulting in van der Waal's repulsion. The electron cloud of a bulky group (hindering group) will tend to reject the electron cloud around the proton in such compounds. As a result, such a proton will be deshielded and will

resonate at a little greater chemical shift value than the expected in the absence of this effect.

3. **Hydrogen Bonding:** In general, hydrogen bonded protons have a greater chemical shift than non-hydrogen bonded protons. Owing to the high electro-negativity of the atom to which proton is hydrogen bonded, the electron cloud around the proton is decreased and thus causes deshielding of the proton. The intensity of the hydrogen bonding determines the downfield shift of the absorption. The greater aproton's degree of hydrogen bonding, the larger downfield shift it has. Because of hydrogen bonding, the chemical shifts of OH, NH, and SH protons vary widely. The degree of hydrogen bonding is unexpected since it is affected by concentration, temperature, solvent, and chemical structure. The OH signals tend to move downfield at higher compound concentration because of increased hydrogen bonding. Also, on increasing temperature, hydrogen bonding decreases and hence OH signals move slightly up field. Both OH and NH signals move downfield in H- bonding solvents like DMSO or acetone. The intermolecular and intramolecular hydrogen bonding can be distinguished by the use of ^{1}H NMR spectroscopy. The intermolecular hydrogen bonding depends on the concentration of the sample and decreases on dilution with a non- polar solvent and also with increasing temperature.

The pure ethanol shows signals near 5 ppm but on dilution with non-hydrogen-bonded solvents (CCl_4, $CDCl_3$, C_6D_6), the OH signal shift up field due to the breaking of intermolecular hydrogen bonds. Because intramolecular hydrogen bonding is unaffected by sample concentration, their absorption position does not change with dilution. Enols of dike tones, salicylates, and carboxylic acids are some classic instances of intramolecular hydrogen bonding. The hydroxyl proton of enol form of 2, 4-pentanedione (4-hydroxypent-3-ene-2-one) shows a peak significantly down field (10-16 ppm) compared to the OH signal in other function groups due to strong intramolecular hydrogen bonding. Similarly, the hydroxyl proton of carboxylic acid displays a very downfield peak at about

10-13 ppm which may be attributed to the favored hydrogen- bonded dimeric association.

4. **Solvent Effects:** Chloroform ($CDCl_3$) is the most common solvent for NMR measurements. Other deuterium labelled compounds, such as deuterium oxide (D_2O), benzene-d_6 (C_6D_6), acetone-d_6 (CD_3COCD_3) and DMSO-d_6 (CD_3SOCD_3) are also used as NMR solvents. The polarity and magnetic susceptibility of all of these solvents varies greatly. As a result, the NMR spectra recorded in one solvent may deviate somewhat from that recorded in another. As a result, the solvent used must be mentioned. Changing the solvent normally causes a minor change in the NMR signals of protons linked to carbon, unless there is strong bonding or dipole- dipole interaction. The changes in chemical shifts due to solvents changes are minor being on the order of ±0.1 ppm. However, in some cases the changes are more. The aromatic solvents benzene and pyridine cause changes in chemical shifts as large as 0.5 to 0.8 ppm compared to less magnetically active solvents like chloroform or acetone.

5. **Shielding and deshielding in Aromatic Protons:** Electron-donating substituents protect aromatic protons by increasing electron density on the benzene ring. The order of shielding is ortho> para> meta because the electron density at ortho and para positions are the higher due to the +M effect. On the other hand, the electron withdrawing substituents cause deshielding of all the aromatic protons. The order of deshielding is in the order of ortho > para > meta because the electron withdrawing effect is maximum at ortho and para positions due to the +M effect.

6. **Anisotropic Effect (space effect):** The chemical shift in some circumstances, such as alkenes, alkynes, carbonyls, and aromatic compounds, cannot be explained only by the facts stated above. The carbon atom in acetylene is more electronegative (sp hybridized) than the carbon in ethylene (sp^2 hybridized) but the chemical shift value for actylenic protons are less (more shielded) than the ethylenic protons. The anisotropic effect induced by the circulation of π-electrons under the influence of an applied magnetic field might explain such unusual

behaviour. Anisotropy refers to an uneven magnetic field in space, which indicates that different regions of space have varied magnetic field strengths. The anisotropic effect is determined by the molecule's direction with respect to the applied field. In fact, a proton experiences three different fields, the applied field, the induced magnetic field generated by σ-electrons and the induced magnetic field generated by π-electrons. The πelectrons are more polarizable than the sigma bond electrons. Therefore, the induced magnetic field due to π-electrons movement is stronger (strong secondary fields that perturb nearby nuclei) than that generated by σ-electrons. Depending on the position of the proton in the induced magnetic field, it can be either shielded (smaller δ) or deshielded (larger δ).

5.6.6 Spin-spin Coupling

Spin-spin coupling is the interaction of the spin magnetic moments of various sets of H atoms in the molecule under study. A minimum of two sets of protons must be present in neighbouring positions.

The magnetic spins of these resonating nuclei interact with one another, influencing their precession frequencies. The effective magnetic field (B_{eff}) experienced by neighbouring protons as a result of magnetic spins thereby affects the chemical shift values. The nature of the peaks in the NMR spectra is also changed, in addition to the chemical shifts.

5.6.6.1 Peak Splitting in NMR Spectroscopy

A closer analysis of an NMR spectrum reveals that each signal on the graph represents one kind of proton present in the molecule. It is commonly observed that this signal is not always a single peak but has multiple peaks. This multiplicity of the signal is a very important determinant for the structure of the molecule. This phenomenon by which the spins of resonating protons cause the peaks on NMR spectrum to multiply is known as peak splitting. The splitting of NMR signal gives precise information about the number of neighbouring protons in a molecule. There is a formula to calculate the multiplicity of the peaks in the NMR spectrum.

$$=2nI + 1$$

n = Number of neighbouring protons

I = spin number of protons Since I is always ½, we can rewrite the formula as n+1.

The other relevant information which comes along with knowing the number of peaks is the intensity of the peaks (which is seen as the height of the peaks). As a general rule, the height of the peaks or in other words, the relative intensities of the peaks can be determined by using Pascal's triangle.

5.6.6.2 Pascal's triangle

This is a number pattern invented by a famous French mathematician, Blaise Pascal. We can use the n+1 rule to determine the number of peaks. The height of the peaks, caused due to spin-spin coupling is in proportion to the values in the row (corresponding to the value n) in Pascal's triangle.

With n = 0 (or 0 neighbouring protons), we get a single peak. This is depicted as 1 at the apex of the Pascal's triangle Similarly, for n=1 (or 1 neighbouring proton), we get a doublet (using the n+1 rule).

This is written as 1 on either side of the second row in the Pascal's triangle. Moving on, for n=2 (or 2 neighbouring protons), we get a triplet. In this case, the number 1 is written at the left and right of the triangle and the sum (1+1) is shown in the middle. For n=3, we get a quartet. In this case, again 1 is written at the ends and the neighbouring numbers are added. Therefore, we end up with the sequence 1331.

Example for peak splitting is CH_3CH_2Cl (Ethyl chloride) First, we calculate the multiplicity for the hydrogen atoms.

There are 2 sets of hydrogen atoms in Ethyl Chloride and we should expect to get 2 peaks in the NMR spectrum. This, however, is not true when it comes to visualizing the actual spectrum. Each of the hydrogen atoms will influence the neighbours in an applied magnetic field and would lead to multiple peaks. To determine how many peaks, we can get for hydrogen atoms in CH_2 or CH_3, we need to apply the above rule of multiplicity determination.

Then we look at the hydrogen atoms in CH_2 which are under the influence of 3 hydrogen atoms of the CH_3 group. Therefore,

$$n = 3 \quad I = 1/2$$

After applying the formula, $2nI+1 = (2 \times 3 \times 1/2) + 1 = 4$

Therefore, there will be 4 peaks for hydrogen atoms in CH_2 Similarly, there would be 3 peaks for hydrogen atoms in CH_3. The position of the split peaks on the chemical shift scale (also known as the delta value) would be further influenced by the presence of the electronegative atom (chloride) in close proximity to hydrogen atoms in CH_2.

5.6.6.3 Factors influencing peak split in NMR spectrum due to spin-spin coupling

It is known that nuclei contain a characteristic called spin. The spinning hydrogen nuclei of a molecule will interact with one another, splitting the signal in the NMR peak. The separation distance between two adjacent peaks in a multiplet is constant as a result of the spin-spin interaction and is known as the coupling constant (denoted by the letter J). The value of the coupling constant depends on the following factors:

5.6.6.3.1 Distance between the protons

The distance between the hydrogen atoms in a molecule is an important determinant in the value of J constant. If the hydrogen atoms involved in the coupling are closer to each other, these give rise to a greater value of J constant than if these atoms are further apart.

5.6.6.3.2 The orientation of the coupled protons

The angle or orientation of the protons with reference to one another is also crucial. The value of the J constant is higher in molecules with H atoms in the c is conformation. When the H atoms are in the trans conformation, it is less.

5.6.6.4 Determination of singlets and doublets

If we, for example, observe peaks in the molecule which are exactly 10 Hz apart and look indistinguishable from each other, it is very hard to decide if they are singlets or doublet.

In order to know whether the peaks are a doublet, we would increase the applied magnetic field. Now, because the coupling constant (J) is constant between the adjacent peaks, the doublet peaks would be unaffected by the change of magnetic field. On the other hand, if the peaks were made of two singlets, then, the individual peaks would shift further apart on the chemical shift scale as shown below:

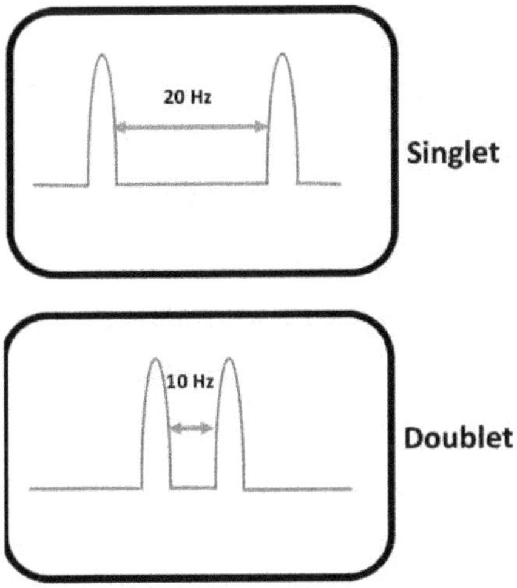

In the above example, if the peaks are doublets then the value of the coupling constant remains 10 Hz.

5.6.6.5 Unit of Coupling constant

The unit of a coupling constant is Hz and it is also referred as Cycles per second (CPS). The value of the coupling constant could be either positive or negative. The value of the coupling constant is a measure of interaction between neighbouring protons. When two spinning nuclei are in the opposite orientation then the energy is lower and the value of the constant is positive. However, if the spinning nuclei are in the same orientation, then, the energy is higher and the value of the constant is negative. The spacing between the split lines or the J constant between coupling protons is of the same magnitude. The J constant can be used for distinguishing, e.g., between two singlets and one doublet or two doublet and one quartet. There is no effect of the external magnetic field on the coupling constant.

5.6.6.6 Different types of couplings and their effects on the coupling constant

Geminal coupling: The word Geminal refers to the binding of two atoms or functional groups to the same carbon atom. J represents the geminal or 2-bond coupling constant. This also indicates that the hydrogens are linked by two bonds. In rare situations, two hydrogen atoms bonded to the same carbon atom might be in totally distinct electronic environments, resulting in different chemical shifts. These protons are referred to as geminal protons.

Vicinal Coupling: Vicinal protons are those which are separated by three bonds. In the molecule shown above, ii and iii are vicinal protons. The vicinal or 3 bond coupling constants is denoted by J. The hydrogen atoms are on the adjacent carbon atoms in vicinal coupling.

Long range coupling: In case the distance between two protons is more than three covalent bonds, the phenomenon of coupling does not occur. Yet, there would be some coupling if unsaturated or fluoro chemicals were present near the protons. Only a highly sensitive and high- resolution NMR spectrophotometer can detect this form of coupling.

5.6.6.7 Complex splitting patterns on NMR Spectrum

The NMR spectrum can sometimes have more complex splitting patterns than the simpler couplings involving equivalent coupling constants (such as doublet, triplet, quartet, quintet etc.). It may sometimes happen that each peak in a doublet (in an NMR spectrum) is further split into another peak. Such cases happen when a hydrogen atom is influenced by 2 adjacent non- equivalent hydrogen atoms. These complex patterns manifest as doublet of doublets, doublet of triplets, triplet of doublets etc.

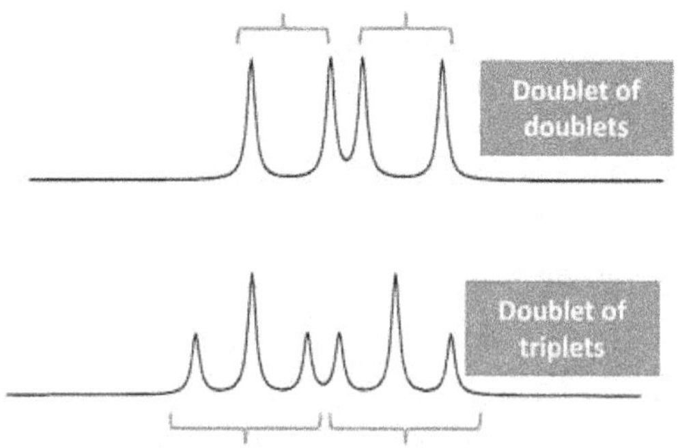

5.7 INTERPRETATION OF NMR SPECTRUM

The number spectrum gives several kinds of information:

1. The number of signals (peaks) tells us how many kinds of protons (protons with different chemical environments) are present in a molecule.
2. The position (chemical shift) of the signal informs about the bonding environment of each proton.
3. The area under each signal tells us how many protons of each kind are in the molecule.
4. All hydrogens with identical environments in a molecule have same chemical shift, e.g., (a) all the three protons of a methyl CH_3; (b) the protons of a methylene - CH_2; (c) one identical.
5. Protons on heteroatoms (H—S, H —N, H—O etc.) show highly variable chemical shifts and sometimes broad peaks.
6. Hydrogen on different carbons yields the same absorptional signal if they are structurally indistinguishable.
7. Sometimes a proton exhibits an absorption signal which is split into several peaks because of coupling with its neighbouring protons. In such cases a coupling constant J is calculated.
8. The number of peaks (N) into which a proton signal is split equals one more than the number of vicinal protons (n) (number of equivalent neighbours causing splitting):

$$N = n + 1$$

N = 2 (one vicinal H) = doublet (d)
= 3 (two vicinal H's) = triplet (t)
= 4 (three vicinal H's) = quartet (q). Example:

5.7.1 Spectrum of Isomers - Dimethyl Ether and Ethanol

The low-resolution spectra of isomers dimethyl ether and ethanol are shown in figures 5 (a) and (b). The spectrum of dimethyl ether shows only one signal because all 6H atoms are equivalent. The 3H atoms in a given CH_3 group are indistinguishable, as are the two CH_3 groups.

The spectrum of ethanol has three signals-one each for CH_3, CH_2 and OH protons. The relative areas under the peak for the ethanol are 3:2:1 for CH_3, CH_2, and OH groups respectively. CH_2 signal is far away than CH_3 signal because of electron withdrawing effect of two adjacent atoms.

In a high-resolution NMR spectrum of ethyl alcohol (CH_3—CH_2—OH), the methyl peak is associated with two peaks, white methylene and OH are associated with four and three peaks respectively.

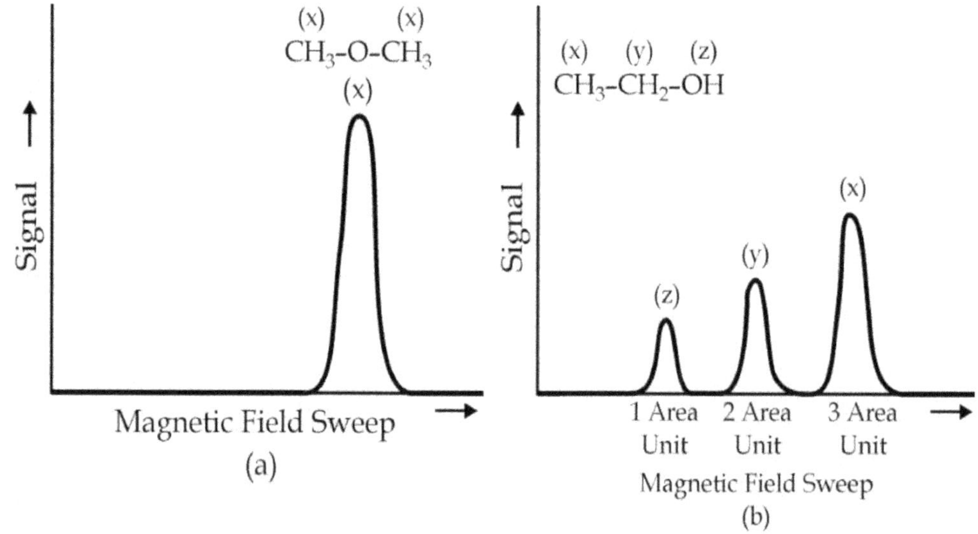

Figure 5.5 (a) and (b): NMR Spectra of Isomers Dimethyl Ether and Ethanol.

The three equivalent methyl protons are split into a triplet (1 + 2) by two equivalent methyl protons. Similarly, two equivalent methylene protons are split into a quartet (1 + 3) by three equivalent methyl protons.

5.8 APPLICATIONS OF NMR SPECTROSCOPY

Applications are summarized in following figure:

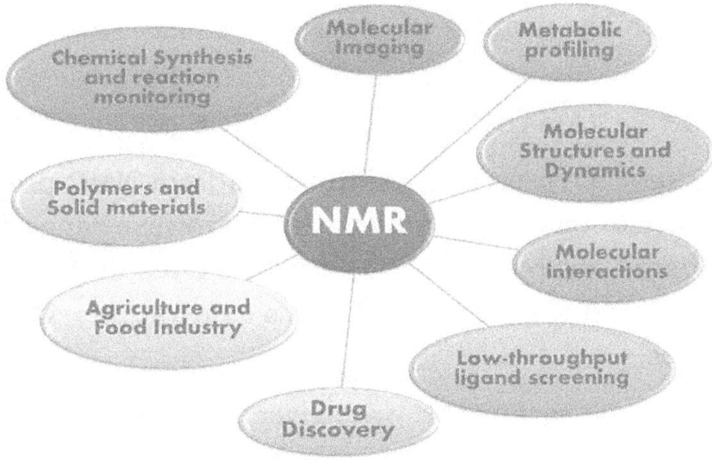

1. Quantitative Analysis:

The area of peak is directly proportional to the number of nuclei responsible for that peak. Thus, the concentration of species can be determined directly by making use of signal area per proton. The signal area per proton can easily be calculated by use of a known concentration of an internal standard.

Similarly, (he concentration of new species formed during the reaction can also be calculated from the spectrum of parent compound.

2. Qualitative Analysis:

The qualitative analysis of the compound can easily be made by knowing:

(i) Chemical shift δ values of hydrogen containing groups,
(ii) The presence of particular functional group,
(iii) The relative position of these groups and
(iv) The relative number of nuclei in these groups.

5.9 NUCLEAR MAGNETIC DOUBLE RESONANCE (NIVIDR)

When two oscillating magnetic fields are delivered to a material at the same time, the experiment is referred to as double resonance, double irradiation, or spin decoupling. A strong rf. field H2 is utilized to irradiate the sample in the standard nuclear magnetic double resonance experiment, whereas a mild rf. field H1 generates the observed transitions. We can sweep the magnetic field while maintaining constant HI and H2.

5.10 ELECTRON PARAMAGNETIC RESONANCE (EPR)

Electron paramagnetic resonance (EPR) varies from NMR primarily in that electron resonance frequencies occur in the microwave range with magnetic fields on the order of several thousand gauss. As a result, for the sample, the EPR spectrometer employs components such as Klystrons, wave guides, and resonance cavities.

The EPR technique is suitable whenever a chemical has at least one unpaired electron, such as in free radicals, crystalline and amorphous materials that have been irradiated, or transition element ions and rare earths that have some chelates. Metals, odd compounds, graphite, and semiconductor contaminants are among more examples.

5.10.1 FT-NMR

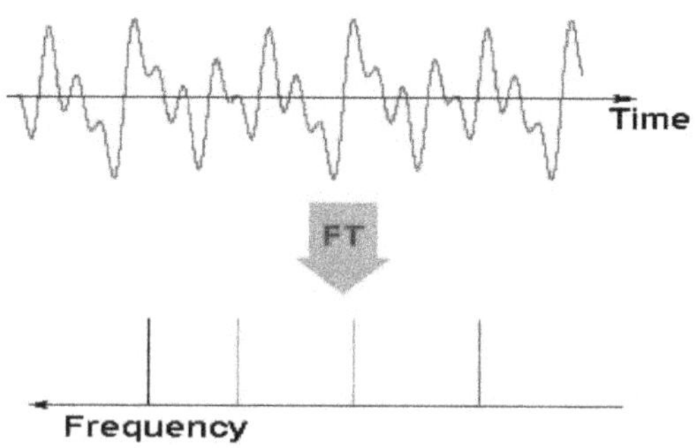

It is mathematical operation in which the complex waveform is broken down into simple mathematical operations. It is the mathematical operation required to convert a time domain spectrum to frequency domain spectrum (or viseversa). Following an S/N ration, digital data must be transformed into the frequency data. FT NMR or pulse NMR the sample irradiated periodically with brief, highly intense pulses of radio frequency radiation, following which the free induction delay signal –a characteristic radio frequency emission signal stimulated by irradiation is recorded as function of time. The frequency domain spectrum can be obtained by Fourier transform employing a digital computer.

5.10.2 C_{13} NMR

Nuclear magnetic resonance concerns the magnetic properties of certain atomic nuclei. It concerns with atom having spin quantum number.

C_{12} is not magnetic active due to zero spin quantum number while C_{13} is magnetic active due to ½ spin quantum number and this NMR technique is quite effective as compared to proton NMR.

CHAPTER 6 MASS SPECTROSCOPY

6.1 INTRODUCTION

Mass spectrometry (MS) is an analytical method for determining the mass-to- charge ratio of particles. It is used to determine particle masses and the elemental composition of a sample or molecule. The MS concept entails ionising chemical compounds to produce charge molecules or molecule fragments and measuring their mass-to-charge ratio using one of many procedures. Mass spectrometry is an effective approach for identifying unknowns, investigating molecular structure, and probing fundamental chemical principles. Mass spectrometry is an effective analytical method used to measure known materials, identify new chemicals within a sample, and elucidate the structure and chemical characteristics of various molecules. The material is transformed into gaseous ions during the whole process, either with or without fragmentation, and these ions are then classified according to their relative abundances and mass to charge ratios (m/z). This method essentially investigates how molecules are affected by ionising radiation. The consumption of sample molecules during the formation of ionic and neutral species depends on chemical reactions occurring in the gas phase.

6.2 PRINCIPLE

Multiple ions are produced from the material under study by a mass spectrometer, which subsequently separates them based on their unique mass-to-charge ratios (m/z) and records the relative abundance of each ion type.

The production of gas phase ions of the compound—basically, via electron ionization—is the initial step in the mass spectrometric examination of substances. This molecular ion undergoes fragmentation.

Fragmentation occurs in turn for each major product ion formed from the molecular ion, and so on. The mass spectrometer separates the ions based on their mass to-charge ratio, and they are detected in relation to their abundance. This leads to the generation of the molecule's mass spectrum. It presents the outcome as a plot of ion abundance against mass- to-charge ratio. Ions reveal details about the makeup and structure of their progenitor molecule. The molecular ion, if present, reveals the molecular mass of a pure substance by appearing in the spectrum at the highest value of m/z (followed by ions with heavier isotopes).

6.3 INSTRUMENTATION

A. Sample Inlet

A pinhole known as a "molecular leak" allows molecules from a large reservoir where a sample is stored to flow steadily and at low pressure into the ionisation chamber.

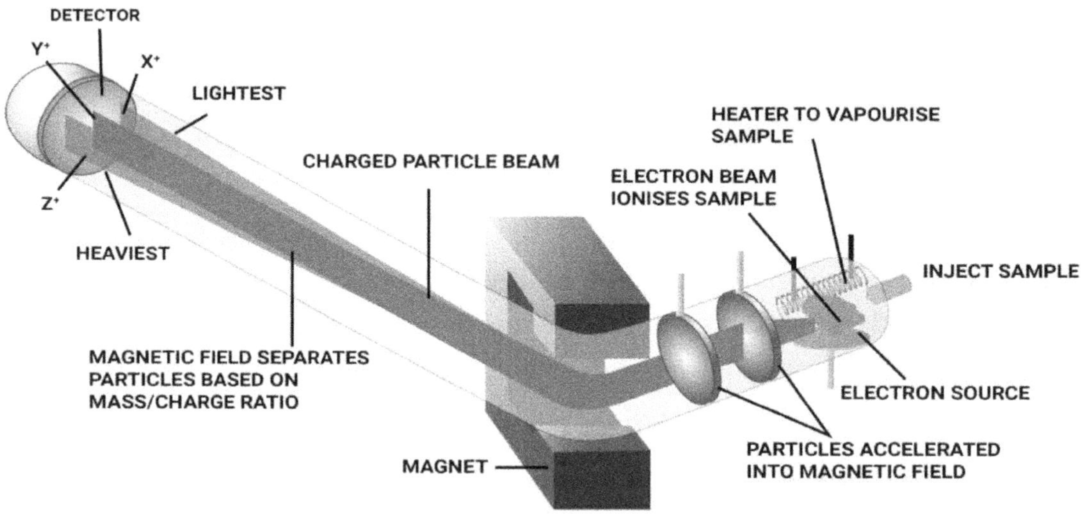

Figure 6.1: Mass Spectrophotometer.

B. Ionization

Atoms are ionised by being bombarded with an electron stream, which removes one or more electrons to produce positive ions. The majority of the newly produced positive ions will have a charge of +1.

Ionization can be accomplished by:

Electron Ionization (EI-MS)

It is the most popular and advanced technique. It is often referred to as electron ionisation or electron bombardment. An ionising chamber that is kept at a temperature of 200 ± 0.25 degrees and a pressure of 0.005 torr makes up an electron impact ionisation source. The location of the electron gun is perpendicular to the chamber.

Thermionic Emission causes a blazing filament to emit electrons, which are then accelerated by a 70 V potential put between the filament and anode. Through positively charged slits in the ionisation chamber, these electrons are pulled. The energy and temperature of the filament determine how many electrons are present. The sample is heated to a level where molecular vapours start to form. The gaseous neutral molecules enter the ionisation chamber after passing through the molecular leaks. In the chamber, the gaseous sample and the electrons collide at right angles, and as a result of the energy exchanged during these collisions between the electron beam and the sample molecules, ions are created.

Chemical Ionization (CI-MS)

Ionization of Chemicals In chemical ionisation, the analyte is made ionised by its molecules interacting with ions of a reagent gas in the source or chamber. A device comparable to an electron impact ion source is modified for chemical ionisation by adding a vacuum pump, for example-

- Addition of a vacuum pump.
- Narrowing of exit slit to mass analyzer to maintain reagent gas pressure of about 1 torr in the ionization chamber.
- Providing a gas inlet.

It involves two steps. Step-I the source of the reagent gas undergoes electron impact ionisation to ionise it. Stabilized reagent ions are created when the main ions of the reagent gas interact with additional gas. Step-II Sample molecules and reagent ions interact to generate molecular ions. In this method, a significant amount of reagent gas is used to dilute the sample. Low molecular weight molecules including methane, tertiary isobutane, ammonia, nitrous oxide, oxygen, and hydrogen are among the gases that are frequently utilised as reagents.

Desorption Technique (FAB)

Fast Atom Bombardment It is an ionization technique in which the analyte and non- volatile liquid matrix mixture is bombarded by a high energy beam of inert gas such as Argon or Xenon. Polypeptides and other polar high molecular weight molecules are ionised using this method. Commonly used matrices include: - Glycerol Monothioglycerol Carbowax 2,4 – dipentyl phenol 3 – nitrobenzyl alcohol (3 – NBA) These solvents easily dissolve organic compounds and do note vaporate in vacuum. The bombarding beam consists of Xenon or Argon atoms of high translational energy. This beam is produced by first ionizing the Xenon (or Argon atoms with electrons to give Xenon radical cations.

A. Acceleration

- Ions are accelerated so that they all have same kinetic e n e r g y.
- Positive ions pass through 3 slits with voltage in decreasing order.
- Middle slit carries intermediate and finals at zero volts.

B. Mass Analyser

Ion separator is another name for a mass analyzer. The heart of the mass spectrometer, the mass analyzer separates ionised masses according to charge to mass ratios. These qualities are necessary for mass analyzers.

i. It should have a high resolution.

ii. It must have a high rate of transmission of ions. Types of mass analyzers.

A. Quadrupole Mass Analyzer

B. Time of Flight Analyzer (TOF)

C. Magnetic Sector Mass Analyzer

D. Single focusing

E. Double Focusing

F. Quadrupole Ion Trap Mass Analyzer

G. Ion Cyclotron Resonances

A. Quadrupole Mass Analyzer

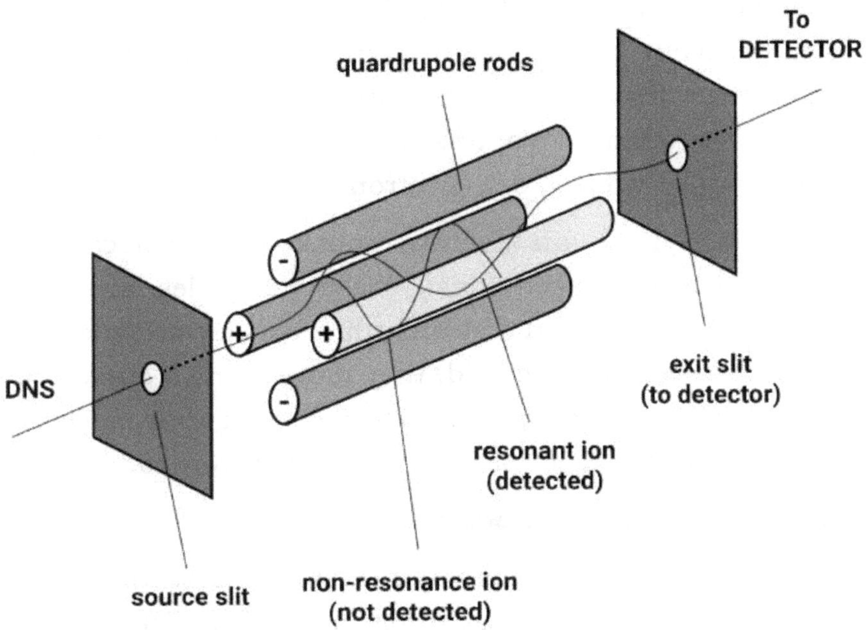

Figure 6.2: Quadrupole Mass Analyzer.

It has 4 rods that carry the voltage. Ions are transferred from one end to the other. The voltage and RF complex oscillations will occur during this application. The single positive charge ions present here exhibits stable oscillations. Mass scanning is carried out by varying each of there and voltage frequencies ratios keeping their ratio constant. It stores the unsorted ions temporarily, they released to the detector by scanning the electric field.

B. Time of Flight Analyzer (TOF)

Ion sorting is carried out in this kind of analyzer without the use of a magnetic field. The ions produced are acquiring different velocities depending on their masses. The particles arrive at the detector in ascending mass order. A detector with an electron multiplier is utilized here. This has a resolution power of 500–600.

C. Single Focusing Magnetic Sector Mass Analyzer

It has an evacuated horseshoe-shaped glass tube with a sample intake, an electron bombardment source, accelerating plates on one end, and a collector slit on the other. There is a facility to apply an electric or magnetic field at the tube's curvature. Vaporized sample is introduced through the intake and bombarded with a 70eV electron beam.

Every molecule is given an electron knockout, which causes them to change into positively charged ions. These molecules are propelled by accelerating plates and move in a straight line as they become +ve charged. By using an electric or magnetic field, they move along a curved route while the molecular ions are sorted and collected based on their masses. Different fragments fall on detector then mass spectrum is recorded.

D. Double Focusing Magnetic Sector Mass Analyzer

This type is employed to distinguish the small mass differences of the fragment. This offers the high resolution. To accomplish better focusing, energy has to be reduced before ions are allowed to enter the magnetic field and increase resolving power can be obtained two mass analyzers in series. In a double- focusing mass analyzer beam is first passes radial Electrostatic field.

E. Quadrupole Ion Trap Mass Analyzers

Similar to the quadrupole analyzer stated above, this analyzer utilizes an electric field to separate the ions according to their mass to charge ratios. An electrode ring with a particular voltage and grounded end cap electrodes make up the analyzer.

Through one of the end caps, the ions get into the space in between the electrodes. Ions with a given m/z value orbit in space after entering the cavity due to the electric field created by the electrodes. As the radio frequency voltage rises, heavier mass ion orbits become more stabilized and the light mass ions become less stabilized, causing them to collide with the wall, and eliminating the possibility of traveling to and being detected by the detector.

F. Ion Cyclotron Resonances

Ions are trapped inside of an ion trap called an ICR by use of a magnetic field. Instead of separation taking place in this analyzer, all the ions in a certain range are trapped within, and an applied external electric field aids in the production of a signal. As mentioned earlier, when a moving charge enters a magnetic field, it experiences a centripetal force making the ion orbit. Again, the force on the ion due to the magnetic field is equal to the centripetal force on the ion.

G. Detector

- The beam of ions passing through the mass analyser is detected by detector on the basis of m/e ratio.
- When an ion hit the metal box, charge is neutralized by an electron jumping from metal on to the ion.
- Types of Detector

1. Faraday Cup Detector

A faraday cup is based on the theory that a change in charge on a metal plate causes an electron flow, which in turn generates a current. A single ion contacting the Faraday cup's surface causes a number of secondary electrons to be expelled and momentarily displaced. When an ion contacts the cup, this brief electron emission causes a current to flow through it and results in a modest signal amplification. Although robust and simple in construction, this detector is rather insensitive.

2. Electron Multiplier or Photo Multiplier

An electron multiplier is composed of a series of surfaces kept at steadily increasing potentials, as opposed to a Faraday cup, which employs a single surface. Ions collide with the surface, releasing electrons as a consequence. A cascade of electrons is finally produced when these secondary electrons are drawn to the subsequent surface, where further secondary electrons are produced. An electron multiplier typically has a current gain or amplification of one million.

Photomultiplier Dynode:

When an electron strikes a phosphorous screen with a photomultiplier conversion detector, photons are released. A photomultiplier, which works in a manner similar to an electron multiplier's cascading action, is then used to detect these photons. The photomultiplier tube is enclosed in a vacuum and is not exposed to the mass spectrometer's internal environment, which is the main benefit of the conversion dynode setup.

3. Micro Channel Plate (Array detector)

An array of glass capillaries (10–25 nm inner diameters) coated on the inside with an electron emissive substance make up a micro channel plate. Similar to the channel tron, the capillaries are biased at a high voltage, and when an ion hits the inside of one of the capillaries, an outburst of secondary electrons occurs. The output of this cascading effect generates a current pulse with a gain of 103–104.

Resolution

The ability of mass spectrophotometer to separate the ions of different mass to charge ratio reaching to the detector is described as resolving power (resolution). The resolution of mass spectrometer depends on two factors: Mass dispersion and beam width at the focal plane. The two beams are said to be resolved, when the beam dispersion is greater than the beam width. The dispersion of mass analyser is determined by its optics which cannot be changed. The beam width can be improved by reducing the width of the source and collector slits. Narrow slits give high resolution but an increase in the resolution is accomplished by a decrease in the sensitivity of the mass spectrometer since the number of ions arriving at the collector is reduced by the use of narrow slit width.

The resolving power of a mass spectrometer necessary to separate two ions of mass M and M+ ΔM giving adjacent peaks of approximately equal intensity is defined as

$$R = \frac{M}{\Delta M}$$

Where, ΔM = difference between the two mass numbers

The peaks are said to be resolved when the valley between them is less a certain percentage of the peaks themselves. Generally, the resolution is expressed for 2% or 10% valley.

6.4 TYPES OF THE ION PRODUCED

The different types of ions are produced in the mass spectrometry for example Molecular ions, fragment ions, rearrangement ions, metastable ions, multiple charged ions, isotope ions and negative ions.

6.4.1 Molecular Ion (Parent Ion)

If the electron beam energy is excess than ionisation potential electrons may be ejected from a lower lying molecular orbital leading to the formation of ions called molecular or parent ion.

$$\mathbf{M + e \longrightarrow M^{+} + 2e^{-}}$$

Thus, molecular ions are formed in the ground state and in electronically excited states. The yield of the molecular ions can be increased by increasing the electron beam energy. The mass of such ions is given the molecular weight of the sample and also it is possible to determine molecular formula. The molecular ion patterns also give information regarding the number and nature of the types of atoms with characteristic isotope abundance present in the molecule. Hence molecular ions are most important of all types of ions in mass spectrum. The molecular ion is located at high mass region of the mass spectrum.

The stability of the parent ion will determine its relative abundance with respect to the fragment ions. Its abundance can be increased by running the spectrum at low ionisation energy. Aromatic compounds give rise to very intense molecular ion peak because of the presence of π electron system. A molecular ion containing unsaturated functional groups will be more stable than that with saturated functional group. In aliphatic compounds branching results in the decrease in the abundance in the parent peak.

6.4.2 Rearrangement Ions

Fragment ions formed by the intermolecular rearrangements involving migration of hydrogen atoms from one part of the ion to another are called rearrangement ions. Rearrangement processes are common in unsaturated compounds and are favoured even at low electron voltage.

The most common type of rearrangement involves intramolecular migration of hydrogen in molecules containing heteroatom. The "McLafferty rearrangement" is a common example. It involves the migration of a ϒ-hydrogen followed by cleavage of β bond and leads to the eliminations of a molecule, ketones, aldehydes, amines, substituted aromatic compounds etc., show this type of rearrangement. Example- in case of carbonyl compound.

6.4.3 Metastable Ions

The peaks produced by ions in mass spectrum are usually sharp and well defined. However, a mass spectrum occasionally shows some diffused, broad, low intensity peaks usually at non-integral masses. These peaks are due to metastable ions.

If the ion m, produced in the ions source is very stable, it remains under composed during its passage through the accelerator, deflector and to the detector. On the other hand, if m is very unstable, it immediately decomposes into smaller fragments in the ion source and each of the fragment ion is deflected and recorded separately according to its m/e ratio. However, when the ions of intermediate stability undergo fragmentation during or immediately after acceleration but prior to magnetic deflection. These ions will give rise to weak and diffused peaks at non- integral masses, called metastable peaks.

A flat top metastable peak show that kinetic energy is released during the fragmentation process.

6.4.4 Multiple Charged Ions

The removal of two or more electrons from a molecule without fragmentation is possible in case of organic compounds with aromatic rings and compounds containing conjugated systems. Thus, the ions may exist with two or three charges instead of the single charge. They are called as double, triple or multi charged ions. The doubly charged parent ions are formed by the loss of two electrons. They appear at half the mass of the molecular ion. A triple charged ions formed by the loss of three electrons from the neutral molecule and will occur at 1/3 of its actual mass since, it carries three positive charges.

6.4.5 Isotope Ions

Most elements are mixture of two or more stable isotopes differing by one or two mass units. Chlorine and bromine have two isotopes (^{35}Cl, ^{37}Cl and ^{79}Br, ^{81}Br) in the ratios 3:1 and 1:1 respectively. Similarly, elements like carbon, hydrogen, oxygen, sulphur etc. have one major isotope which is more than 90% abundant and a minor abundant. Fluorine, phosphorous and iodine are monoisotopic elements. The presence of these elements in a molecule is often recognized by the characteristic isotopic clusters observed in the spectrum. Thus, in the spectrum of methyl bromide the molecular ion peak is a doublet consisting of two equally intense peaks one at m/e 94 ($CH_3\,^{79}Br$) and the other at m/e 96 ($CH_3\,^{81}Br$). These isotopic clusters are referred to as isotopic peaks. They are helpful in determining the presence of such elements in a molecule.

6.5 MASS SPECTRUM

The plot of relative abundance or intensity on the ordinate vs the m/e ratio on the abscissa represents the mass spectrum of an organic molecule. The intensity of other peaks is stated relative to the base peak, which is the most intense peak in the mass spectrum and is given the value of 100. The base peak in most of the cases is due to the molecular ion and helpful in determining the molecular weight of the compound. Following are some example of mass spectrum. Mass spectrum of ethylbenzene

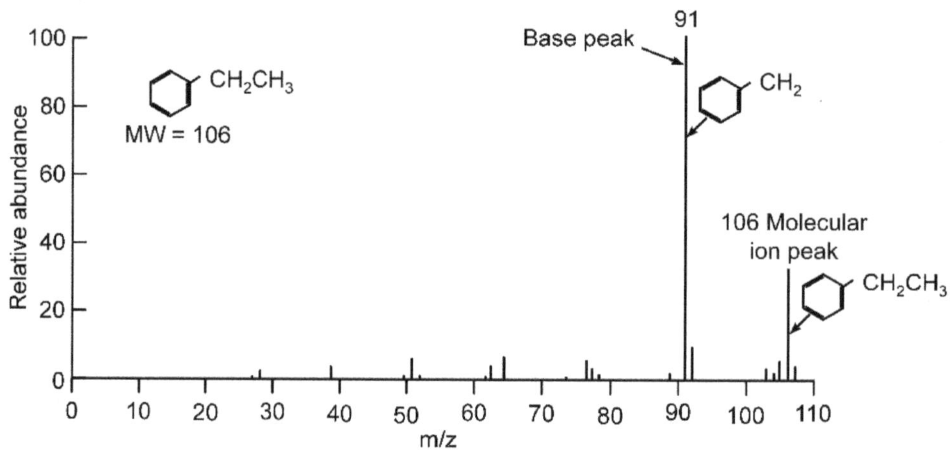

6.5.1 Fragmentation Patterns

A stream of electrons is directed towards the vaporised organic sample as it enters the mass spectrometer's ionisation chamber. These electrons are powerful enough to remove an electron from an organic molecule, resulting in the formation of a positive ion. This ion is called the molecular ion – or sometimes the parent ion and is often given the symbol M^+ or $M^{+\bullet}$. The dot in this second version represents the fact that somewhere in the ion there will be a single unpaired electron. That's one half of what was originally a pair of electrons - the other half is the electron which was removed in the ionization process.

Due to their energy instability, some of the molecular ions will fragment into smaller parts. A molecule ion can split into two components in the simplest situation, one of which is another positive ion and the other is an uncharged free radical.

$$M^{+}_{\bullet} \longrightarrow X^{+} + Y\bullet$$

A line on the mass spectrum won't be produced by the neutral free radical. The mass spectrometer will only accelerate, deflect, and detect charged particles. These uncharged particles will only float around in the device until the vacuum pump ultimately removes them.

The ion, X^{+}, will travel through the mass spectrometer just like any other positive ion - and will produce a line on the stick diagram. All sorts of fragmentations of the original molecular ion are possible - and that means that you will get a whole host of lines in the mass spectrum. For example, the mass spectrum of pentane looks like this:

Simplified mass spectrum of pentane- $CH_3CH_2CH_2CH_2CH_3$

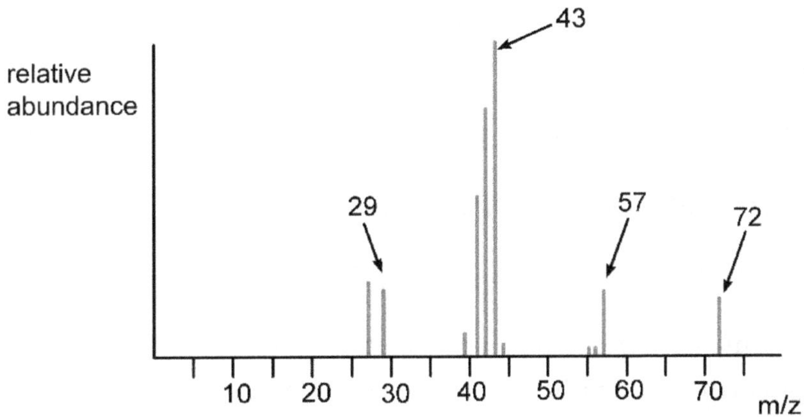

In the above diagram showing the mass spectrum of pentane, the line produced by the heaviest ion passing through the machine (at m/z = 72) is due to the molecular ion. The tallest line in the stick diagram (in this case at m/z = 43) is called the base peak. This is usually given an arbitrary height of 100, and the height of everything else is measured relative to this. The base peak is the tallest peak because it represents the commonest fragment ion to be formed-either because there are several ways in which it could be produced during fragmentation of the parent ion, or because it is a particularly stable ion. Again, we take the example of n-pentane C_5H_{12}

Solution of mass spectrum of n-pentane by using fragmentation pattern.

Question 1: What causes the line at m/z = 57?

Question 2: How many carbon atoms are there in this ion?

There cannot be 5 because 5 × 12 = 60. What about 4? 4 × 12 = 48. That leaves 9 to make up a total of 57. How about $C_4H_9^+$ then?

$C_4H_9^+$ would be $[CH_3 CH_2 CH_3 CH_2]^+$, and this would be produced by the following fragmentation:

$$[CH_3CH_2CH_2CH_2CH_3]^{+\bullet} \longrightarrow [CH_3CH_2CH_2CH_2]^+ + \bullet CH_3$$

The methyl radical produced will simply get lost in the machine.

The line at m/z = 43 can be worked out similarly. If you play around with the numbers, you will find that this corresponds to a break producing a 3-carbon ion:

$$[CH_3CH_2CH_2CH_2CH_3]^{+\bullet} \longrightarrow [CH_3CH_2CH_2]^+ + \bullet CH_2CH_3$$

The line at m/z = 29 is typical of an ethyl ion, $[CH_3CH_2]^+$:

$$[CH_3CH_2CH_2CH_2CH_3]^{+\bullet} \longrightarrow [CH_3CH_2]^+ + \bullet CH_2CH_2CH_3$$

The other lines in the mass spectrum are more difficult to explain. For example, lines with m/z values 1 or 2 less than one of the easy lines are often due to loss of one or more hydrogen atoms during the fragmentation process.

Another Example Pentane-3-one

This time the base peak (the tallest peak-and so the commonest fragment ion) is at m/z =57. But this is not produced by the same ion as the same m/z value peak in pentane.

Simplified mass spectrum of pentan-3-one – $CH_3CH_2COCH_2CH_3$

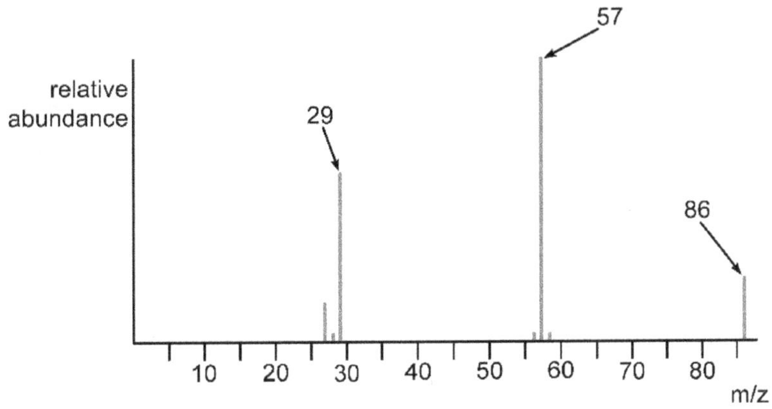

Fig: 6.3

If you remember, the m/z = 57 peak in pentane was produced by $[CH_3CH_2CH_2CH_2]^+$. If you look at the structure of pentan-3-one, it's impossible to get that particular fragment from it.

Work along the molecule mentally chopping bits off until you come up with something that adds up to 57. With a small amount of patience, you'll eventually find $[CH_3CH_2CO]^+$ - which is produced by this fragmentation:

$$[CH_3CH_2COCH_2CH_3]^{+\bullet} \longrightarrow [CH_3CH_2CO]^+ + \bullet CH_2CH_3$$

You would get exactly the same products whichever side of the CO group you split the molecular ion. The m/z = 29 peak is produced by the ethyl ion - which once again could be formed by splitting the molecular ion either side of the CO group.

$$[CH_3CH_2COCH_2CH_3]^{+\bullet} \longrightarrow [CH_3CH_2]^+ + \bullet COCH_2CH_3$$

6.5.2 McLafferty Rearrangements

Few fragments are the consequence of several bonds being broken. One example is the removal of water from an alcohol. The nitrogen rule can be used to spot peaks that result from a rearrangement. If a molecular ion has an even molecular weight, then a rearrangement often produced peaks with an even molecular weight. A molecule's rearrangement peaks will also be odd if it has an odd molecular weight. The removal of water from a primary alcohol is one rearrangement. But anol is used to demonstrate the mechanism. The low energy transitions in these rearrangements are preferred because they aid in product stabilization.

Examples of McLafferty Rearrangement

An example of McLafferty rearrangement is the fragmentation of 2-hexanone, producing acetone enol radical cation and a neutral molecule of propene. Other examples include carboxylic acid and ester

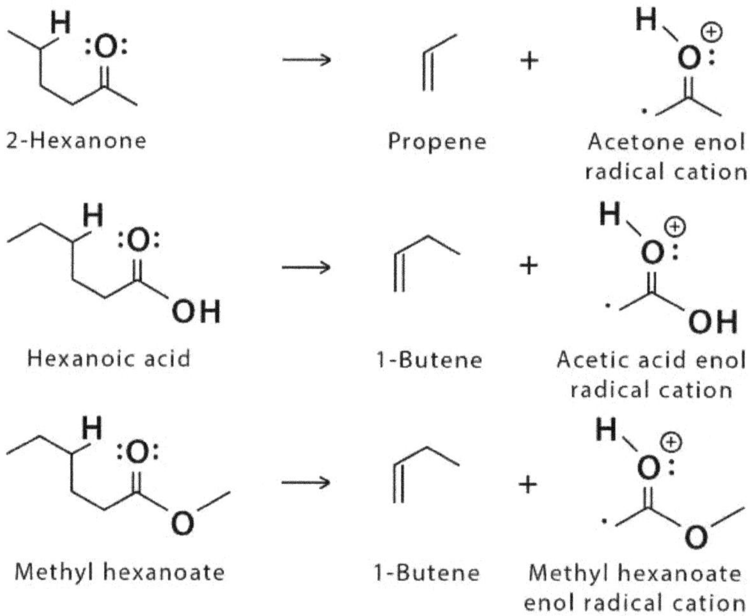

6.6 APPLICATION OF MASS SPECTROSCOPY

- **Analysis of Biomolecules using Mass Spectrometry:** Mass spectrometry is rapidly becoming a must-have tool for studying biomolecules. Until the 1970s, the only analytical procedures that offered comparable data were electrophoretic, chromatographic, or ultracentrifugation. Because the conclusions were dependent on factors other than molecular weight, they were not absolute. As a result, the only way to determine a macromolecule's actual molecular weight was through a computation based on its chemical structure.

The introduction of desorption ionisation techniques based on the emission of pre-existing ions, such as plasma desorption (PD), rapid atom bombardment (FAB), or laser desorption (LD), enabled mass spectrometry to be used to analyse complex biomolecules.

- **Analysis of Glycans:** Oligosaccharides are molecules that are generated by the joining of multiple monosaccharides connected by glycosidic linkages. The full structure of oligosaccharides is more difficult to determine than that of proteins or oligonucleotides. It entails the identification of extra components as a result of the isomeric character of monosaccharides and their ability to create linear or branched oligosaccharides. The structure of an oligosaccharide must be determined not only by its monosaccharide sequence and branching pattern, but also by the isomer position and anomeric configuration of each of its glycosidic linkages. Glycobiology advances encompass a thorough examination of the structure, biosynthesis, and biology of sugars and saccharides and mass spectrometry is developing as a transformative technique in glycomics and glycobiology.
- **Analysis of Lipids:** Numerous kinds of distinct compounds that are soluble in organic solvents make up lipids. A significant component of metabolomics is lipidomics, which is the comprehensive study and global characterization of the structure and function of lipids (the lipidome) inside a biological system, both spatially and temporally.

CHAPTER 7 CHROMATOGRAPHY

7.1 INTRODUCTION

The Russian-Italian botanist M. S. Tswett devised chromatography, a physicochemical technique for separating complicated mixtures, at the very beginning of the 20th century. Few reliable chromatographic techniques were commercially accessible for laboratory scientists until the 1970s. In the 1970s, a number of methods, such as open-column chromatography, paper chromatography, and thin-layer chromatography, were used to perform the majority of chemical separations. These chromatographic methods, however, could not provide sufficient resolution between similar compounds or for compound quantification.

Nowadays, chromatography is a very flexible technology that can separate gases, volatile substances, and in-volatile chemicals from materials with extremely high molecular weights (including biopolymers) using GC, in-volatile chemicals, and materials using LC, and if necessary, very cheaply using TLC.

7.2 VARIOUS TYPES OF CHROMATOGRAPHY

Chromatography can be categorized in several ways.

(I) Techniques based on solute-stationary phase interaction,

(II) Techniques based on chromatographic bed shape, and

(III) Techniques based on mobile phase physical state.

7.3 TECHNIQUES BASED ON SOLUTE-STATIONARY PHASE INTERACTION

7.3.1 Adsorption Chromatography

One of the most traditional forms of chromatography is likely the adsorption chromatography. It makes use of a mobile liquid or gaseous phase that has been adsorbed onto a surface of stationary solid phase. The separation of various solutes is caused by the equilibrium between the mobile and stationary phases.

7.3.2 Partition Chromatography

This chromatography technique is based on the formation of a thin film by a liquid stationary phase on the surface of a solid support. Between the stationary liquid and the mobile phase, the solute reaches equilibrium.

7.3.3 Ion exchange Chromatography

Anions or cations are covalently attached to a resin (the stationary solid phase) in this form of chromatography. Electrostatic forces cause solute ions with the opposite charge in the mobile liquid phase to be drawn to the resin.

7.4 ON THE BASIS OF CHROMATOGRAPHIC BED SHAPE

7.4.1 Column Chromatography

In the separation method known as column chromatography, the stationary bed is contained inside a tube. The mobile phase may have an open, unconstrained passage through the center of the tube while the solid stationary phase or support covered with a liquid stationary phase fills the whole interior volume of the tube (packed column) or is centered or along the interior tube wall (open tubular column). Different retention durations for the sample are determined based on variations in sample movement speeds through the medium.

7.4.2 Paper Chromatography

A little dot or line of sample solution is applied to a strip of chromatography paper as part of the paper chromatography procedure. The paper is put inside a sealed jar with a thin coating of solvent. The sample mixture begins to ascend the paper with the solvent as it climbs through the paper and meets it. Because the cellulose in this paper is polar, non- polar compounds within the mixture move more slowly. More polar chemicals easily bind with the cellulose paper and hence do not travel quite far.

7.4.3 Thin Layer Chromatography

Similar to paper chromatography, thin layer chromatography (TLC) is a common laboratory method. However, it uses a stationary phase comprising a thin layer of adsorbent like silica gel, alumina, or cellulose over a flat, inert substrate, in contrast to employing paper as the stationary phase. Faster runs, better separations, and the option of multiple adsorbents are advantages over paper. High-performance TLC can be employed for even better resolution and for enabling quantification.

CHAPTER 8 PAPER CHROMATOGRAPHY

8.1 INTRODUCTION

Paper chromatography is a sort of chromatography method that takes place on a sheet of specialized paper. It is a planar chromatography technique in which cellulose filter paper serves as a stationary phase for chemical separation.

8.2 PRINCIPLE OF PAPER CHROMATOGRAPHY

The underlying principle is partition chromatography, in which the compounds are spread or partitioned between liquid phases. Water is held in two phases: the stationary phase, which travels over the filter paper, and the mobile phase, which is held in the pores of the paper. When the mobile phase moves under the capillary action of paper pores, the compounds in the mixture separate as a result of variations in their affinities for water (in the stationary phase) and other solvents (in the mobile phase). The concept can be adsorption chromatography also, in which thestationary phase is the solid surface of paper and the mobile phase is the liquid. However, the majority of paper chromatography applications use the partition chromatography concept, which partitions the sample into two liquid phases.

8.3 USES AND APPLICATIONS OF PAPER CHROMATOGRAPHY

1. Paper chromatography is particularly useful for polar and non-polar chemical separation in mixtures.
2. For amino acid separation.
3. It is employed to identify organic substances, biochemicals, etc., in urine.
4. It is employed in the pharmaceutical industry to determine hormones, drugs, etc.
5. It is occasionally used to evaluate inorganic substances like salts and complexes.

8.4 TYPES OR MODES OF PAPER CHROMATOGRAPHY

We have, generally, five different types of chromatography based on the methods used to develop chromatograms on paper.

1. **Ascending Chromatography:** The chromatogram ascends, just like its name suggests. Here, the movement of the solvent or upward movement on the paper causes the development of the paper. The beaker's bottom contains the solvent reservoir. The sample areas on the paper tip just barely touch the bottom of the solvent, keeping them considerably above it. Figure 1 depicts the ascending chromatography procedure.

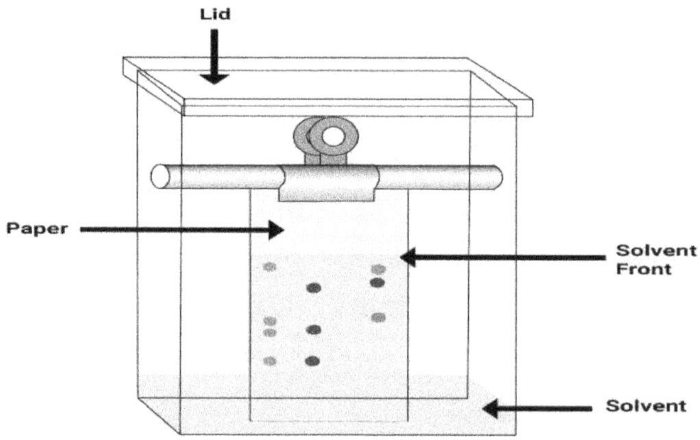

Figure 8.1: Ascending Paper Chromatography.

2. **Descending chromatography**: In this, the paper develops as a result of solvent moving downwardly across the paper. The reservoir for the solvent is at the top. In addition to capillary action, gravity also aids in the transport of the solvent. Here the development of paper occurs due to solvent travel downwards on the paper.

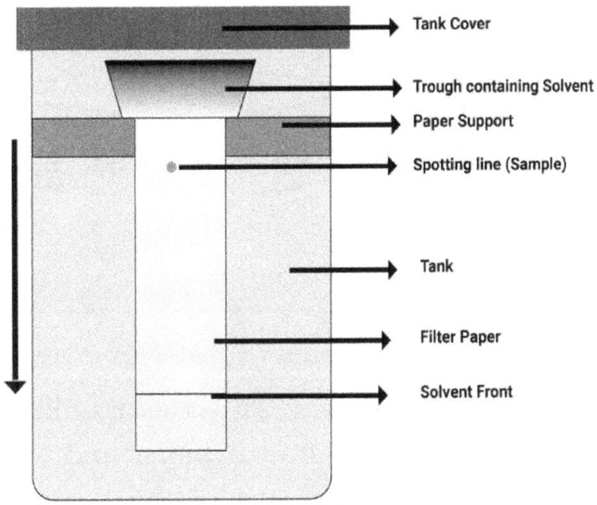

Figure 8.2: Descending Paper Chromatography.

3. **Ascending-descending mode**: Here solvent first travels upwards and then downwards on the paper.

4. **Radial mode**: Here, the solvent moves outward from the middle (midpoint) of the circular chromatography paper toward the edges. The entire setup is placed in a covered petri dish to facilitate the chromatogram development.

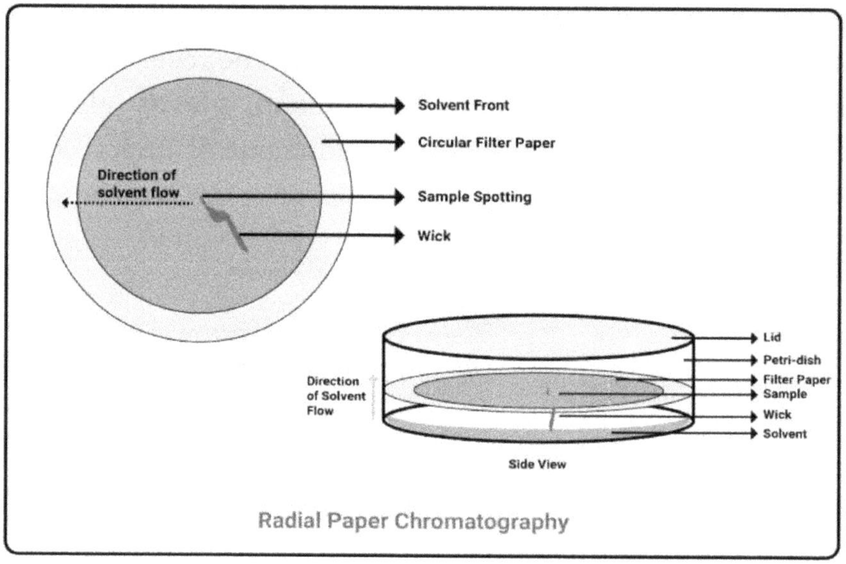

Figure 8.3: Radial or Circular Paper Chromatography.

The paper's central wick is dipped into the mobile phase of a petri dish, causing the solvent to drain onto the paper and transport the sample radially to produce concentric rings out of the sample spots of various compounds.

5. Two-dimensional Chromatography

The chromatogram develops in two directions at right angles here.

Samples are spotted on one corner of rectangle paper and allowed to develop for the first time in this mode. For the second chromatogram, the paper is submerged in mobile phase again, this time at a right angle to the previous development.

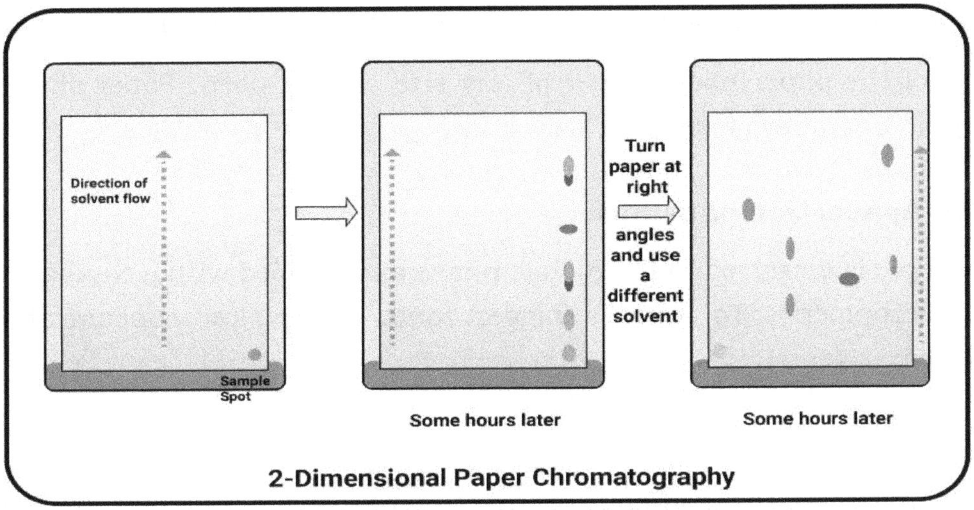

Figure 8.4: 2-Dimensional Paper Chromatography.

8.5 PROCEDURE IN PAPER CHROMATOGRAPHY

8.5.1 Selection of Papers and Stationary Phase Used

Chromatographic grade paper is composed of α-cellulose-98.99%, β-cellulose 0.3-1%, pentosans-0.4-0.8%, ether soluble matter- 0.015-0.02%, ash-0.01-0.07%. Whatmann filter papers consist of different grade like No.1, No.2, No.3, No.4, No.17, No. 20 etc. are used. These papers are differing in sizes, shapes, porosities and thickness.

- Choice of filter paper depends upon thickness, flow rate, purity, technique etc.
- Modified papers- acid or base washed filter paper, glass fibre type paper
- Hydrophilic papers- papers modified with methanol, formamide, glycol, glycerol etc.
- Hydrophobic papers- acetylation of OH groups lead to hydrophobic nature, hence can be used for reverse phase chromatography. Silicone pre-treatment and organic non-polar polymers can also be impregnated to give reverse phase chromatographic mode.

- Impregnation of silica, alumina or ion exchange resins can also be made.
- Size of the paper used: Paper of any size can be used. Paper should be kept in chamber of suitable size

8.5.2 Application of Sample

The sample is dissolved in the mobile phase and applied with a capillary tube or a micropipette. To avoid a bigger zone, a very low concentration is employed.

8.5.3 Mobile Phase

The solubility of the compounds to be separated influences the solvent selection. The compounds to be separated can be classified based on their functional groups.

8.5.3.1 Strongly Hydrophilic Groups

hydroxyl, carboxyl, and primary amino groups,

8.5.3.2 Moderately Hydrophillic Groups

Carbonyl, ether, ester and tertiary amino groups,

8.5.3.3 Hydrophobic Groups

alkyl groups and aromatic nuclei.

If a substance with a hydrophillic group moves too slowly, the hydrophillic character of the solvent must be increased for instance by using a solvent mixture which contains acetic acid

If the substance moves too rapidly, a loss hydrophillic system has to be selected e.g., light petroleum methanol-water mixtures. Some of the examples of mobile phase are- Isopropanol: Ammonia: Water - 9:1:2 n-Butanol: Glacial acetic acid: water- 4:1:5Methanol: water- 3:1 or 4:1

8.5.3.4 Development Technique- The following different techniques are applied for the development of the chromatograms.

8.5.3.4.1 Descending

8.5.3.4.2 Ascending

8.5.3.4.3 Circular

8.5.3.4.4 Two-dimensional ascending or descending techniques.

The ascending technique pioneered by Williams and Kirby is far simpler. The lower end of a strip of paper holding one or more spots of solution is immersed in the solvent, which rises up in the paper due to capillary action. The typical solvents can rise from 20-25 cm in 3-10 hours. The approach is called the descending method if the prepared strip of paper is hung over the edge of the tray filled with the solvent. The substances to be separated are applied point by point in a circle around the centre of the paper in circular Paper Chromatography. A paper wick held above the centre of the filter paper is used to apply the solvent. This approach provides relatively quick separation with high resolution. In the test, circular filter paper is inserted between the tray's bottom and the lid. When a single solvent does not provide sufficient separation, two- dimensional paper chromatography is used. Several spots may be applied to the bottom of the paper in one dimensional Paper Chromatography, but in two-dimensional PC, a single spot is applied in a corner of the paper and chromatographed with the first solvent in one direction, after which the paper is dried, turned 90°, and treated with the second solvent.

8.5.4 Detecting or Visualizing Agent

After the development of chromatogram, the spots should be visualized. Detecting colored spots can be done visually. But for detecting colorless spots, any one of the following techniques can be used.

(a) Nonspecific methods: detect the quantity of spots but not the actual nature or type of substance. Examples

I. **Iodine chamber method:** when the paper is kept in a chamber with a few iodine crystals at the bottom, brown or amber coloured spots appear.

II. **UV chamber for fluorescent compounds:** Fluorescent substances can be detected when viewed in a UV chamber at 254 nm (short λ) or 365 nm (long λ). The bright spots stand out against the dark background.

Examples: -

- Ferric chloride- for phenolic compounds and tannins
- Ninhydrin in acetone- for amino acids
- Dragendroff's reagents- for alkaloids
- 3,5-dinitro benzoic acid- for cardiac glycosides
- 2, 4-dinitrophenyl hydrazine- for aldehydes and ketone. The detecting techniques can also categorized as

III. **Destructive Technique:** example. Specific spray reagent, etc. where the sample are destroyed before detection ex. Ninhydrin solution.

IV. **Non-destructive Technique:** like iodine chamber method, densitometric method, UV chamber method etc. where even after detection, the sample is not destroyed.

V. For radioactive materials, detection is by autoradiography or Geiger muller counter.

VI. For antibiotic the chromatogram is laid on nutrient agar inoculated with appropriate strain and zone of inhibition is compared.

8.6 QUANTITATIVE ANALYSIS

Direct Technique: A densitometer is a device that measures the density of spots quantitatively. The amount of substance can be calculated after determining the optical density of spots in the standard and test solutions.

To obtain the compounds, the papers are neither damaged nor eluted with solvents. This technique is also known as the in-situ method.

In this procedure, spots are divided into pieces and eluted using solvents. The solution can be studied using any usual technique, such as spectrophotometry, electrochemical methods, and so on.

8.7 QUALITATIVE ANALYSIS

8.7.1 R_f Value

The R_f value (Retardation factor) is calculated in qualitative analysis to detect the spots. The R_f value is the ratio of the solute's distance travelled to the distance travelled by the solvent front.

R_f values vary between 0 and 1. However, optimum values range from 0.3 to 0.8. Every compound in a specific combination of stationary and mobile phase has the same R_f value. When the R_f values of a sample compound and a reference compound are the same, the compound is identified by its standard. When the R_f value differs from the reference standard, the compound may be different.

8.8 APPLICATIONS OF PAPER CHROMATOGRAPHY

In the area of analytical chemistry, the use of chromatographic techniques is significant. They abound in the literature. A full list of their applications is neither possible nor desirable. Here are a few examples of applications.

1. Separation of the Mixture of the Sugars:

A large number of examples are available in the literature in regard to the separation and identification of the sugars. Both monosaccharide and disaccharide mixtures have been separated. The polysaccharide has been hydrolyzed and the hydrolysate has been examined by Paper chromatography for its sugar components. The following solvent systems have been effective in the separation of the sugars:

(a)n-butanol: ethanol: water (4:1:5 v/v)

(b)pyridine: ethyl acetate: water: acetic acid (5:5*3*1 v/v)

(c)othyl acetate: acetic acid: butanol: water (4:3:2:2 v/v)

(d)othyl acetate: pyridine: water (10:4:3) (v/v)

(e)ethyl acetate: pyridine: water (5:2:7 v/v) (f) n-butanoi: acetic acid: water (4:1:5 v/v)

The following spray reagents have been successfully applied for the location of the sugars - (i) alkaline silver nitrate solution, (ii) p-anisidine phosphate, (iii) aniline hydrogen phthalate, and (iv) benzedine trichloro acetic acid.

2. Resolution of Amino Acid Mixtures:

Amino acids are the building materials of both the plant and animal body. Proteins isolated from the living organisms are hydrolyzed to amino acids and the compositions of the amino acids are studied by the chromatographic technique. The interesting colour reaction with ninhydrin helps in locating the amino acids separated over the paper. Several solvent systems have been chosen for the purpose but the most promising among them is 11-butanols acetic acid: water (4:1:5v/v).

Two dimensional Paper chromatography is a more efficient technique for detecting a number of amino acids present in the protein hydrolysate, n-butanolsacetic acid:water(4:1:5) in the/dimension and phenol:m-cresol(1:l) in the second dimension have proved to be quite successful.

3. Separation of mixtures of drugs of chemical or biological origin, plant extract etc.

4. Separation of carbohydrates, vitamins, antibiotics, proteins, alkaloids, glycosides etc.

5. Identification of drugs like erythromycin, gentamycin, vancomycin

6. Identification of impurities like hydroxocobalamin

7. Identification of related compounds like Phen form in HCl, Ergotamine injection and vitamin A.
8. Identification of foreign substances in drugs
9. Identification of decomposition products
10. Analysis of metabolites of drugs in blood, urine etc.

CHAPTER 9 THIN LAYER CHROMATOGRAPHY

9.1 INTRODUCTION

Thin layer chromatography (TLC) is a type of chromatography used to separate mixtures. Thin layer chromatography is carried out on a sheet of glass, plastic, or aluminium foil that has been covered with a thin layer of adsorbent material, most often silica gel, aluminium oxide, or cellulose (blotter paper). The stationary phase refers to this adsorbent layer. Following the application of the sample to the plate, a solvent or solvent combination (known as the mobile phase) is dragged up the plate by capillary action. Separation occurs because different analytes ascend the TLC plate at different rates. Thin layer chromatography may be used to: monitor the progression of a reaction, identify chemicals contained in a given sample, and assess a substance's purity. Compound separation is based on the competition of the solute and mobile phase for binding sites on the stationary phase. For example, if normal phase silica gel is employed as the stationary phase, it is polar. Given two polar compounds, the more polar molecule has a stronger interaction with the silica and is hence more capable of dispelling the mobile phase from the binding sites.

9.1.1 Principle of Thin Layer Chromatography

In thin layer chromatography, the solid phase is a thin glass plate coated with either silica gel or aluminium oxide. A solvent is selected for the mobile phase based on the characteristics of the mixture's constituent parts. The distribution of a component between a liquid mobile phase (eluting solvent) that is moving across the solid phase and a solid fixed phase (the thin layer) placed to a glass or plastic plate is the basis of TLC. A small amount of a compound or mixture is applied to a starting point just above the bottom of TLC plate. In the developing chamber, which has a small pool of solvent immediately below the level at which the sample was applied, the plate is then developed Through capillary action, the solvent is pulled up through the plate's particles; as it passes over the mixture, each component either stays in the solid phase or dissolves in the solvent and moves up the plate. Whether a compound climbs the plate or lags behind depends on its physical characteristics and, consequently, on its molecular structure, particularly its functional groups. The "Like Dissolves Like" solubility rule is obeyed. The longer a compound stays in the mobile phase, the more physically similar its properties are to those of the mobile phase. The most soluble substances will be carried up farthest by the mobile phase on the TLC plate. The substances that have a higher affinity for the particles on the TLC plate and are less soluble in the mobile phase will remain.

R*f* values: The behavior of an individual compound in TLC is characterized by a quantity Known as R*f* and is expressed as a decimal fraction. The R*f* is calculated by dividing the distance the compound traveled from the original position by the distance the solvent travelled from the original position (the solvent front).

9.2 PROCEDURE OF THIN LAYER CHROMATOGRAPHY

9.2.1 Requirements in Thin Layer Chromatography

1. **Nature of Adsorbent:** For the same solvent, different adsorbents will produce different R values. Only an adsorbent with a consistent particle size and binder may be reproduced. Before usage, plates should be kept over silica gel in desiccators, and samples should be applied rapidly to avoid the plate absorbing atmospheric water vapour. It is much preferable to use plates that have been stored at room temperature rather than

activating them due to the challenges involved in the activation operations. The mobile phase: The purity of solvents and quantity of solvent mixed should be strictly controlled. It should be made freshly for each run if one of the solvents is very volatile or hygroscopic. Example- acetone.

2. **Temperature:** While exact temperature control is not required, the chamber should be maintained away from heat sources, such as direct sunshine, etc. Volatile solvents evaporate more quickly as the temperature rises, solvents move through the system more quickly, and R*f* values generally fall.

3. **Thickness of Layer:** Standard plates approximately 250 micrometers are the preferable thickness of layer. Below 200, the R*f* values vary considerably. In individual compounds, the layers may have a larger or lower thickness.

4. **Developing Tank:** Saturated conditions must be established before running TLC plates. The ideal way to do this is to use small tanks with filter paper liners and enough solvent.

   You should also give the tank at least 30 minutes to equilibrate before running the plates. A tight-fitting lid is necessary.

5. **Mass of Sample:** A drug's R*f* is frequently increased by adding more samples to the plate, especially if the substance typically exhibits a tail in the body. However, if a plate is seriously overloaded, this will also result in a tailing spot and will appear to lower the R value. The intensity of the spot typically makes it simple to distinguish between the two situations.

6. **Chromatographic Technique:** The R*f* value varies for the same solvent system depending on the development method employed, such as ascending, descending, horizontal, etc.

9.3 PROCEDURE

9.3.1 Plate Preparation

Commercially available TLC plates often have specified particle size ranges to increase reproducibility. They are made by combining an inert binder, such as calcium sulphate (gypsum), a little amount of water, and an adsorbent, such as silica gel. On a non-reactive carrier sheet, typically made of glass, thick aluminium foil, or plastic, this combination is applied as thick slurry. The finished plate is heated in an oven for 30 minutes at 110 °C to dry and activate it. For analytical purposes, the adsorbent layer is typically between 0.1-0.25 mm thick, while for preparative TLC, it is between 0.5 and 2.0 mm thick.

9.3.2 Capillary Spotters

Hold a melting point capillary in the Bunsen burner's dark blue flame. Keep it in place until it becomes soft and begins to sag. Pull the capillary out of the flame as quickly as possible, lengthening it by around 2-3 times. However, you won't have a decent spotter if you draw the capillary inside the flame. After the capillary has cooled, split it down the middle. Make sure you cut off one of them at the closed end.

9.3.3 Spotting the Plate

The spotter's thin end is inserted into the diluted solution, causing the solution to rise up the capillary (capillary forces). At the starting line, briefly touch the plate. Spot in the same location once the solvent has completely evaporated. You will achieve a concentrated and small spot in this manner. Avoid spotting too much material since this will greatly reduce the separation's (or "tailing's") quality. The spots need to be sufficiently spaced from the edges and from one another. If at all possible, mark the compound or mixture on the plate beside the raw components and any potential intermediates.

9.3.4 Location of Spots

There are several ways to locate the positions of different solutes that have been separated using TLC. When viewed against a stationary phase, coloured compounds are immediately apparent, but colourless substances cannot be seen without the aid of a spraying agent that creates coloured regions in the area they occupy. The following can be utilized to spray the invisible places in TLC specifically:

1. Since they are entirely inorganic, corrosive agents can also be sprayed on the invisible places.
2. Potassium dichromate solution in concentrated sulfuric acid. Most organic chemicals, especially those used for sugars, decrease potassium dichromate (yellow) to chromic sulphate (green) during the process.
3. Sulfur trioxide vapours, produced by heating fuming sulfuric acid, char organic compounds, making them noticeable as dark spots.
4. Potassium permanganate solution Iodine vapours Saturated hydrogen sulphide solution, 0.2N aqueous ammonium sulphide, 0.1 percent alcoholic quercetin, 0.2 percent methanolic 1-(2-pyridylazo)- 2- napthol, 1 percent methanolic oxine, and 0.5 percent aqueous sodium rhodizonate are other common reagents. If the TLC plate adsorbent contains a fluorescing material, the solutes can be viewed under ultraviolet light.

9.3.5 Development Solvents

The nature of the substance and the adsorbent placed on the plate influence the selection of a suitable solvent. A development solvent should not react chemically with the compounds in the mixture under investigation. Carcinogenic solvents (benzene, for example) and ecologically hazardous solvents (dichloromethane, for example) should be avoided at all costs. Non-polar to polar solvents are used in solvent systems. Because highly polar solvents promote adsorption of any component of the solvent combination, non-polar solvents are often utilized. Petroleum ether, pyridine, carbon tetrachloride glycol, glycerol, form amide, diethyl ether, ethanol, methanol, n-propanol, and acetone are common developing solvents.

9.3.6 Mobile Phase

The mobile phase in silica gel chromatography is an organic solvent or a combination of organic solvents. The analyte is transported through the particles of the stationary phase while the mobile phase travels over the surface of the silica gel. The analyte molecules, on the other hand, are only free to travel with the solvent if they are not attached to the surface of the silica gel. Thus, the retention factor of the analyte is determined by the proportion of time the analyte is bonded to the surface of the silica gel relative to the time it spends in solution. An analyte's capacity to attach to the surface of silica gel in the presence of a certain solvent or mixture of solvents may be seen as the total of two competitive interactions. For starters, polar groups in the solvent can compete with the analyte for binding sites on the silica gel's surface. As a result, if a highly polar solvent is utilized, it will significantly interact with the surface of the silica gel, leaving few sites on the stationary phase free to bind the analyte. As a result, the analyte will migrate swiftly past the stationary phase. Similarly, polar groups in the solvent might significantly interact with polar functionality in the analyte, preventing the analyte from interacting with the silica gel surface. This action also causes the analyte to migrate quickly past the stationary phase. The polarity of a solvent for chromatography can be determined by measuring its dielectric constant (κ) and dipole moment (Σ). The greater the difference between these two figures, the more polar the solvent. Furthermore, the solvent's hydrogen bonding capacity must be noted. Methanol, for example, is a powerful hydrogen bond donor and will substantially restrict the ability of all but the most polar analytes to attach the silica gel surface.

9.3.7 Developing a Plate

In a beaker or tightly closed jar, a TLC plate may be created. Fill the container with a small amount of the solvent (mobile phase). On a plate, a little spot of solution with the sample is applied one centimetre from the bottom. The plate is then dipped in to a suitable solvent, such as hexane or ethyl acetate, and placed in a sealed container. The solvent moves up the plate by capillary action and meets the sample mixture, which is dissolved and is carried up the plate by the solvent. Different compounds in the sample mixture travel at different rates due to the differences in their attraction to the stationary phase, and because of differences in solubility in the solvent. It is possible to alter the separation of components (as determined by the Rf value) by altering the solvent or possibly using a combination. The solvent level must be lower than the TLC's starting line in order to prevent the spots from dissolving. The plate's lower edge is then submerged in a solvent. Due to their varying degrees of contact with the matrix (stationary phase) and solubility in the developing solvent, the components of the samples move at different speeds as the solvent (eluent) ascends the matrix through capillarity. Because non-polar compounds dissolve easily and do not interact with the polar stationary phase, non-polar solvents will push non-polar compounds to the top of the plate. Up to about 1 cm from the top of the plate, let the solvent rise. Remove the plate and make a mark on the solvent front right away. Do not let the solvent spill over the plate's edge. Next, let the solvent to entirely evaporate.

Precautions During Sample Application-

1. Since polar solvents tend to spread out at the starting location, the sample should be dissolved in a nonpolar solvent.
2. The solvent used to dissolve the sample must be volatile.
3. When applying the sample, the adsorbent's surface should not be disturbed since doing so would cause the spots on the produced chromatogram to have distorted forms, which will reduce the precision of the quantitative measurements.
4. The sample spot's diameter should fall between 2 and 5 mm.

9.3.8 Visualization

The plate should be withdrawn from the developing chamber, the location of the solvent front should be noted, and the solvent should be allowed to evaporate after it has moved to about 1 cm of the top end of the adsorbent (after 15 to 45 minutes). If the sample's constituent parts are coloured, it is possible to see them clearly. If not, they can occasionally be seen by putting ultraviolet light on the plate or by letting the plate stand for a short period of time in a closed container with an iodine-vapor-rich environment. Spraying the plate with a reagent that will react with one or more of the sample's components might occasionally help you see the spots.

9.3.9 Analysis

By comparing the distances, the components have travelled with those of the known reference materials, the components, which are visible as isolated spots, are identified. Calculate the separation between the solvent front and the starting line. Then calculate the distance from the spot's centre to the starting line. Subtract the distance the solvent travelled from the distance travelled by each location. The ratio that results is known as the R*f*-value. Many techniques exist to visualize the spots since the compounds being separated could be colourless. Frequently, a little quantity of a fluorescent substance is added to the adsorbent to enable the detection of spots under a black light, typically manganese activated zinc silicate (UV254). Iodine vapours are a generic, non-specific colour reagent. Specific colour reagents exist, into which the TLC plate is dipped or which are sprayed over the plate, quenching this fluorescence when spots of analyte are present. Once each spot is visible, the R*f* value, or retention factor, may be calculated by dividing the product's travel distance by the solvent's overall travel distance (the solvent front). These numbers are not physical constants and depend on the type of TLC plate and solvent being used.

9.3.10 Preparative TLC

TLC may also be used to separate mixtures of up to a few hundred milligrammes on a modest, semi-preparative scale. Instead of "spotting" the mixture as spots on the TLC plate, the mixture is placed to the plate as a thin, even layer that extends to and just above the solvent level. Instead of horizontally separated spots, the compounds separate in horizontal bands when developed with a solvent. The backing material is scraped off one band at a time (or the desired band). Once the backing material has been extracted using a suitable solvent (like DCM), it is filtered to produce the isolated substance. Preparative TLC can be a far more effective method for small-scale reactions with easily separable products in terms of cost and time than doing chromatography. It's evident that the entire plate cannot be chemically developed since the product would be ruined. Consequently, this method works well with substances that are coloured or visible under UV light. As an alternative, a tiny portion of the plate can be chemically developed, for example by cutting out a bit and doing so, or by covering most of the plate and exposing a small portion to a chemical developer like iodine.

9.4 APPLICATIONS OF THIN LAYER CHROMATOGRAPHY

The use of thin layer chromatography has proved beneficial in several pharmaceutically significant applications.

i. **TLC of amino acids:** Because amino acids are colorless, TLC of amino acids is more challenging than TLC of inks. As a result, once the plate has fully developed and dried, the spots are invisible to the human sight. To observe the spots, either ninhydrin or black-light visualisation methods must be used. Amino acids, proteins, and peptides, for example: Using silica gel plates, a combination of 34 amino acids, proteins, and peptides was effectively separated and extracted from urine. These compounds were all discovered to be ninhydrin positive. The development was carried out first using chloroform-methanol-20% ammonium hydroxide (2:2:1) and subsequently with phenol-water.

ii. **Pharmaceuticals and drugs:** TLC are utilized in drug and drug preparation identification, purity testing, and concentration determination of active components, auxiliary compounds, and preservatives, as well as process control in synthetic production processes. Various pharmacopoeias have recognized the TLC technique for detecting impurities in a medicine or chemical, for example, antibiotics. The penicillins were separated on silica gel 'G' using two solvents, acetone- methanol (1:1) and isopropanol- methanol (1:1). (3:7). The iodine-azide reaction was used as the detecting agent by spraying the dry plates with a 0.1 percent iodine solution containing 3.5 percent sodium azide.

iii. **Multicomponent pharmaceutical formulation separation:** It is also utilized in the separation of multicomponent pharmaceutical formulations.

iv. **Qualitative analysis of alkaloids:** It is employed in the qualitative examination of alkaloids in both pharmaceutical formulations and vegetable medicines during the control phase. TLC has been employed in toxicology for the isolation and determination of alkaloids, where the 30-60-minute runs provide a significant advantage over the 12-24 hours necessary for paper chromatography. TLC was used to separate purine alkaloids on silicic acid, silica gel, and aluminium oxide. The spots are visible by spraying an alcoholic iodine-potassium iodine solution first, followed by a 25 percent HCl-96 percent ethanol solution (1:1).

v. **Clinical chemistry and Biochemistry:** Diagnosis of metabolic diseases such as phenylketonuria, cystinuria, and maple syrup illness in neonates by determining active chemicals and their metabolites in biological matrices. It is a valuable method in the examination of several urine components produced from lipids, including steroids, amino acids, porphyrins, and bile acids. Urinary TLC analysis works best when combined with other chromatographic procedures, allowing small metabolites to be discovered and resolved totally free of other components.

vi. **Cosmetology:** Preservatives, surfactants, fatty acids, and scent components are all identified as dye source ingredients and end products.

vii. **Food Analysis:** Pesticides and fungicides in drinking water, residues in vegetables, salads, and meat, vitamins in soft drinks, illegal additions in Germany (e.g., sandalwood extracting fish and meat products), and compliance with limit values are all determined (e.g. polycyclic compounds in drinking water, aflatoxins in milk and milk products).

CHAPTER 10 ION EXCHANGE CHROMATOGRAPHY (OR ION CHROMATOGRAPHY)

10.1 INTRODUCTION

Ion exchange chromatography is a distinct type of column chromatography. Chromatography is the process of separating molecules from a mixture. This separation is performed based on differences in the sample's adsorption or partition coefficient with the stationary phase.

The ion displacement hypothesis, on the other hand, determines the separation of molecules in ion exchange chromatography. Ions and polar molecules can be separated using this approach based on their affinity for the ion exchanger. Almost any charged molecule, including large proteins, small nucleotides, and amino acids, can be used. In contrast, ion exchange chromatography segregates molecules based on ion displacement theory. It is a procedure that permits ions and polar molecules to be separated depending on their affinity for the ion exchanger. It may be used to charge practically any molecule, including huge proteins, tiny nucleotides, and amino acids. This can be seen by the example below:

When Magnesium is allowed to react with hydrochloric acid, it forms a salt of Magnesium Chloride and Hydrogen gas.

$$Mg + 2HCl \downarrow\downarrow MgCl_2 + H_2$$

As seen in the above reaction, more reactive ion Mg replaces less reactive ion H to form $MgCl_2$.

10.2 ION EXCHANGE CHROMATOGRAPHY PRINCIPLE

The charged molecules in the sample are separated by the electrostatic forces of attraction when passed through an ionic resin at particular pH and temperature.

The separation occurs by reversible exchange of ions between the ions present in the solution and those present in the ion exchange resin which is shown in figure 1 and figure 2.

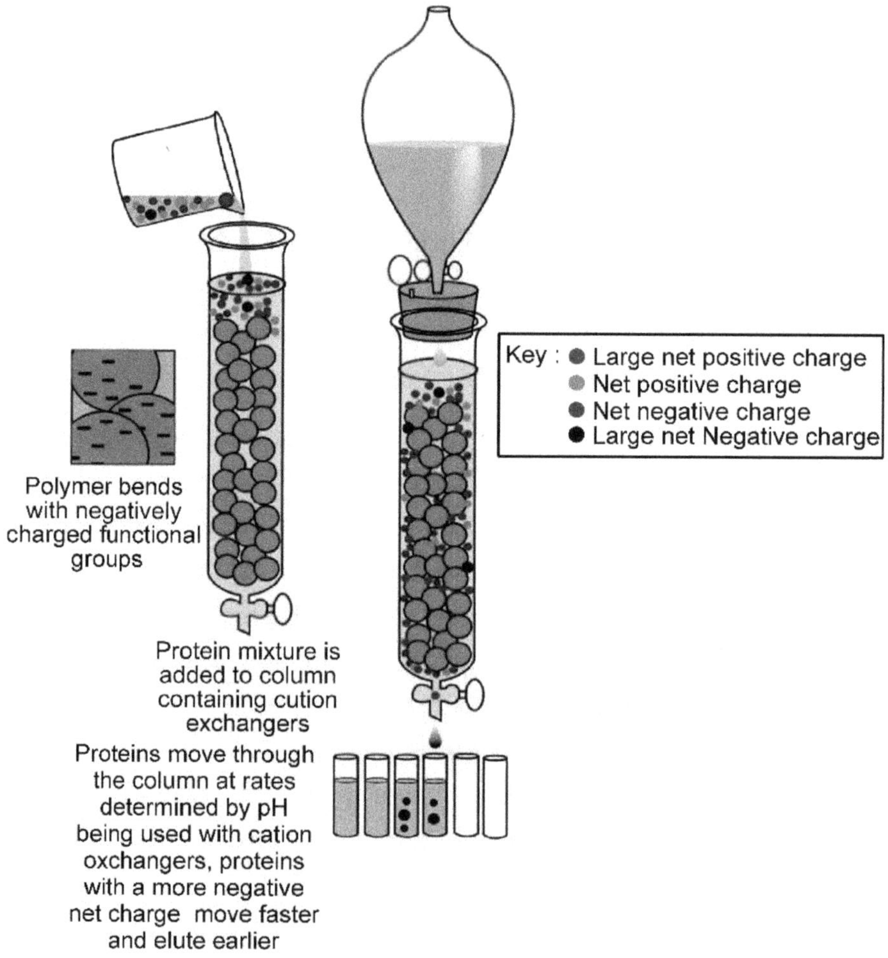

Figure 10.1: Ion Exchange Resin.

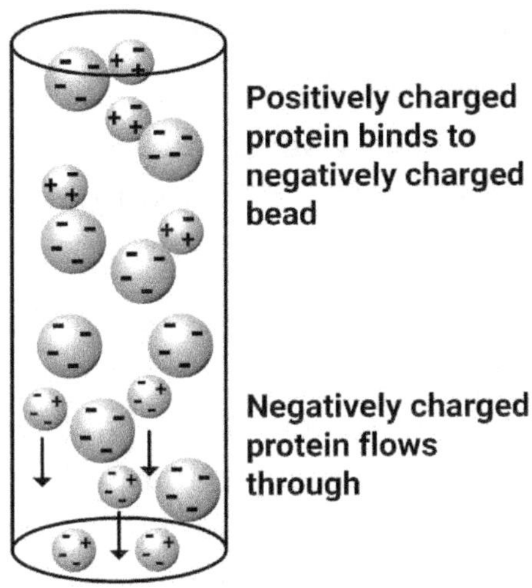

Figure 10.2: Ion Exchange Resin.

Two types of exchangers, cationic and anionic exchangers, can be utilized in this operation. Cationic exchangers have positively charged groups that attract positively charged cations. Because their negative charges come from the ionisation of an acidic group, these exchangers are also known as "Acidic ion exchange" materials.

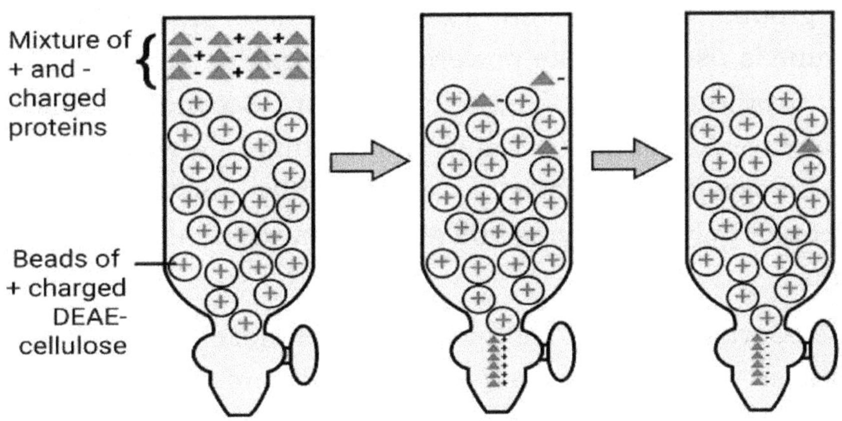

Figure 10.3: Ion Exchange.

Anionic exchangers have positively charged groups that will attract negatively charged anions. These are also called “Basic ion exchange” materials.

10.3 TYPES OF ION EXCHANGE RESINS

Ion exchange resins are made from two types of materials: polystyrene and cellulose. The flow characteristics, ion accessibility, chemical and mechanical stability of resins manufactured from both of these components differ.

Polystyrene resins are postulated as a result of a polymerization reaction between styrene and divinyl benzene. Cross connections increase as the concentration of divinyl benzene increases. Polystyrene resins are excellent for separating substances with low molecular weight. Increased cross linking enhances the stiffness, decreases swelling, decreases porosity, and decreases the solubility of the polymeric structure.

Sulfonic acids are strong acids with excellent proton dissociation properties. Acidic Functional groups are readily linked to practically every aromatic nucleus via the sulfonation process. sulfonic acid-substituted resins are excellent cationic exchangers.

Carbohydrate groups can be linked to aromatic rings instead of sulfonic acid groups to create weekly acidic exchanger. With the addition of basic functional groups, the resin may exchange anions rather than cations. A tertiary amine is used to make powerful anion exchangers, which results in a strongly basic quaternary ammonium group. Secondary amines can be used to make weak anionic exchangers, resulting in a weakly basic tertiary amine. Cellulose resins have a substantially higher permeability to macromolecular polyelectrolytes and a lower charge density than polystyrene exchangers.

Example: Carboxy methyl cellulose (CM-cellulose) – Cationic exchanger DEAE cellulose – Anionic exchanger Preparation of the exchange medium: There are three steps are of absolute importance:

1. Swelling of medium: (Pre-cycling):

Swelling makes the functional groups to be exposed for ion exchange. Swelling of anion exchangers is usually carried out by treating it. First with an acid (0.5N HCl) and then with base (0.5N NaOH).

Exactly the reverse is the case with cationic exchangers. The matrix can be treated with EDTA for impurity eliminations.

2. Removal of very small particles:

These fines will decrease flow rate and unsatisfactory reaction. To remove fines, the exchanger is repeatedly suspended in a large volume of water and after the larger polymers have settle down, the slow sedimenting materials decanted.

3. Equilibration with counter ions:

This is accomplished by washing the exchanger with different reagents depending upon the desired counter ion to be introduced.

NaOH counter ion to be introduced is "Na+". HCl counter ion to be introduced is "H+". NaNO3 counter ion to be introduced is "NO3" Choice of Buffers:

- Anionic exchange Chromatography should be carried out with cationic buffers.
- Cationic exchange Chromatography should be carried out with anionic buffers.
- The pK of the buffer should be as near as possible to the pH at which the system is buffered. These results in high buffer capacity, which can with stand the local changes of pH in the column easily.

Buffers	**PH range**
Ammonium acetate	4 to 6
Ammonium format	3 to 5
Pyridinium format	3 to 6
Pyridinium acetate	4 to 6
Ammonium carbonate	8 to 10

10.4 FACTORS AFFECTING ION EXCHANGE SEPARATIONS

The factors affecting ion exchange separations are

A. Nature and properties of ion exchange resins

B. Nature of exchanging ions

A. Nature of ion exchange resins: Crosslinking and swelling are essential factors that are affected by the ratio of cross-linking agent (divinyl benzene) to polystyrene. When there is more cross-linking agent present, they become stiffer yet swell less. When swelling is low, it is difficult to separate ions of different sizes because they cannot flow through the pores present, and it becomes selective to ions of different sizes. They are less stiff and swell more when there is less cross-linking agent present. When swelling is greater, separation is inefficient because exchange of functional groups does not occur due to the large pore. As a result, the optimal amount of cross-linking agent should be applied to the polymeric ion exchange resins for successful separation.

B. Nature of exchanging ions:

i. **Valency of ions:** At low concentrations and at ordinary temperatures, extent of exchange increases with increase in valency.

$$Na+ < Ca+2 < Al+3 < Th+4$$

ii. **Size of ions:** For similar charged ions, exchange increases with decreases in the size of hydrated ion.

$$Li^+ < H^+ < Na^+ < NH^+ < K^+ < Rb^+ < Cs^+$$

iii. **Polarizability:** Exchange is preferred for greater polarizable ion **example** $I^- < Br^- < Cl^- < F^-$

iv. **Concentration of solution:** In dilute solution, polyvalent anions are generally adsorbed preferentially.

v. **Concentration and charge of ions:** If resin has higher +ve charge and solution have lower +ve charge, exchange is favoured at higher concentration. If resin has lower +ve charge and solution has high +ve charge. Then exchange is favoured at low concentration.

10.5 APPLICATIONS OF ION EXCHANGE CHROMATOGRAPHY

1. **Softening of water:** Removal of monovalent and divalent ions like sodium, potassium, calcium, magnesium etc.
2. **Demineralization or deionization of water:** Removal of different ions to get demineralized water.
3. **Separation of inorganic ions:** Cations and anions
4. Purification of some solutions to be free from ionic impurities.
5. Biochemical separations like isolation of some drugs or metabolites from blood, urine etc.
6. It is extremely used in the analysis of amino acids. The amino acid "Auto analyzer" is based on in exchange principle.
7. To determine the base composition of nucleic acids. Chargaff used this technique for established the equivalence of Adenine and Thymine; Guanine and Cytosine.
8. This is most effective method for water purification. Complete deionization of water (or) a non- electrolyte solution is performed by exchanging solute cations for hydrogen ions and solute anions for hydroxyl ions. This is usually achieved by method is used for softening of drinking water.
9. Proteins are also successfully separated by this technique.
10. It is also used for the separation of many vitamins, other biological amines, and organic acids and bases.
11. One of the main disadvantages of ion exchange chromatography is its buffer requirement: because binding to IEX resins is dependent on electrostatic interactions between proteins of interest and the stationary phase, IEX columns must be loaded in low-salt buffers. For some applications, this restriction may require a buffer exchange step prior to ion exchange chromatography.

CHAPTER 11 COLUMN CHROMATOGRAPHY

11.1 INTRODUCTION

Column chromatography is a method of separation in which the stationary bed is contained within a tube. The particles of the solid stationary phase or the support coated with a liquid stationary phase may fill the whole interior volume of the tube (packed column) or be concentrated on or along the inner tube wall, leaving an open, uncontrolled passage for the mobile phase in the tube's centre (open tubular column). Different retention durations of the sample are computed based on differences in rates of movement through the medium.

W.C. Still invented flash column chromatography, a modified version of column chromatography, in 1978. The method is essentially similar to classic column chromatography, with the exception that the solvent is forced through the column by providing positive pressure. Most separations could now be completed in less than 20 minutes, with better separations than the previous approach. Modern flash chromatography systems are sold in the form of pre-packaged plastic cartridges, with the solvent pushed through the cartridge. Detectors and fraction collectors can also be attached to systems to provide automation. Gradient pumps resulted in faster separations and reduced solvent use. Instead of a solid phase produced by a packed bed, a fluidized bed is employed in expanded bed adsorption. This enables the removal of preliminary cleaning procedures for culture broths or slurries of broken cells, such as centrifugation and filtering.

11.2 PRINCIPLE

Adsorption is the primary method of separation, which involves a liquid mobile phase and a solid stationary phase. When a combination of substances that have been dissolved in the mobile phase is added to the column, depending on their relative affinities, the constituent components travel at varying speeds. The compounds are so divided. The interaction between the solute and the stationary phase (adsorbent) is reversible in nature.

The following is a description of how quickly a component (R) moves:

$$R = \frac{\text{Rate of movementof a component}}{\text{Rate of movementof mobilephase}}$$

This equation can be simplified as follows:

$$R = \frac{\text{Distancemovedhe solute}}{\text{Distancemovedby thesolvent}}$$

When a liquid mobile phase is used, the equation is written as

Where α is the partition co-efficient

$$R = \frac{Am}{Am + \alpha As} = \frac{\text{Concentration in stationaryphase}}{\text{concentration in movilephase}}$$

A_m is the average cross section of mobile phase A_s is the average cross section of stationary phase

11.3 PROCEDURE IN COLUMN CHROMATOGRAPHY

1. **Stationary Phase (Absorbents):** An adsorbent used in column chromatography should meet the following criteria.

A. Particle size and geometry: the particles should have uniform size distribution and have spherical shape. Particle size: 60-200μ.

B. Should be inert and should not react with the solute or other components.

C. Insoluble in the solvents or mobile phase used.

D. It should be colourless to facilitate observation of zones and recovery of components.

E. It should allow free flow of mobile phase.

F. It should be useful for separating for wide variety of compounds. Types of adsorbents-

Weak	Medium	Strong
Sucrose	$CaCO_3$	Activated Mg Silicate
Starch	$Ca_3(PO_4)_2$	Activated Alumina
Insulin	$MgCO_3$	Activated Charcoal
Talc	MgO	Activated Magnesia
Na_2CO_3	$Ca(OH)_2$	Fuller's earth

The most commonly used adsorbent is silica gel of 80-100 mesh or 100-200 mesh size which has a particle size of 60-200μ.

2. Selection of Stationary Phase

The success of Chromatography depends upon the proper selection of stationary phase. The selection of stationary phase in column chromatography depends upon the following:

- **Removal of impurities:** When a small quantity of impurity is present and there is difference in affinity when compared to the major component, a weak adsorbent is sufficient.

- **No. of components to be separated:** When few components are to be separated, weak adsorbent is used. When more components are to be separated, a strong adsorbent is selected.
- **Affinity differences between components:** When components have similar affinities, a strong adsorbent will be effective. When there is more difference in affinities, a weak adsorbent is selected.
- **Length of the column used:** When a shorter column is used, strong adsorbent has to be used. When a long column is used, a weak column can be used.
- **Quantity of adsorbent used:** 20 to 30 times the weight of the adsorbent is used for effective separation.

3. Mobile Phase

Mobile phase is very important and they serve several functions. They act as solvent, developer and as eluent. The function of a mobile phase is-

- To introduce the mixture into the column- As solvent
- To develop the zones of separation- As developing agent
- To remove pure component out of the column- As eluent
- Example- Petroleum ether, Carbon tetrachloride, Cyclohexane, Ether, Acetone, water, pyridine etc.

4. Column characteristics

The material of the column is mostly good quality neutral glass since it should not be affected by solvents, acid and bases. An ordinary burette can also be used as column for separation. The length of the column depends upon:

- ❖ Affinity of compounds towards the adsorbents used.
- ❖ Number of compounds to be separated.

- Type of adsorbent used.
- Quantity of the sample.

5. Preparation of column

Above the packing of the column of adsorbent is a bottom layer of cotton wool, glass wool, or- in certain cases-an asbestos pad. Another option is a whatmann filter paper disc. A similar paper disc is retained on top of the column once the adsorbent has been packed within, preventing any disruption of the adsorbent layer during the addition of the sample or mobile phase. Uneven bands result from disruption in the adsorbent layer.

When packing a column, there are various suitable techniques. These include the slurry technique and dry packing (two types of dry packing are covered here). The best packing results are often obtained by the slurry approach, however there are certain situations when the dry packing method works just as well if not better.

Dry packing method

The preferred technique for a micro scale column is dry packing. Start by adding a nonpolar solvent to the column. Add the powdered alumina or silica gradually, touching the column's side lightly with a pencil as you go. Should the bottom of the column, the solid ought to "float." A poor separation will result from fractures, air bubbles, and uneven packing of the column; try to avoid them as much as you can. The stationary phase is placed in the column prior to the solvent in the second dry pack technique. In this instance, pour the stationary phase into the column to the desired height before adding the nonpolar solvent gradually. Slowly adding the solvent will prevent unequal channelling.

Slurry Method

For macro scale separations, the slurry approach is frequently employed. In a beaker, mix the solid stationary phase with a tiny quantity of nonpolar solvent. Mix the two ingredients well together until a smooth paste forms that can still flow. Using a spatula to remove the solid as you pour the liquid, gently pour this uniform mixture into the column. Although the slurry approach is more challenging to learn, it often results in the best column packing. The most crucial step in packing the column, whether using the dry or slurry approach is producing a uniformly distributed and packed stationary phase. As already established, poor separation will result from fractures, air bubbles, and channelling. Open the stopcock once the column has been loaded, allowing the solvent level to fall to the top of the packing, but do not let it descend below this level. Always avoid letting the column "run dry," which is when the solvent level drops below the stationary phase. Since it enables the production of air bubbles and channels, it results in a poor separation.

Addition of Sample

After packing is finished, the sample can be put straight onto the column's top. The combination is typically dissolved using 5–10 drops at the very least of a polar solvent. Using a pipette, the solution is then slowly fed to the column's top without disturbing its smooth top surface. For the optimum separation, a narrow horizontal band of sample is ideal. The top of the column is then covered with a thin coating of white sand once the sample has been loaded. When adding solvent eluent, this will assist in keeping the top of the column level. When adding solvent eluent, this will aid in maintaining the level of the column's top. After the combination has been introduced and the sand barrier has been established, add the solvent eluent continually while collecting tiny fractions at the bottom of the column. To prevent disturbing the column and dilution of the sample, add the initial quantity of solvent using a pipet on top of the packing, sample, and sand. Your column separation will be more successful if you collect tiny fractions (1-3 ml). Fractions that are too tiny can always be pooled together, but if they are too huge, you can end up with many compounds in each fraction. If this occurs, the only way to complete the separation is to redo the chromatography. Since column chromatography is time consuming, collecting large fractions is discouraged.

6. Monitoring the Sample

The column may be easily monitored if the mixture to be separated contains colourful chemicals. Along with the solvent, the coloured bands will descend the column, and as they near the bottom of the column, they will begin to gather the colours in separate containers. Make use of the colour as a guide. However, the majority of organic compounds lack colour. TLC must be used in this situation to monitor the response. Put one fraction at a time on a TLC plate. On one TLC plate, four or five fractions can be detected. To identify which chemical is present in each of the fractions of the collected samples, develop the plate and utilise the observed spot or spots. It will be easier to identify the initial material or product if you can see some of it on the TLC plate as a benchmark.

Isolation and Separation of Compounds

The colours of the materials or the TLC findings should show which fractions contain the compound(s) you are interested in isolating once all the materials have been taken out of the column. Evaporate the solvent before combining similar or identical portions. There will remain a residue of the pure separated component. A solid product may be further purified through recrystallization. On a milligram me scale, however, there is typically insufficient material to do this. The colours of the materials or the TLC findings should show which fractions contain the compound(s) you are interested in isolating once all the materials have been taken out of the column. Evaporate the solvent before combining similar or identical portions. There will remain a residue of the pure separated component. A solid product may be further purified through recrystallization. On a milligramme scale, however, there is typically insufficient material to do this

7. Detection of components

The detection of coloured components can be done visually. Different coloured bands are seen moving down the column which can be collected separately. But for colourless compounds, the technique depends upon the properties of the components. Different properties which can be used are

1. Absorption of light (UV/VIS)- using UV/VIS detector
2. Fluorescence or light emission characteristics- using fluorescence detector
3. By using flame ionization detector
4. Refractive index detector- based on the refractive index difference between the mobile phase and mobile phase + component
5. Evaporation of the solvent and weighing the residue
6. By monitoring the fractions by thin layer chromatography
7. Any one of the above techniques can be used for detection of compounds so that it can be used for qualitative analysis and for detection of compounds.

11.4 FACTORS AFFECTING COLUMN EFFICIENCY

Particle Size of the Stationary Phase: Particle size reduction boosts surface area and enhances separation. However, a smaller particle size will result in a slower flow of the mobile phase. To get extremely excellent separation in HPLC, we employ very small particles. The employment of high-pressure pumps to force the mobile phase through the stationary phase solves the flow rate problem. To resist the intense pressure, columns are built of stainless steel.

Adsorbent activity: The choice of the suitable adsorbent is very important.

Uniformity if packing of the column: If the stationary phase is not packed uniformly then the bands will be irregular and less uniform resulting in poor separation.

Selection of the proper mobile phase: Very polar mobile phase will wash out all components without any separation. On the other hand, very non, polar mobile phase will result in broad band and poor separation.

Concentration of the mixture: the proper ratio between sample to be separated and the amount of stationary phase is very important too much samples resulted in bad separation.

Rate of flow: Slower flow rate usually resulted in a better separation and narrower bands.

Consistency of flow: The continuous flow of the mobile phase during the whole experiment gives better separation than interrupting the flow then continues it later.

Column dimensions: Increasing the length of the column improve separation. However, that usually leads to slower flow rate. Also increasing the column length sometimes is impractical.

Column temperature: Increasing the temperature usually reduces the adsorption power of the stationary phase and increase elution speed. This may lead to decrease in the efficiency separation.

11.5 APPLICATION OF COLUMN CHROMATOGRAPHY

I. Separation of Different Mixture of Compounds

- Separation of inorganic compounds like copper, cobalt and nickel
- Separation and purification of organic compounds–sudan blue, methylene blue etc.
- Separation of diastereoisomers, tautomers and racemic mixtures
- Separation of cis and trans isomers of pyrazoline
- Separation of geometric isomers, cis and trans isomers of bixin and crocetin dimethyl ether using alumina

II. Removal of Impurities

- Purification of steroids, carotenoids, chlorophyll, xanthophylls.

III. Isolation of Active Constituents

- Separation of alkaloids and glycosides

IV. Isolation of Metabolite from Biological Fluids

- Purification of vitamin B12
- Purification of oxytetracycline and oleandomycin
- Separation of 17-keto steroids
- Separation of cortisol from plasma
- Separation of amino acids, proteins, phospholipids, cholesterol and triglycerides

V. Estimation of drugs in formulations

- Determination of % W/W of strychnine in syrup of ferrous phosphate with strychnine and quinine
- Determination of primary and secondary glycosides in digitalis leaf
- Determination of phytome and ione in injection and tablets.
- Determination of fluocinolone acetonide or betamethasone 17- valerate in formulated products.

11.6 ADVANTAGE OF COLUMN CHROMATOGRAPHY

1. Any type of mixture can be separated by column chromatography
2. Any quantity of the mixture can be separated (μg to mg of substance)
3. Wider choice of mobile phase.
4. In preparative type, the sample can be separated and reused.

CHAPTER

12

GAS CHROMATOGRAPHY

12.1 INTRODUCTION

In analytical chemistry, gas-liquid chromatography (GLC) is one of the most effective methods. In 1946, Class on published one of the key early works on gas liquid chromatography. Gas-liquid chromatography is a type of partition chromatography in which an inert gas, such as nitrogen (N2), is used as the carrier gas and flows in a regulated manner across the surface of a liquid film as the stationary phase. The sample being analysed is vaporised in high-temperature programming condition. The partitioning between a mobile gaseous phase and a stationary liquid phase contained in a column causes the components of the vaporised sample to be separated.

12.2 PRINCIPLE

The constituent components of a sample mixture separate based on their partition coefficient between the stationary gas and liquid phases when the vapours of the sample mixture migrate between the stationary phase (liquid) and the mobile phase (gas).

$$\text{Partition coefficient (Kg)} = \frac{\text{Concentation of solute in liquid}\left(\text{w/cc}\right)}{\text{Concentration of solute in gas}\left(\text{w/cc}\right)}$$

It is a common belief that if the partition coefficient is low, the component will emerge quickly, and the opposite is also true. Low boiling point (B.P.) compounds will elute or emerge sooner because they are more concentrated in the mobile phase, which has a higher vapour pressure and more volatility. For instance, lower chain fatty acids emerge before long chain fatty acids because they have a higher vapour pressure, higher volatility, and lower B.P than higher carbon number molecules. As a result, less polar compounds elute more quickly than polar ones. In comparison to less polar compounds, which flow more quickly, more polar substances are more retained in the column and travel slowly. There are two frequently used terminologies in chromatographic analysis: (i) Retention Time and (ii) Retention volume.

The time it takes for a solute peak (the peak of specific component) to enter the detector in a gas chromatographic column. The retention time (tR) of that component is characteristic, and the area beneath the peak is proportional to its amount. These factors produce qualitative and quantitative data. The characterisation of a combination in an unknown sample is accomplished by comparing retention times to those of reference chemicals. The relative proportion of distinct components in a mixture is calculated by first calculating their peak areas and then calculating the percentage of peaks obtained from the total area of various peaks produced.

Retention volume (VR) is defined as the volume of the gas required to carry a component maximum through the column. VR = tR×Fc Where Fc is the volume flow rate of the gas at outlet.

12.3 THEORETICAL PLATES (PLATE THEORY)

A theoretical plate is a hypothetical or imaginary unit of a column in which the solute distribution between stationary and mobile phases has reached equilibrium. A theoretical plate is also known as a functional column unit.

HETP- Height Equivalent to a Theoretical Plate

The height of a theoretical plate determines the deficiency of separation. The column is more efficient when HETP is low. Column is less efficient as HETP increases. The following formula can be used to compute HETP:

$$\text{HETP} = \frac{\text{Lenght of the coloum}}{\text{No. of theoretical plates}}$$

HETP is given by the Van Demeter equation

$$\text{HETP} = \frac{A+B}{\mu + Cu}$$

Where

A = Eddy diffusion term or multiple path diffusion

B = Longitudinal diffusion term or molecular diffusion which depends on flow rate

C = Effect of mass transfer which depends on flow rate

u = Flow rate or velocity of the mobile phase

Efficiency (No. of Theoretical Plate)

The number of theoretical plates is used to represent a column's efficiency. It may be calculated using the formula:

$$N = \frac{16Rt^2}{W_2}$$

Where

N = no. of theoretical plates

Rt = retention time

W = peak width at base

Rt and W are measured in common units (mm or cm or minutes or seconds) and are proportional to the distances marked on chart paper.

The column is regarded to be very efficient if the number of theoretical plates is large. The column is believed to be less efficient if the number of theoretical plates is minimal. A value of 600/metre is adequate for gas chromatographic columns. However, in HPLC, high values such as 40000 to 70000/metre are preferred.

12.4 INSTRUMENTATION

The basic components of a typical gas chromatograph (GC) are as:

1. Carrier Gas Supply:

The inert gaseous mobile phase is necessary. Helium is the most commonly utilized mobile phase, but argon, nitrogen, and hydrogen are also employed. The majority of these gases, including mixes such as nitrogen and hydrogen, are accessible in cylinders. In general, the gases used in GC must be completely dried since moisture in the gases causes background noise. Nowadays, GC providers include desiccant cartridges and other filters in addition to the equipment that handle these and other contaminants. Otherwise, a molecular sieve active at 200 -300°C is the finest desiccant. The pressure gauges and flow metres regulate the flow rate of these gases.

Detector	Carrier Gas
Thermal conductivity	Helium
Flame ionization	Helium or nitrogen
Electron capture	Very dry nitrogen

2. Sample injection Systems:

Whether a sample is gaseous, liquid, or solid will determine the method of injection. In GLC, it is necessary to inject the appropriate amount of sample as a "plug" of vapours.

Band spreading and poor resolution have been seen to be caused by oversized samples or slow injection. The sensitivity of the detector determines the appropriate sample size; for an ionisation detector, the liquid sample volume should not be larger than 0.5 µl.

Liquid Samples: At the top of the column, a heated sample port is placed, and tiny needles are used to inject liquid samples via a silicon septum. Typically, the sample port is 50°C or more above the boiling point of the least volatile components in the sample. The sample sizes for analytical columns that are packed routinely range from a few tenths of a microliter to 20 l. For capillary columns, sample sizes must be lowered by a factor of 100 or more. Here, a sample splitter is typically required to only transmit a tiny known proportion (1:100 to 1:500) of the injected material, with the remainder going to waste.

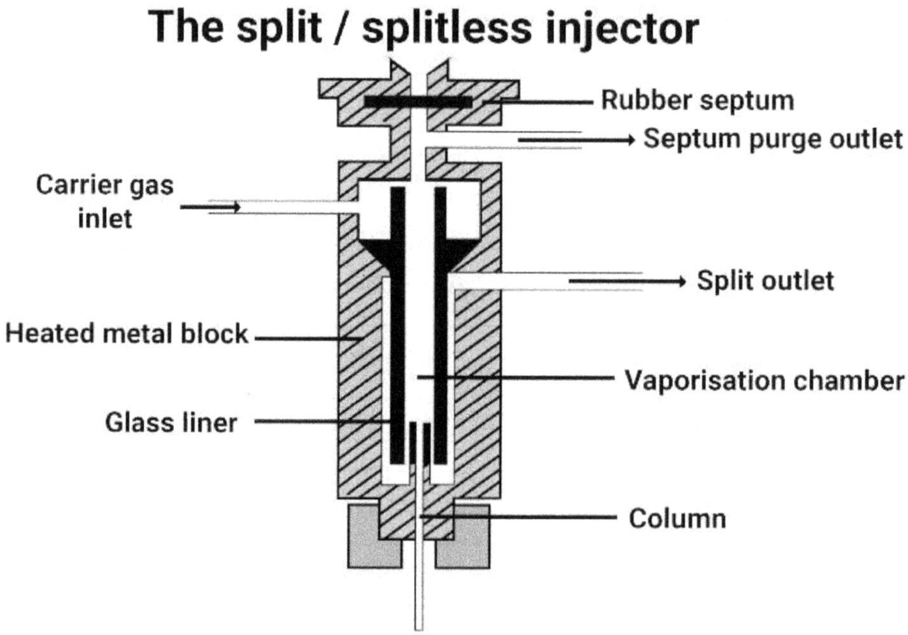

Figure 12.1: Sample Injection System.

Solid samples: Solid samples are typically weighed into thin glass ampules before being put into the gas stream and smashed.

3. Columns:

Any gas chromatograph's efficiency is greatly dependent on the columns used in GLC, which can be composed of glass or metal. Columns are classified into two types: packed columns and open tubular (capillary) columns.

Packed columns: These columns may accommodate more samples and are typically more convenient to use. They are generally 2 to 3 m long and have inner sizes ranging from 2 to 4 mm. To allow for simple thermo stating in an oven, the tubes are often built as coils with diameters of roughly 15cm. A column's packing or support holds the liquid stationary phase in place, increasing the surface area exposed to the mobile phase. For gas chromatography, the optimal particle size of packing material is 60 - 80 mesh (250 – 170μm) or 80 - 100 mesh (170 – 149μm).

Capillary Columns: Capillary columns are frequently made from glass or fused silica. The interior diameters of these columns range from 0.25 to 0.50 mm and their lengths range from 25 to 100 metres. The outside diameter of silica capillaries, which have far thinner walls than glass or metal equivalents, is around 0.3 mm.

4. Column Oven:

A high precision thermostat is commonly used to control the temperature of the column mounted within the GLC oven in order to achieve a predictable retention time. Temperatures can range from 0 to 400°C.

5. Detectors:

Because of its great sensitivity, detectors may respond quickly to even trace quantities of solutes exiting the columns. Detectors provide linear responses that are stable and consistent for a wide variety of chemical species. There are several kinds of detectors (a) Thermal conductivity (b) Gas density (c) Flame ionization (d) ß – ray ionization (Cross section, Argon, Helium, Electron capture, Electron mobility) (e) Photo ionization. (f) Glow discharge (g) Flame temperature (h) Dielectric constant. The two detectors described above are the ones that are most frequently utilized.

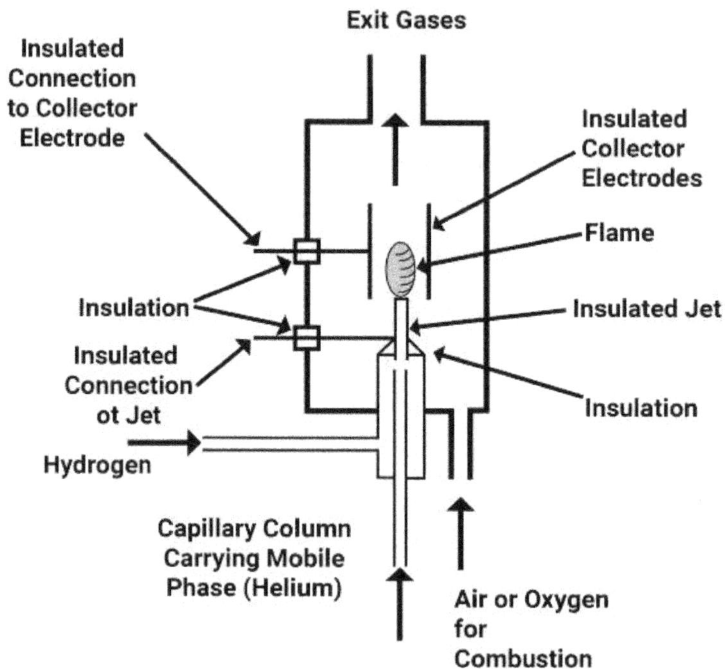

Figure 12.2: Detector System in GLC.

Thermal Conductivity Detector (TCD):

This is sometimes referred to as a Katharometer. This is made up of four filaments connected by an electrical bridge network. The carrier gas travels around these filaments via cavities. The temperature of the filament is determined by the rate of heat transfer through the carrier gas. When the components of the gas elute from the column, the composition of the gas changes, causing the thermal conductivity to change. This changes the temperature of the filaments, causing the bridge circuit to generate electrical output.

Merits: (i) Simple (ii) can be used in all applications (iii) non-destructive and thus suitable for preparative fraction collection work.

Limitation: (i) Low resistance ii) Low sensitivity (10 –9 g/ ml carrier).

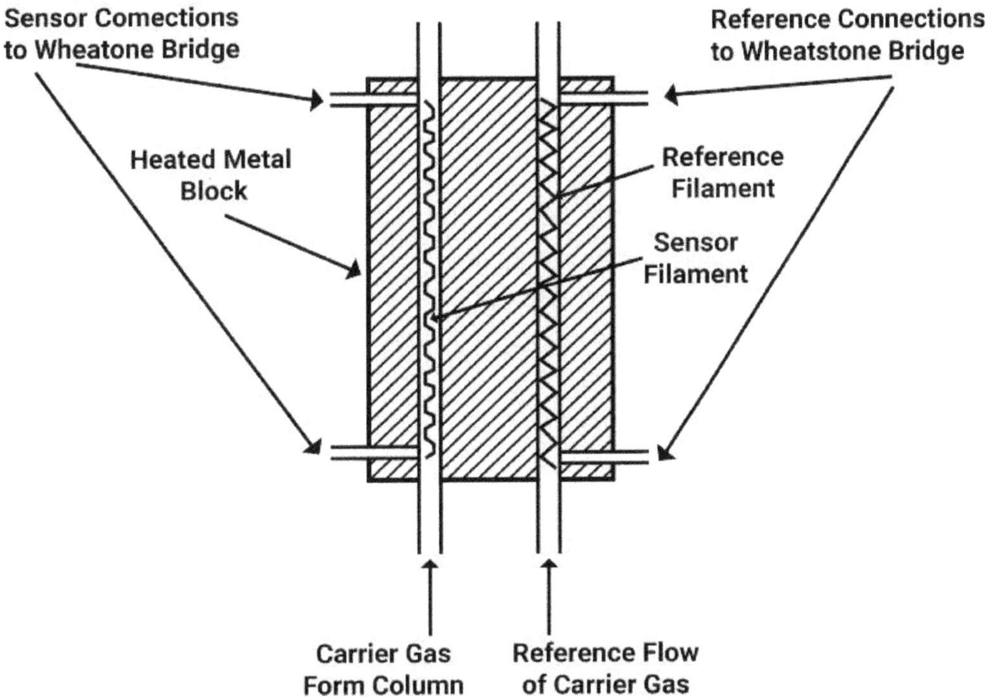

Figure 12.3: Thermal Conductivity Detector (TCD).

❖ Flame Ionization Detector (FID):

Because of its excellent sensitivity, wide working range, and good dependability, it is the most commonly used detector. It only interacts with organic compounds. It works on the principle that when most organic molecules pyrolize in a hot flame, ionic intermediates are formed that allow electricity to pass through the flame. It consists of a tiny hydrogen flame surrounded by an electric field and burning in an abundance of air. Before entering the burner, hydrogen and column effluent are mixed. The organic molecules eluted from the column are burnt, producing CO_2. As an intermediate consequence of this oxidation process, some ionising particles and electrons are created. The amount of carbon in the original compounds is proportional to the number of these ionising particles. These ionizing particles are quantitatively proportional to the amount of carbon in original compounds. The polarising electrodes gather and neutralise these ionising particles, producing an electric current that is detected by the electrometer and shapes a peak on their cording chart. The ionisation detector has a broad linear response, low noise, and high sensitivity (10–13 g/mL). It is also user-friendly and robust. It only reacts to organic substances.

Detection limit: 10 picograms for higher organic liquids and gases and 5 ppb for light hydrocarbon gases. The realistic detection limit when using a column with a temperature of 200°C or above is approximately 1 nanogram (10-7 - 10-8g.). Disadvantage: It destroys the sample.

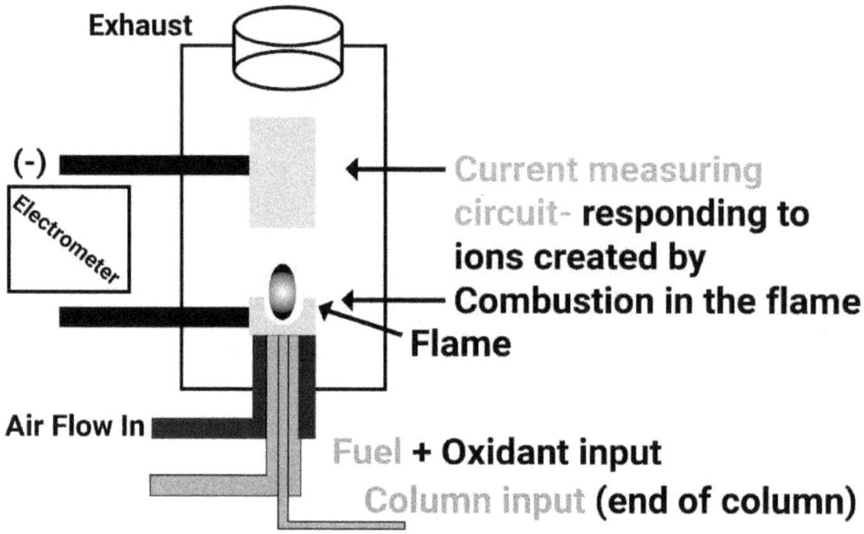

Figure 12.4: Flame Ionization Detector (FID).

❖ Modified Flame ionization detector (FID):

Another term for it is the thermo ionic alkali flame detector (TID). An alkali metal salt is added to the flame in this example to promote ionisation of compounds comprising P, Cl, and N. Salts, typically PO_4, and halides of Na, K, Rb, or CS, are fed into the flame through a fixed wire, a heated capillary, and a pallet connected to the jet. When salt is used, it should be replenished.

❖ Electron Capture Detector (ECD):

It operates on the basis of electron capture by various identified chemicals, resulting in a drop-in ion current. Electrons are drawn to electronegative elements or groups in chemistry. In the gaseous form, they tend to capture electrons and produce negative ions. Exposing these compounds to a low energy electron source forms the foundation of an extremely sensitive selective detector for such chemicals.

The radioactive sources utilized in ECD include tritium (H3) and Ni63. As a quench gas, methane or argon are used to reduce energy (combined with a carrier gas). Non-radioactive sources: high sensitivity and operational temperature helium glow discharge (400°C). In all types of ECD, specificity or selectivity is more important than sensitivity. Non-capturing compounds (those without an electronegative group) should remain unnoticed.

Advantages: Oxygen, halogens, and halogen-containing compounds have very high sensitivity and specificity.

❖ The Nitrogen Phosphorus Detector (NPD):

This detector is very sensitive and specific. It is extremely sensitive to organic compounds containing nitrogen and/or phosphorus. This detector's sensor is a rubidium or cesium bead enclosed inside a small heating coil. The anode is situated on one of the detector's sides. The heated alkali Rubidium Sulphate generates electrons that are collected at the anode and hence form ions through thermionic emission. When a solute containing nitrogen or phosphorus is eluted, the partially combusted nitrogen and phosphorus components are adsorbed on the surface of the bead. This deposited material decreases the work function of the surface, increasing electron emission and hence increasing anode current. The NPD has a sensitivity of around 10-12g/ml for nitrogen.

6. Stationary Phases for GLC:

Hundreds of liquids have been proposed as stationary phases in the development of GLC. A liquid phase's polarity and operational temperature range are critical factors in its selection. Tables or the provider can be used to derive the latter. In practice, the stronger the polarity of the liquid stationary phase, the greater the retention of a polar solute over anon-polar solute with the same boiling point. The fundamental rule is that like dissolves like. As a result, if the chemical structures of the sample components are equivalent but the volatilities differ, a non-polar liquid phase is frequently desirable. Polar phase, on the other hand, is frequently more suited when the components have unique functional groups but comparable boiling temperatures. There are two kinds of stationary phases: polar and non-polar.

Polar stationary phases (selective): They contain functional groups such as -CN, -CO, and -OH. Polyethylene glycol and polyester are two of these polar solute-retaining phases. These phases categorise solute molecules based on their functional groups. In some stationary phases, carbon-carbon double bonds are preferentially preserved. These phases are used to separate carbonyls, lactones, and fatty acid esters.

In nature, non-polar (non-selective) phases are often hydrocarbons (dialkyl siloxane), such as methyl silicon's, Apiezen greases, and squalene. They have a proclivity to fractionate solutes based on their boiling points. Generally used to describe triglycerides. All stationary phases have the same characteristics:

(1) Low volatility (ideally, the liquid's boiling point should be 100°C higher than the column's maximum working temperature)

(2) Thermal stability

(3) Chemical inertness

(4) Solvent properties

Some Common Liquid Stationary phases: Polydimethyl siloxane, Phenyl – polydimethyl siloxane, Polyethylene glycol, Cynopropyl – polydimethyl siloxane.

Selection of stationary phases depend upon the compounds

Stationary phase	Type	Analyte type
100% Dimethyl polysiloxane	Non-polar	Petroleum products, Solvents, saturated hydrocarbons, flavors
Diphenyl: dimethyl polysiloxane	Non-Polar	es, flavors, aromatic hydrocarbons
100% Diphenyl: dimethyl polysiloxane	Medium polarity	Nitrogen containing pesticides
Polyethylene glycol	Polar	Fatty acids, fatty acid methyl esters, flavours, alcohol

7. Conditioning of Column:

To eliminate low molecular weight residues from stationary phase in order to maintain liquid phase bleeds to a minimum over the temperature range of operation. This is commonly accomplished by heating the column to roughly 20-30°Cover its acceptable operating temperature while passing a carrier gas stream across it. This is required to ensure complete removal of any solvent, water, and volatile contaminants that may have been retained during the production of the column material. GLC derivatives include the following: The most common derivatization occurs prior to G.C., which increases the volatility of the sample; for example, 1. Methyl esters: Acidic and basic catalysts are used in the esterification of fatty acids and fats.

12.5 APPLICATIONS OF GLC

i. **Qualitative Analysis** - When two substances produce coincident peaks (one known and one unknown), it is inferred that the compounds are the same. The retention properties of an unknown chemical are determined by:

(a) **Specific Retention Volume (Vg)-** Carrier Gas Flow Rate X Adjusted Retention Time). However, there is very little repeatability in this on account of the variable packing density, liquid loading, support activity, age, etc.

(b) **Relative Retention (rA/B)-** Adjusted retention volume of drug A in comparison to reference standard B. Reproducibility is high in this case.

1. Presence of impurities.
2. Used in the quality control of:
    - ❖ Antibiotics - Penicillin, Gentamycin
    - ❖ Anti T.B drugs - Isoniazid, Ethambutol
    - ❖ Antivirals - Amantadine, Idoxuridine

i. Residual solvent analysis

ii. Analysis of various functional groups

iii. For the analysis of drugs of abuse

iv. In pharmaceutical R & D's to determine the identity of natural products which contains complex mixture of similar compounds

v. In the metabolomics studies.

CHAPTER 13 HIGH PERFORMANCE LIQUID CHROMATOGRAPHY

13.1 INTRODUCTION

Liquid chromatography (LC) was discovered in late 1890s by the Russian botanist, Tswett while he was trying to separate various plant pigments. The colored bands as produced on the adsorbent bed evoked the term chromatography (Chroma = color) for this type of separation. Later 1930s a primitive form of liquid-liquid chromatography by supporting the stationary phase water, on silica gel in the form of a packed bed and was demonstrated for the separation of acetyl amino acids. Ever since, liquid chromatography slowly transformed into gas chromatography and liquid chromatography as major divisions. The slow speed of separation in normal gravity based liquid chromatography was converted into high performance by the technological development of bonded phase columns with small particle size of 2-10-micron silica surface derivated with various chemistry making it polar to non- polar of various grades. The pressure required to extrude mobile phase was achieved by reciprocating pumps which can work at higher pressures such as 3000 psi (pounds per square inch). These machines are called High performance liquid chromatography (HPLC). Ever since, several developments in this area lead to lowering the particle size of particle in decreased further down to reach 1.5-2-micron particle size thereby necessitated to opt for mobile phase delivery pumps capable of delivering the required flow rate even at the pressure of 15000LBS. These machines are called ultrahigh performance liquid chromatography (UPLC or UHPLC). These UPLCs are capable of reducing the runtime with a finer separation of compounds. These machines are preferred for connecting it to mass spectrometers for precise analysis of compounds.

13.2 CHROMATOGRAPHY - A SEPARATION SCIENCE

In a broad objective, chromatography is separation science; in which precise knowledge of the compound help us to make an appropriate analytical method for its quantification. Apart from this lower pressure chromatography techniques are also routinely used for isolation of compounds from a crude mixture. In this chapter, we will understand the basic components of HPLC and its working principle.

- **(A) Types of Chromatography**
- **(B) (i) Modes of Separation in HPLC**
  - **(ii) Principle of Separation in HPLC**
- **(C) Basic Construction of HPLC**
- **(D) Working Principle of HPLC**
- **(E) Quantitative Analysis**

(A) Types of Chromatography

❖ Adsorption Chromatography

Adsorption chromatography is the of the primitive type for separation in which the stationary phase (adsorbent) is solid and the mobile phase (adsorbate) can either be liquid or gaseous in nature. Mobile phase molecules adsorb over the active site of the stationary phase and forms hydrogen bond with its hydroxyl groups. Alumina and silica are the most common adsorbents used because of their inert and porous nature which gives large surface area for adsorption.

Solute molecules are dissolved in the solution of mobile phase and travels through the length of stationary phase. Each solute molecule has differential equilibrium towards the solution of mobile phase and stationary phase. In a mixture of solute molecules to be separated from a solution the one with more affinity towards stationary phase and less towards mobile phase will form a band first followed by the one with lesser affinity towards stationary phase. Most often polar compounds are separated by this technique based on their differential distribution towards stationary phase. Thin layer chromatography, column chromatography and gas chromatography come under adsorption chromatography.

❖ Partition Chromatography

In partition chromatography partitioning of the solute molecules between two immiscible liquids take place. The stationary phase is a liquid (non-volatile) which forms a thin layer over the surface of an inert matrix. The mobile phase is liquid or gaseous and analyte to be separated are present in it. Differential distribution of solute molecules between two immiscible liquids leads to separation. Solute molecule having high affinity towards mobile phase will be eluted first and the once with higher affinity towards stationary phase will be eluted at the end. Non-polar and polar both molecules can be separated. Paper chromatography and high-performance liquid chromatography comes under partition chromatography.

❖ Ion-exchange Chromatography

In Ion-Exchange chromatography, retention of the analytes is based on the attraction of solute ion towards the charge sites (anionic or cationic) bound to the stationary phase. Solute ions of the opposite charge to the charged sites of the column are retained on the column and can be eluted from the column by using the mobile phase such as (salts, NaCl, ammonium acetate)/charged stationary phase (resin) charged solutes.

❖ Size Exclusion

In size exclusion chromatography compounds are separated on the basis of their molecular weight and are also known as permeation or gel chromatography. Hence, the affinity of solute towards the stationary phase is not the driving force towards the separation of compounds. The column is porous in nature and like a molecular sieve. Size exclusion works by trapping these smaller molecules in the pores of a particle. The larger molecules simply pass by the pores as they are too large to enter the pores. Larger molecules therefore flow through the column quicker than smaller molecules, that is, the smaller the molecule, the longer the retention time. This is mainly use for the separation of proteins, carbohydrates and polymers.

(B) (i) Modes of separation in HPLC

❖ Affinity

In affinity chromatography the stationary phase consists of a solid material made of cellulose beads usually of different grades of agarose on which a ligand (co-enzyme or substrate) is bound covalently in such a way that is active sites are exposed. The specific protein of interest to be purified specifically has affinity towards the bound ligand. The stationary phase consisting of ligand packed in a column and the buffer containing mixture of proteins is passed through the length of column only the specific protein of interest to be purified is retained in column as it gets bound to its specific ligand and all other proteins get eluted in the void volume. The ligand of stationary phase and protein interaction is reversible. As soon as buffer strength is changed in the mobile phase the desired protein gets eluted. This technique is mainly used in protein purification, antigen-antibody reaction, separation of hormone receptor, enzyme purification.

❖ Normal Phase

Normal phase HPLC is the one readily used type of HPLC, this method of HPLC separates analytes based on their affinity for the polar stationary phase such as silica. The analytes polar interaction with the stationary phase happens due to hydrogen bonding or dipole- dipole type of interactions. In this type of HPLC, the mobile phase is non-polar and thus works effectively for separating analytes readily soluble in non-polar solvents. The analyte associates with and is retained by the polar stationary phase. Adsorption strength increases with increased analyte polarity. The interaction strength depends not only on the functional groups present in the structure of the analyte molecule, but also on steric factors. The effect of steric hindrance on interaction strength allows this method to resolve (separate) structural isomers.

❖ Reverse Phase

Reverse phase HPLC consists of a non-polar stationary phase and a moderately polar mobile phase. Stationary phase primarily consists of silica with additional straight chain alkyl groups attached to its silanol groups so as to render hydrophobicity. The alkyl chain length ranges from C2 to C18 carbon and based on custom made requirements additional groups can be added to modify the column chemistry such as amino, cyano, phenyl, phenyl-hexyl, zwitterions. Non- polar compounds can be well separated by such a stationary phase as they are well retained by the column and based on their affinity are eluted from the column. Polar molecule is difficult to separate through such stationary phase because they are having very less affinity towards the stationary phase without special modifications.

❖ Ion-exchange & Size Exclusion/Gel Filtrate

Multimode or mixed mode of chromatography is the advancement to the chromatographic separation modes available. In other words, it is a combination of normal phase, reverse phase and ion–exchange chromatographic separation. The stationary phase comprised of two or more material based on the application for example silica based stationary phase with additional groups attached like long chain alkyl with octane-ethiol, gold nanoparticles, Nano polymer silica hybrids, cystamine, SIELC, RP/WAX-AQ, RP/WAX-AT, dionex, HILIC etc. In the conventional ion exchange technique either anionic or cationic analyte can be separate but with the multi-mode a mixture of cationic and anionic molecules can be separated together. Also, polar molecules with or without charge can be separated along with their non-polar counterpart together by multi-mode. For protein, enzyme and peptide separation multimode can be adopted in place of ion-exchange or affinity chromatography. Separation of an active drug molecule along with its metabolite is more successful with multimode as metabolites are polar in nature and the active drugs are either polar or non- polar. The method development in case of multimode is its key to the separation. Based on the compounds of interest to be separated the mobile phase selection and composition is crucial step and sometime cumbersome.

(B) (ii) Principle of Separation in HPLC

❖ Isocratic and Gradient Elution

They differ based on the composition of mobile phase. In isocratic mobile phase is same throughout the run. The mobile phase may comprise of either one solvent or a fix ratio of two solvents. In the gradient elution the ration of mobile phase changes with respect to time throughout the run.

❖ Derivatization

The derivatization of analyte of interest is usually done to increase the sensitivity and selectivity. In this the analyte bound to another molecule by chemical reaction so as to increase its detection intensity, decrease instability etc. There are pre and post derivatization techniques available based on the chemistry of analyte of interest.

(C) Basic Construction of HPLC

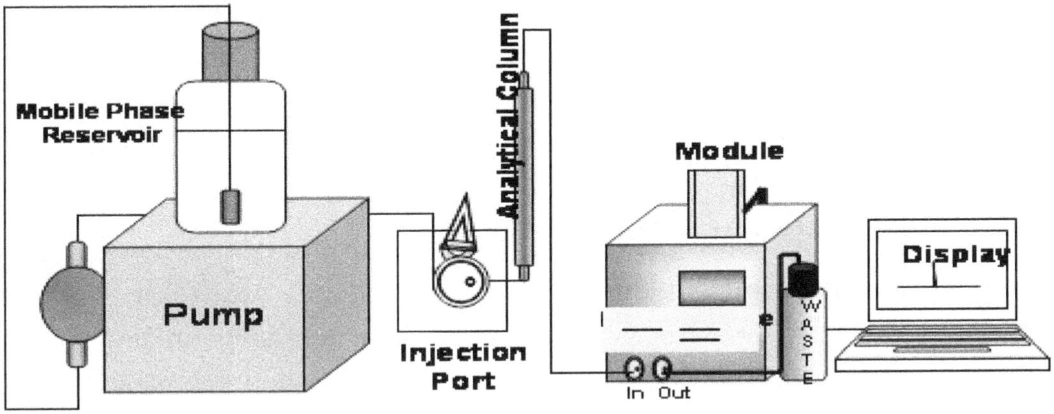

Figure 13.1: A typical HPLC system consisting of Mobile phase reservoir, pump, injector, column, detector and integrator.

As shown in the figure, a simple HPLC would be having a solvent dispenser, pump, injector, analytical column, detector and integrator. Due to several technological advancements, most of them are modified according to the performance.

(a) Mobile Phase: He phase that elutes the sample from the stationary phase Mobile phase in a HPLC system consists of solvent system that passes through the length of HPLC system. There are two types of Mobile phase that includes isocratic and gradient. In an isocratic mobile phase one solvent system ratio is used while in gradient system ratio of mobile phase composition changes with respect to time.

Based on the chemistry of analyte of interest the mobile phase composition is selected. Non- polar analytes are separated by the use of organic solvents that includes methanol, acetonitrile, n-hexane, dichloromethane, tetrahydrofuran, frifluoro acetic acid etc.

For the separation of polar molecules buffers are added in the mobile phase because of their ionizable nature. For their best separation pH of mobile phase has to be adjusted to make themun- ionized. The un-ionized state of such molecule is well retained by the column leads to peak separation and better retention.

Derivatizing agents are added in some of the analyte of interest for their enhanced resolution in HPLC system. The process can be pre-derivatization or post-derivatization based on the requirement. Ion-paring reagents are added in the mobile phase to enhance its affinity towards column that leads to their better resolution.

Sometimes organic modification in the mobile phase is essential because of tailing in reverse phase separation which is by ionization of the packing surface. Hydrolytic degradation of packing material leads to free silanol groups formation and react with the amine group present in the mobile phase. Older the column more the free silanol exists. To overcome this problem nonyl amine addition to the mobile phase is advised. Addition of varied amount of methanol or acetonitrile to the polar mobile phase increase retention of compounds in reverse phase column and hence leads better chromatographic resolution. □ Water for HPLC system

This is the water which is suitable for HPLC applications. Ultrapure water is prepared by subjecting distilled water (less in organic impurity with ions) or water made by reverse osmosis for the removal of organic and inorganic impurities by using ion exchange resins.

This grade of water can have a maximum resistance up to 18.2 MΩ·cm, compared to around 15 kΩ·cm for common tap water.

(b) Pump

It is made up of corrosive resistant metal fitted with a piston connected with a motor gear system to increase or decrease the flow of mobile phase.

(c) Injector

Injector for HPLC is connected in between the pump and the analytical column. At the load mode the flow of mobile phase by-passes the injector loop and in the inject mode the loop filled with the sample containing analyte is injected in line for separation in the column. Most of the modern day HPLCs are fitted with Rheodyne (Cotati, California, US) injector. Samples are introduced onto column with an injection valve or loop or more frequently with a micro syringe.

(d) Analytical Column

Stationary Phase: The media in which the separation of analyte takes place with respect to its affinity for the mobile phase.

The heart of HPLC system is HPLC columns, where separations of sample components take place.

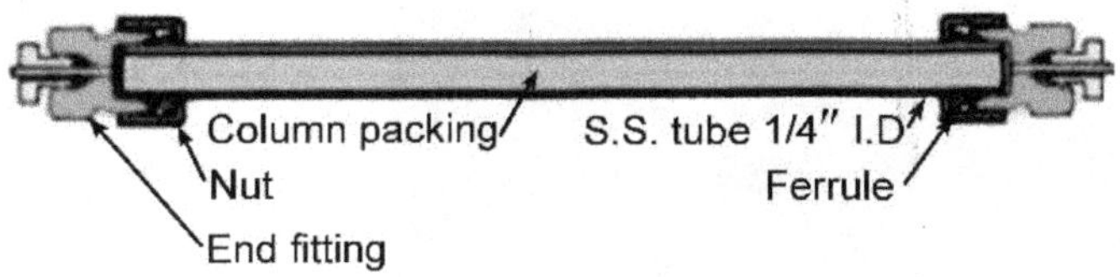

Columns are subjected to natural wear mainly due to irreversible adsorption of injected sample matrix or mechanical or chemical instabilities of stationary phase. HPLC columns are packed with very fine particles (usually a few microns in diameter). The very fine particles are required to attain the low dispersion that give the high plate counts expected of modern HPLC. Particle sizes generally range between 3 and 50 microns, with 5 μm particles being the most popular. Plate counts in excess of 25,000 plates per column are possible with modern columns.

- Bonded Phase Column
- Silica Based Columns

Artificial or refined packed silica is used as the column packing material. For the normal phase column high grade silica is used and for the reverse phase column silanol groups of silica are blocked by the alkyl straight chains. Varies length of alkyl side chains can be added ranging from C2 to C32. Most commonly C4, C8 and C18 length carbon chains are added. End-capping is usually performed in the columns so as to give additional hydrophilicity and better separation.

In this process additional alkyl chains are added so as to block the end silanol groups by a process called carbon loading. Carbon loading renders more hydrophobicity to a HPLC column. Customer made modifications are also made to the stationary phase by addition of phenyl, nitro, amino, cyano, phenyl–hexyl groups or even zwitterions to the silica for a wide variety of analyte separation.

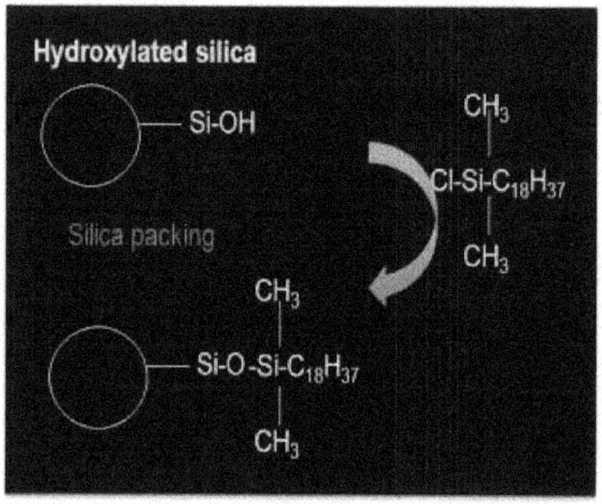

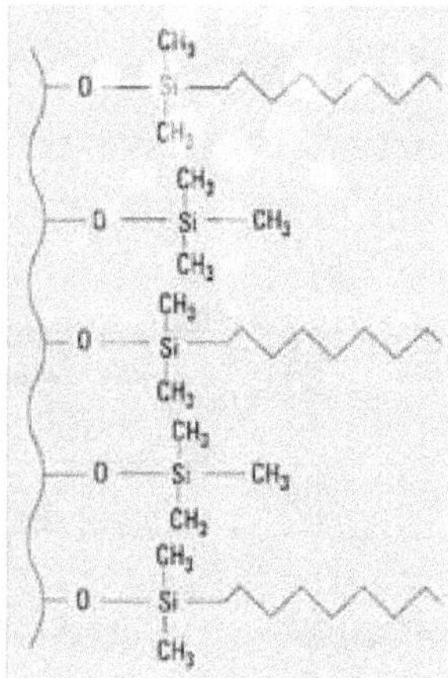

Polymer Based Columns

Polymer based column have higher pH stability compared to silica-based column. The pressure and solvent compatibility may vary with the type of polymer used. General rules followed for silica-based column care are not followed for polymer-based column. Manufacturer instructions need to be followed for such columns. These columns are compromised on mechanical stability as compared to silica-based column and leads to low column age.

Chiral Columns

Chiral separation is based on retention of one enantiomer over another in the sample mixture and cause enantio-selective separation. Chiral columns are used for separation of proteins, polysaccharides, antibiotics, chiral synthetic polymers, dextrin etc.

Carbohydrate Column

These are used for analysis of carbohydrates especially dietary products. It is based on ligand- exchange chromatography on polymeric phases based on sulphated polystyrene divinyl benzene, loaded with Ca^{2+}, Na^{+} or Pb^{2+}. Furanoses and pyranoses are bound to the metal cations via co-ordination complexes. The affinity for carbohydrates increases in the order of $Na^{+}<Ca^{2+}<Pb^{2+}$. Separation is carried out at 80-90° C, using water as solvent.

(e)Integrators

These are various types of integrators available for interpretation of the signal from the detector to quantify the response. Initially, calculations were made from the tracings of the chart recorders but it has been replaced with modern data integrators and computer aided software.

(f) Detector

The success of the high-pressure technique depends on the use of highly sensitive detectors because of small sample sizes. This requires the use of small-volume detectors, typically 10-100µl. The most widely used detectors are the refractive index monitor and the ultraviolet absorption photometer. The former detector monitors are refractive indices of the column effluent and pure solvent. Although RI detectors respond to most substances, they are not highly sensitive. Ultraviolet (UV) detectors can be 1000 times more sensitive than RI detectors. These UV detectors can be of continuously variable or fixed wavelength. Radioactivity detectors are extremely useful for β- emitting labelled compounds. Fluorescence properties of the compounds are also utilized for its successful detection. Electrochemical detectors are helpful in the estimation of neurotransmitters at the level of picograms.

Type of detectors used in HPLC

- **Refractive Index (RI) Detector**

Detection is based on refractive index of analyte as compared to mobile phase. They are the low sensitivity detectors and are mostly used for carbohydrate analysis.

- **Ultraviolet – Visible Detector**

Detection of analyte is based on the UV absorbance of the analyte of interest. The absorbance of the molecule in UV detector is based on the molar extinction coefficient of the molecule.

Absorbtion of UV radiation at a particular wavelength by the molecule causes its detection. More the amount of sample higher will be its UV absorbance. For molecules having low UV absorbance derivatization technique is employed. Derivatization leads to attachment of particular group having better UV absorbance to the analyte of interest and hence detection. For the detection of colored compounds UV absorbance at the visible range is used.

Deuterium light source (wavelength ranges from 200-400nm) and tungsten light source (wavelength ranges from 400-800nm) are employed in UV-Visible detector.

- **Photodiode array (PDA) detector**

It is a hybrid detector which is capable of monitoring all the visible to ultraviolet wavelengths of the incident beam continuously. The detector is having array of diodes instead of photomultiplier tube or photodiode, which is capable of monitoring from 200nm -800nm. The bundle of data generated is transformed into three-dimensional plot having time in 'x' axis, absorbance in 'y' axis and wavelength in 'z' axis. This detector is slightly less sensitive to single wave length UV or tunable UV-visible detector, however, capable of matching the peak spectrum with the standard to confirm the peak purity.

- **Fluorescent Detector**

Excitation induced emission property of analyte of interest is used in such detectors. It is more sensitive than UV detector. There limitation being detection of compounds having fluorescence. It is often powered with xenon light source which is capable of emitting light both in ultraviolet as well as in visible range.

- **Evaporation Light Scattering Detector**

The detector is based on the light scattering by the solid analyte after evaporation of mobile phase. The analyte must have low volatility as compared to the mobile phase. Size of droplet from the nebulizer and the particle size formed thereafter determine its light scattering intensity. Physical property of liquid and relative velocity and flow rate of gas and liquid determines droplet formation by nebulizer. More temperature is required to evaporate larger droplets thus formed and more light scattering intensity required. They are mainly used for lipid detection.

- **Electrochemical Detector**

The detection is based on the electric current through the electrodes from the chemical reaction of oxidisables or reducible analyte. Working electrode, auxiliary electrode and reference electrode are three part of electrochemical detector. There are two modes of operation coulometric detection and ampiometric detection. If the reaction at the electrode surface exhausts all the reactant and the current become zero, the total charge that passes will be proportional to the mass of solute detected. For obvious reasons this process is called coulometric detection. If the mobile phase is flowing past the electrodes, the solute will be continuously replaced as the peak passes through the detector. While there is solute present between the electrodes, a current will be maintained (albeit varying in magnitude). The process is called ampiometric detection. There are a number of electrode configurations, each having claims to special attributes; the electrochemical detector has been reported to be very flow sensitive for compounds like catecholamines etc.

- **Mass detector**

LC-MS is a powerful technique used for many applications which has very high sensitivity and specificity. Generally, its application is oriented towards the specific detection and potential identification of chemicals in the presence of other chemicals (in a complex mixture).

(D) Working Principle of HPLC

Mobile phase varies according to the column chemistry and type of analyte undergoing separation using that column. As adsorption and partition principles are employed in the separation in bonded phase silica columns, appropriate combination of solvents must be selected based on their miscibility index and viscosity. If it is aqueous based separations, additional factors such as ion paring reagents and buffers for maintaining the pH can be added to enable the fine separation of analyte of interest from the complex matrices like blood, urine, plant, tissue extracts and environmental samples.

Prepared mix of mobile phase is allowed to come back to room temperature as mixing Acetonitrile and water would be an endothermic event and mixing methanol with water would be an exothermic event which is expected to alter the final volume of the resultant mixture. These mobile phases are usually sonicated or vacuum filtered to reduce dissolved oxygen as its low solubility is expected to produce microbubbles during high pressure generated against the resistance of the column resulting in increased baseline noise.

Mostly silica (artificial or regenerated) based columns are used for HPLC in normal and reverse phase HPLC columns due to the advantage of silica in giving required tensile strength against the pressure, chemical inertness, porous nature, having sialinol groups which enable for chemical modification of the surface while converting its nature into various hydrophobic modifications (C2, C4, C8, C12, C18, C32 phenyl, amino, cyano, phenyl-hexyl etc). Due to this possibility, application of silica-based columns is having tremendous support in separation chemistry. The silica beads or particles are generally characterized by particle and pore size. Particle sizes generally range between 2 and 50 microns, with 5 μm particles being the most popular for peptides. 2μm particles are used for quantification experiments.

Larger particles will generate less system pressure and smaller particles will generate more pressure.

The smaller particles generally give higher separation efficiencies. The particle pore size is measured in angstroms and generally range between 100-1000 angstroms. 300 angstroms are the most popular pore size for proteins and peptides and 100 angstroms is the most common for small molecules.

The efficiency of the column for the analytical separation is expressed by the factor called Height Equivalent to Theoretical Plates (HETP). Plate counts more than 25,000 plates per column has been achieved in modern columns, however, these very high efficiencies are rarely found with real samples because of the dispersion or distortion due to instrument design. Maintaining the flow rates of 0.5-1ml in 2μm columns for very high HETP is complicated with the generation of high pressure at room temperature. Therefore, column oven heating systems are used by some instrument manufacturers to reach such limits. However, the most successful model is increasing the capability of the pump to reach pressures up to 15000 psi while maintaining the flow rate of 0.5-1ml per minute in ultrahigh performance liquid chromatography systems.

Van Deemter equation (1956) explains the plat number as a function of column property and the experimental conditions employed (Equation 1).

$$HETP = A + B/u + Cu \qquad ...(1)$$

HETP = Height of the theoretical plate

A = Eddy's diffusion (multi path effect of the solvent inside the column)

B = Random molecular diffusion

C = Mass transfer with in particle caused by mobile phase

u = Velocity of the mobile phase passing through the column

Although, silica is the most common particle material used for analytical separations, it is not free of some conditions. For example, silica dissolves at a higher pH, therefore, it is not recommended for using solvents exceeding pH 8. Recent modifications in the column chemistry introduced silica-based technologies which are more resistant to high pH, temperature and pressure however, it if it is important that one must read the manufacturer's instructions well before using them for analytical use.

Mechanism behind the separations in reverse phase chromatography

As already mentioned, the column chemistry in reverse phase columns is having modified surface bonded phases. For most of the analytical applications revere phase columns are widely developed and employed due to its versatility. Let us take a common example of octadecyl (C_{18}) column for understanding the separation. Let us select the mobile phase as methanol in which an analyte like cyclosporine having higher logP value is injected. The separation would be based on the property of the analyte's affinity towards the hydrophobic C_{18} chains. The differential distribution between hydrophobic interacting C_{18} chains and mobile phase makes the molecule to crawl on the stationary bed thereby a considerable delay caused. This delay is called as retention time of that particular analyte.

Whereas a mixture of methanol and water is used, a layer of methanol is artificially formed on the silica particles derivate with C_{18} making it as a methanol layer, upon which then gliding biphasic water and methanol mobile phase increases the delay time of a particular analyte based on its hydrophobicity in the mobile phase. The hydrophobicity of the compounds (salts of organic acids or bases) can be induced by altering the pH of the mobile phase and making it unionized in the given pH.

(E) Quantitative Analysis

Quantification of compounds are performed on the basis of either considering peak height or peak area. In a well resolved chromatographic peak the peak area/height increases with respect to the increase in concentration and is then analyzed. There are two methods for sample analysis that includes external calibration and internal calibration.

External calibration: In this method known concentration of analyte is injected with respect to the increase in the concentration. Intensity of peak area or height will increase with respect to time in a linear manner. The concentration of unknown analyte can then be plotted by following equation:

$$\text{Conc.}_{\text{unknown}} = \left(\frac{\text{Area}_{\text{unknown}}}{\text{Area}_{\text{known}}} \right) \text{conc.}_{\text{known}}$$

Internal calibration: In this method analyte of interest is plotted with a known internal standard. The internal standard concentration is kept constant throughout the experiment.

The increase peak area or height if analyte with increase in concentration for the analyte is plotted with respect to the internal standard. The concentration of unknown analyte can then be plotted by following equation

$$\text{Conc.}_{\text{unknown}} = \left(\frac{\text{Area}_{\text{Internal Std.in known}}}{\text{Area}_{\text{Internal Std.in unknown}}} \right) \times \left(\frac{\text{Area}_{\text{unknown}}}{\text{Area}_{\text{known}}} \right) \times (\text{Conc.}_{\text{known}})$$

CHAPTER 14 AFFINITY CHROMATOGRAPHY

14.1 INTRODUCTION

- 1930s Affinity Chromatography was developed for the study of enzymes and other proteins.
- **Affinity Chromatography (AC)** - is the purification of a biomolecule with respect to the specific binding of that biomolecule due to the chemical structure.

History of Affinity Chromatography

- 1930s, first developed by A. Wilhelm Tiselius-a Swedish biochemist, won the Nobel Prize in 1948.
- Used to study enzymes and other proteins.
- Relies on the affinity of various biochemical compounds with specific properties.

14.2 AFFINITY CHROMATOGRAPHY

- Affinity Chromatography is essentially a sample purification technique, used primarily for biological molecules such as proteins.
- It is a method of separating a mixture of proteins or nucleic acids (molecules) by specific interactions of those molecules with a component

known as a ligand, which is immobilized on a support. If a solution of, say, a mixture of proteins is passed over (through) the column, one of the proteins binds to the ligand on the basis of specificity and high affinity (they fit together like a lock and key).

- The other proteins in the solution wash through the column because they were not able to bind to the ligand.

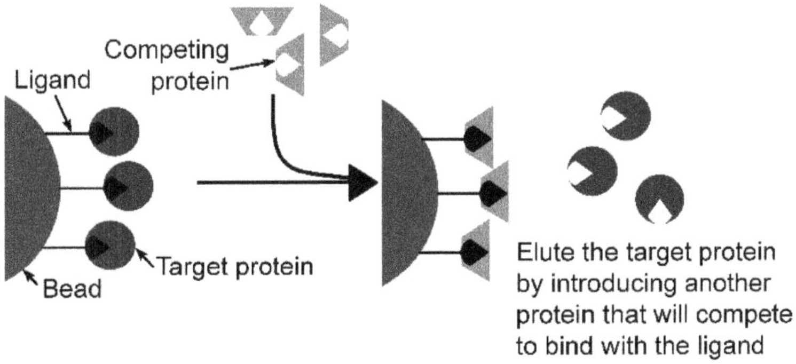

14.3 PRINCIPLE

- Affinity chromatography is one of the most diverse and powerful chromatographic methods for purification of a specific molecule or a group of molecules from complex mixtures
- It is based on highly specific biological interactions between two molecules such as interactions between enzyme and substrate, receptor and ligand, or antibody and antigen.
- These interactions which are typically reversible are used for purification by placing one of the interacting molecules referred to as affinity ligand onto a solid matrix to create a stationary phase while a target molecule is in the mobile phase.
- Many of the commonly used ligands coupled to affinity matrices are now commercially available and are ready to use.

14.4 CHROMATOGRAPHIC MEDIA

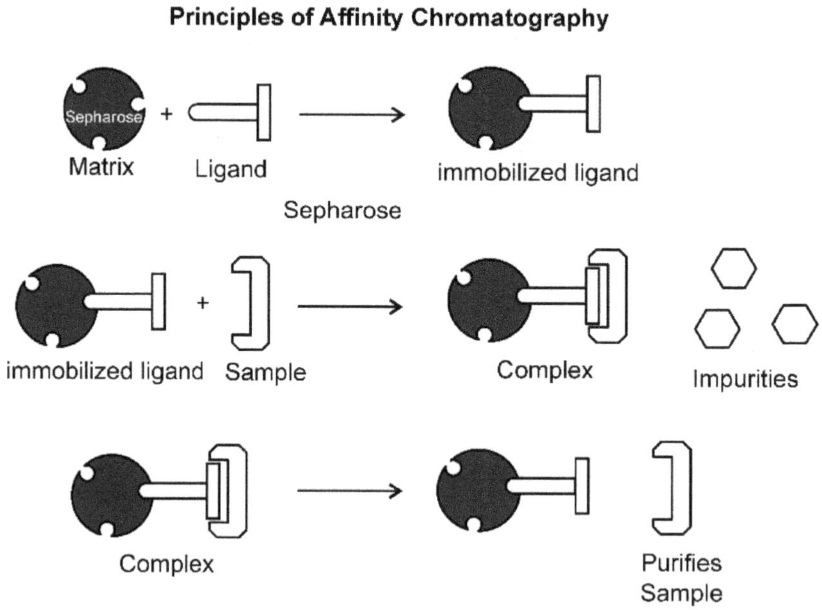

- A matrix in its use here is a substance, usually in bead form to which a specific ligand is covalently bound.
- In order to for the matrix to be effective it must have certain characters:
- It must be insoluble in solvents and buffers employed in the process
- It must be chemically and mechanically stable...
- It must be easily coupled to a ligand or spacer arm onto which the ligand can be attached.
- It must exhibit good flow properties and have a relatively large surface area for attachment

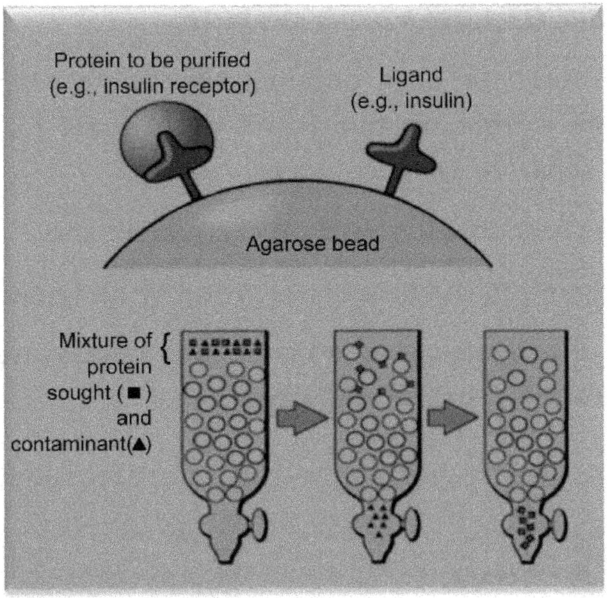

14.5 IMMOBILIZED LIGAND

- The ligand can be selected only after the nature of the macromolecule to be isolated is known.
- When a hormone receptor protein is to be purified by affinity chromatography, the hormone itself is an ideal candidate for the ligand.
- For antibody isolation, an antigen or happen may be used as ligand.
- If an enzyme is to be purified, a substrate analog, inhibitor, cofactor, or effector may be used as an immobilized ligand.

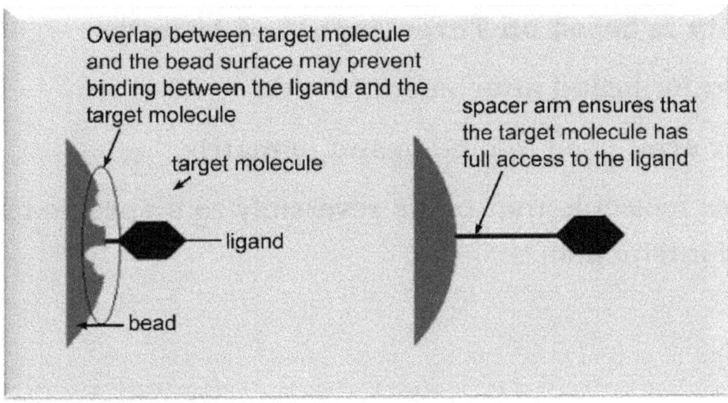

14.6 ATTACHMENT OF LIGAND TO MATRIX

- Several procedures have been developed for the covalent attachment of the ligand to the stationary phase. All procedures for gel modification proceed in two separate chemical steps:
- Activation of the functional groups on the matrix and
- Joining of the ligand to the functional group on the matrix.

A wide variety of activated gels is now commercially available. The most widely used are described in the following:

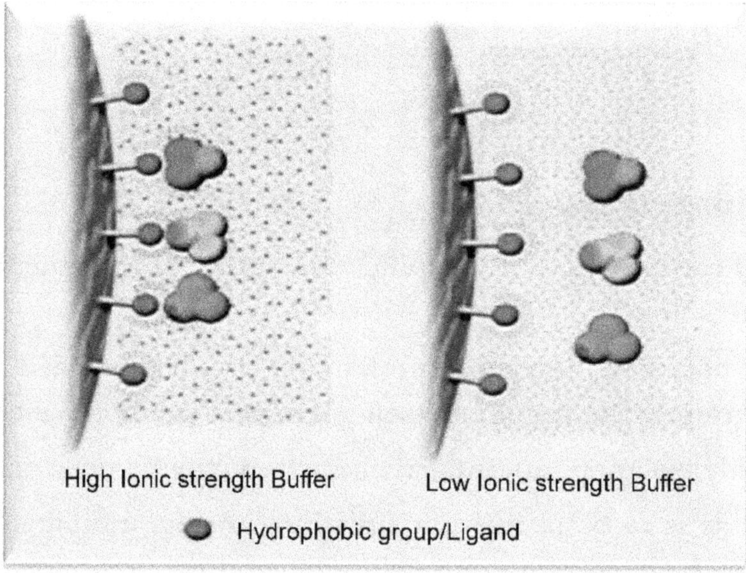

1. Specificity is based on Three Aspect of Affinity

1. **Matrix:** for ligand attachment.
2. **Spacer arm:** used to bind ligand to matrix.
3. **Ligand:** molecule that binds reversibly to a specific target molecule (site of interaction)

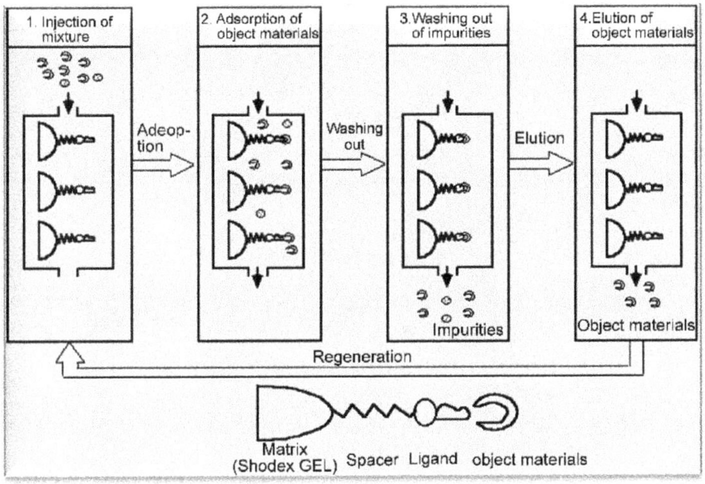

2. Examples

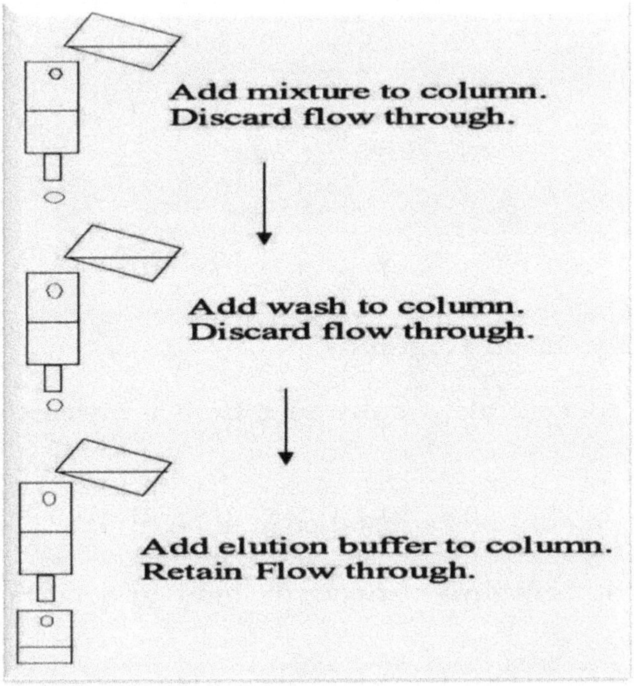

- Antigen → Antibody
- Antibody → Antigen

- Substrate → Enzyme
- DNA → Histon
- Hormone → Binding Protein/Receptor

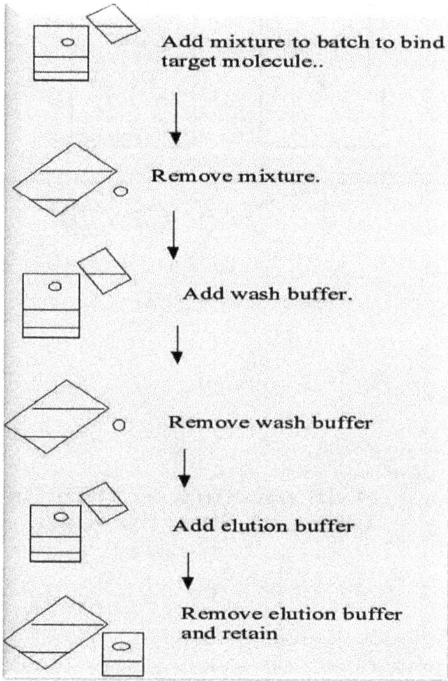

3. Used of Affinity Chromatography

- ❖ Purify and concentrate a substance from a mixture into a buffering solution
- ❖ Reduce the amount of a substance in a mixture
- ❖ Discern what biological compounds bind to a particular substance, such as drugs
- ❖ Purify and concentrate an enzyme solution

4. Advantages of Affinity Chromatography

1. Extremely high specificity

2. High degrees of purity can be obtained
3. The process is very reproducible
4. The binding sites of biological molecules can be simply investigated

5. Disadvantages of Affinity Chromatography

1. Expensive ligands
2. Leakage of ligand
3. Degradation of the solid support
4. Limited lifetime
5. Non-specific adsorption
6. Relatively low productivity

6. Applications

1. It is used for isolation and purification of all biological macromolecule.
2. It is used to purify nucleic acid, antibodies, and enzymes etc.
3. To notice which biological compounds bind to a particular substance.
4. To reduce an amount of substance in a mixture.
5. Used in Genetic Engineering - nucleic acid purification.
6. Production of Vaccines - antibody purification from blood serum.
7. And Basic Metabolic Research - protein or enzyme purification from cell free extract.

CHAPTER 15

ELECTROPHORESIS

15.1 INTRODUCTION

The surface area grows and separation is improved when the particle size is reduced. The mobile phase's flow rate will, however, be slower when the particle size is reduced.

In HPLC, we employ extremely small particles to achieve excellent separation. High pressure pumps are used to force the mobile phase through the stationary phase in order to address the flow rate problem. To resist the extreme pressure, columns are constructed from stainless steel. As a result, at any given pH, many significant biological compounds, including amino acids, peptides, proteins, nucleotides, and nucleic acids, exist in solution as electrically charged species, either as cations or anions. Depending on the makeup of their net charge, these charged particles will migrate either to the cathode or to the anode under the influence of an electric field. All kinds of molecular biology and RDT investigations employ this as one of the most essential processes.

The Rate of migration of charged molecules depends upon following factors:

(a) The strength of electric field, size and shape.

(b) Relative hydrophobicity of the sample.

(c) Ionic strength and temperature of the buffer.

(d) Molecular size of the taken biomolecule.

(e) Net charge density of the taken bio molecule.

(f) Shape of the taken biomolecule.

In the process of electrophoresis large molecules have more difficulty in moving through the supporting medium (i.e., gel) whereas the smaller medium has more mobility through it.

15.2 CLASSIFICATION OF ELECTROPHORESIS

These days, supporting media are a part of every electrophoretic device. A supporting medium is a material that serves as a physical barrier through which charged molecules are separated. Adsorption and molecular sieving of the taken molecules that are intended to be separated are its two main uses.

The question now is why use a supporting medium instead of employing an electrophoretic tank with two electrodes and applying the fundamentals of electrochemistry to separate these charged molecules. This is how things had been in the beginning. Tiselieus *et al* 1948's ground breaking electrophoresis research was limited to free solution. However, it soon became clear that this method had a number of drawbacks, most notably the negative consequences of convection currents (Current brought on by the expansion of a liquid, solid, or gas as its temperature increases.

By stabilising the medium, this distortion and relatively random arrangement of the dispersed molecules might be reduced. By performing electrophoresis on a porous mechanical support, this was accomplished. The supporting medium's viscosity (which is lacking in free solution) slows down the conventional currents, separating the molecules into sharp zones. Starch, agar, polyacrylamide, and agarose are a few of the widely utilized supporting media. The electrophoresis may be divided into two categories: free electrophoresis and zone electrophoresis, depending on whether supporting media are present or absent.

A. Free Electrophoresis:

A free electrolyte is used in place of supporting medium in this form of electrophoresis. These days, this kind of electrophoresis is largely employed in non-biological investigations and has gone out of date.

It mainly consists of two types: moving boundary electrophoresis, which has long been used for quantitative analysis of complex mixtures of macromolecules, particularly proteins, and micro- electrophoresis, which is primarily used in calculating Zeta potentials (a colloidal property of cells in a liquid medium).

B. Zone Electrophoresis:

This is the most prevalent electrophoretic technique of these days. In this type of electrophoresis, the separation process is carried out on a stabilizing media as discussed above. The zone electrophoresis is of following types;

(a) Paper electrophoresis

(b) Cellulose acetate electrophoresis

(c) Capillary electrophoresis

(d) Gel electrophoresis – which further includes Agarose gel electrophoresis, SDSPAGE, PFGE and two-dimensional electrophoresis. Paper electrophoresis

Introduction

Von Klobusitzky and Konig successfully used an electrophoretic field to separate components of snake venom on paper strips saturated with an electrolytic solution, although the majority of the early electrophoretic investigations of biomolecules were conducted in liquid phase. This "paper electrophoresis" predates the method of "paper chromatography," with which it is typically connected, by a number of years. This solid phase electrophoresis was utilized in the late 1940s and early 1950s to describe a wide range of physiologically significant compounds, including the amino acids. The capacity of the solid support to sustain migration is what gives solid support electrophoresis an edge over free solution electrophoresis.

Definition

The electrophoresis procedure used on filter paper is known as paper electrophoresis. In this process, charged particles move through a colloid under the influence of an electric field; positively charged particles go toward the cathode and negatively charged particles toward the anode.

This type of electrophoresis uses filter paper (similar to chromatography paper) as the supporting medium to separate samples under the influence of an applied electric field. The filter paper has a little adsorption capacity and consistent pore size. A strip of filter paper used for paper electrophoresis is soaked with buffer and its ends are dipped into buffer reservoirs that include electrodes. After applying a high voltage and spotting the samples in the paper's centre, the spots move in accordance with their charges. Depending on their chemical identity, the electrophoretically separated components can be found using a number of staining procedures.

15.3 PRINCIPLE OF PAPER ELECTROPHORESIS

The pH of the medium affects the charge that each molecule carries. Because of diffusion, low voltage electrophoresis is often not used to separate low molecular weight substances, however amino acids make a better example of the link between charge and pH than proteins or other macromolecules do.

Components of Paper Electrophoresis

(i) Paper: In paper electrophoresis, Paper is used as the supporting medium. But in other types, agar gels, polyacrylamide gels (PAGE), starch blocks or cellulose acetate strips are used as medium for separation. Normally whatmann filter paper (No. 1) of suitable dimension (2.5 cm to 5 cm width) with a length so that both ends of the strip of paper touches the buffer solution, kept in the electrode vessels. The paper to be used is washed with distilled water followed by 0.1 M HCl or 0.01M EDTA to remove impurities.

(ii) **Electrode & Voltage to be Applied:** The electrode in the form of a thin wire, is made up of carbon or platinum. A DC voltage of about 8-15 V/cm length of paper is normally applied. In low voltage electrophoresis, the voltage across two electrodes is about 100-300 V, with a current of 0.4 m Amp per cm width or 1.5 m Amp/strip.

In High voltage electrophoresis, a potential of about 50-215V/cm (Total 10,000V/strip) is applied across the electrodes.

(iii) **Electrolyte/buffers used:** In the separation process, buffers of various pH and ionic strengths are employed. The kind of substances to be separated determines the pH of the buffer that should be employed.

Compound migration velocities in paper electrophoresis are influenced by the ionic strength of the buffer employed. Ionic strength has an inverse relationship with compound migration. Migration moves more quickly at low ionic strength, although the divided bands look diffused. In most separations, ionic strengths between 0.05 and 0.5 are often utilized, pH 3.0–6.8 example Citrate buffer.

Types of Paper Electrophoresis

There are two types of Paper electrophoresis based on the voltage applied, i.e. low voltage or high voltage Paper electrophoresis. In high voltage paper electrophoresis voltage is having range of 50-215V/cm while Low voltage paper electrophoresis is having range of 8-15V/cm.

High voltage paper electrophoresis has the following advantages.

- Separation is faster. hence less time is required for separation.
- Sharp bands are obtained, since there is less diffusion of bands.

- As sharp bands are obtained, separation of closely related compounds can be achieved.
- More number of samples can be analyzed simultaneously.

Horizontal/Vertical/ Continuous Electrophoresis

There are different types of electrophoretic instruments based on the design of the instrument.

The diagrams of these 3 types of instruments are shown in figure 1 to 3.

Analytical scale uses horizontal and vertical modes, whereas preparative scale uses continuous electrophoresis.

Although the fundamentals of each mode are the same, each instrument's design is unique.

Two beakers are filled with a buffer solution that has a known pH and ionic strength (Figures 1 and 2), horizontally and vertically. Cut into practical sizes (2.5–5 cm wide and adequate length), Whatmann filter paper of the appropriate grade is submerged in buffer solution. The centre of the paper is covered with 10 to 20μl of sample solution, which is then fixed in place.

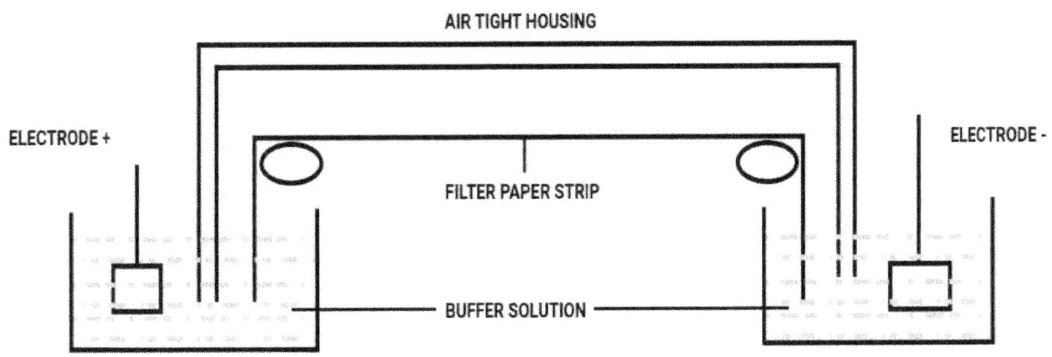

Figure 15.1: Horizontal Paper Electrophoresis.

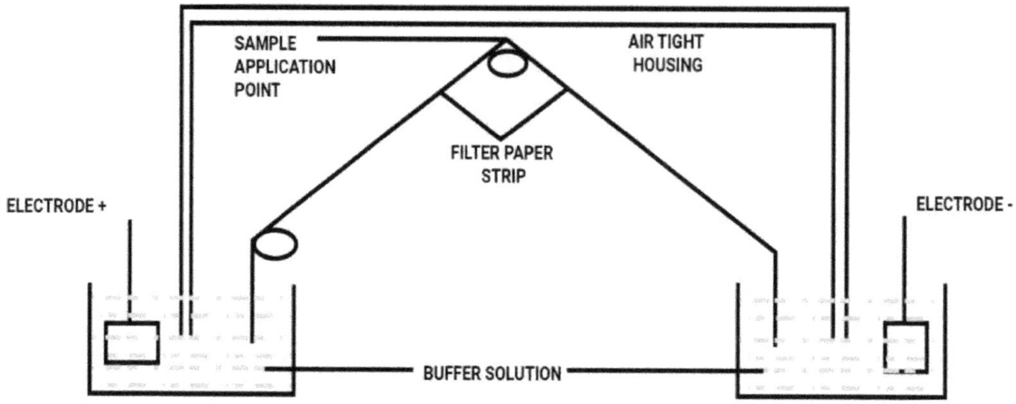

Figure 15.2: Vertical Paper Electrophoresis.

Electrophoresis: Two electrodes immersed in buffer solution are subjected to an appropriate potential (100- 300V). Anions and cations move toward the anode and cathode, respectively, when such a voltage is provided across two electrodes. Neutral/non-ionizable compounds remain stationary. As a result, chemicals are separated from the mixture.

Because gravity has an impact on ion migration in the vertical mode, separation takes a long time. The paper is removed and dried to fix the spots or bands after an appropriate amount of migration. The molecules, bands, or spots can then be seen visually, much as in paper chromatography. Densitometers can be used for spot quantitation as well. The horizontal mode is similar to the vertical mode, in principle. However, the paper is placed on a flat bed, as shown in figure 2. The procedure to be

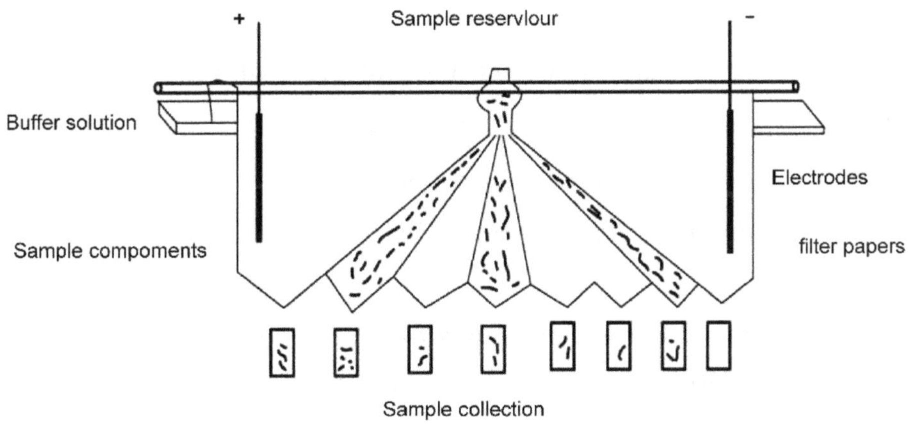

Figure 15.3: Continuous Electrophoresis.

Followed is same as that of vertical type. In horizontal mode, it takes about 10-12 hours for separation.

Continuous electrophoresis (Figure 3) is meant for preparative samples, where a predetermined sample volume through a valve device is applied continuously on the centre of a paper. The application of voltage causes migration of samples and hence compounds are separated as bands. Thus, each band is made to fall down and pure compounds are collected in separate containers. The solvent is evaporated and fractions are reused.

The rate of migration (Separation of particles) during electrophoresis will depend on the following factors:

Factors affecting migration of ions

1. The Sample
2. The Electric Field
3. The Medium
4. The Buffer

1. **The Sample:** Charge/mass ratio of the sample dictates its electrophoretic mobility. The mass consists of not only the size (molecular weight) but also the shape of the molecule.

a. **Charge:** The higher the charge, greater is the electrophoretic mobility. The charge is dependent on pH of the medium.

b. **Size:** The bigger molecules have a small electrophoretic mobility compared to the smaller particles.

c. **Shape:** The globular protein will migrate faster than the fibrous protein

2. **The Electric Field:** The rate of migration under unit potential gradient is referred to as "Mobility of the ion". An increase in potential gradient increases the rate of migration.

3. **The Medium:** The inert medium can exert adsorption & molecular sieving effects on the particle, influencing its rate of migration.

(a) **Adsorption:** It means retention of a component on the surface of supporting medium. The rate and resolution of the electrophoretic separation can be efficiently reduced by adsorption.

(b) **Molecular sieving:** Media such as "Polyacrylamide", "Agar", "Starch" & "Sephadex" have cross-linked structures giving rise to pores within the gel beads. Sephadex, molecules larger than the pores are excluded from entering the gel beads & these molecules migrate faster.

Polyacrylamide, Starch & Agarose the larger molecules also are made to squeeze through the pores. The smaller molecules pass through the pores easily, but the larger molecules are retarded.

4. **The Buffer:** The buffer can affect the electrophoretic mobility of the sample in various ways.

(a) **Composition:** Commonly used buffers are "Format", "Acetate", "Citrate", "Phosphate", "EDTA" "Acetate" "Pyridine", "Tris" (2-amino, 2-hydroxymethyl, 1,3-diol pentane) and "Barbitone" etc. The choice of buffer depends upon the type of sample being electrophoresed.

(b) **Ionic Strength:** "Ionic Strength (I) is a measure of the electrical environment of ions in a sol". When increase ionic strength of the buffer means a larger share of the current being carried by the buffer ions & meager (small quantity) proportion carried by the sample ions. When decrease ionic strength, a larger share of the current being carried by the sample ions leading to a faster separation. Note: The ionic strength used is usually between 0.05 to 0.1M.

c) **pH:** The pH determines the degree of ionization of organic compounds; it can also affect the rate of migration of these compounds. When increase pH, increases ionization of organic acids. Decrease in pH, increases ionization of organic bases. E.g.: an Ampholyte (Amino acid) - The amino acid has both acidic & basic properties

Applications:

1. Serum analysis for diagnostic purpose is carried out by paper electrophoresis.
2. Muscle protein (Myosin), egg protein (albumin), milk protein (casein), snake and insect venoms have been satisfactorily analysed using paper electrophoresis.
3. Separation of enzymes in blood
4. Separation of alkaloids and antibiotics

Advantages:

1. The technique is easy to follow
2. The cost of the instrument is low
3. Operational costs are less
4. Number of samples can be separated on a single paper

Disadvantages:

It is very time-taking. Around 14-16 hours are needed for the process of complete separation.

15.4 GEL ELECTROPHORESIS

Introduction

Gel is used as a supporting medium in gel electrophoresis, which separates DNA, RNA, or proteins under the influence of an electric charge. The majority of the time, it is carried out for analytical purposes, but it may also be employed as a pre-processing technique to partly purify molecules before they are utilized in other techniques like mass spectrometry, PCR, cloning, DNA sequencing, and immuno-blotting.

This form of electrophoresis is the one that is most often employed in biotechnology labs and is utilized in practically all RD research.

Principle:

The molecules (proteins or nucleic acids) are pushed or pulled through the gel matrix by the electromotive force (EMF) produced across the electrodes. If the molecules are positively charged or negatively charged, they migrate toward the cathode, respectively.

A typical gel electrophoresis apparatus is of two kinds:

(a) **Vertical Gel Apparatus:** It is used for the separation of proteins in SDS-PAGE.

(b) **Horizontal Gel Apparatus:** It is used for immune-electrophoresis, isoelectric focusing and electrophoresis of DNA and RNA in the agarose gel.

Types of Gel-Electrophoresis:

Agarose Gel Electrophoresis:

The supporting medium in this type of electrophoresis is agarose gel. This is used for the electrophoresis of Nucleic acids like DNA and RNA.

1. **Principle:** Biomolecules (such as nucleic acids) are loaded into a horizontal electrophoretic tank containing agarose gel and electrodes. When a potential difference is applied across the electrodes, the

biomolecules separate into larger and smaller molecular sizes and move to the electrodes that correspond to those sizes. In this case, agarose gel serves as a filter.

In the gel, the bigger and bulkier molecules stay behind while the smaller molecules travel swiftly and quickly towards their respective electrodes, just as in a sieve, the large particles stay above and the smaller particles that are smaller than the pore size pass through it.

Instrumentation:

1. Physical Apparatus:

This includes the physical body of the experimental set-up. It is of following three types:

(a) **Electrophoretic Apparatus:** The Horizontal Gel Electrophoresis System is made to separate DNA restriction fragments on agarose gels extremely quickly and clearly. Gel equipment varies depending on the brand. Flatbed horizontal equipment is the most basic device. This device comprises of two buffer chambers, an agarose wick that is poured into one, and a horizontal bed of agarose with tiny wells for sample loading.

(b) **Power supply:** For a standard agarose gel electrophoresis a voltage of 5 volts per cm of gel is applied (the cm value is the distance between the two electrodes, not the length of the gel).

(c) **Trans illuminator:** This is an ultraviolet light box which is used to visualize ethidium bromide-stained DNA in gels.

2. Chemical Components:

This includes all the chemical components which are involved in the electrophoresis of the biomolecule.

(a) **Supporting Media:** Agarose is a polysaccharide extracted from seaweed. It is a linear polymer composed of alternating isomers of the sugar D- and L-galactose. Agarose melts approximately at 90°C and gels approximately at 40°C (Fig. 4). This gelation results in a mesh of channels with a diameter varying form 50-200nm. The diameters of these channels determine the final porosity of the gel and acts as the sieve.

By using gels with different concentrations of agarose, one can resolve different sizes of DNA fragments. Higher concentrations of agarose facilitate separation of small DNAs, while low agarose concentration is maintained during the separation of DNA having higher molecular weight. It is typically used at concentrations of 0.5 to 2%.

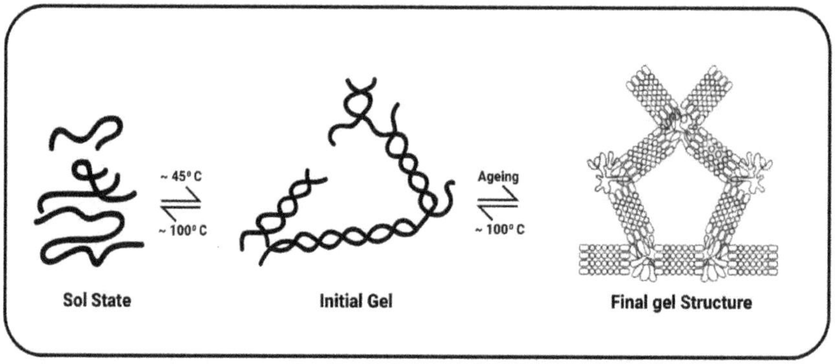

Figure 15.4: Gel Structure of Agarose (b) Buffer.

The gel is submerged in an electrophoresis buffer, which offers ions to conduct a current and some sort of buffer to keep the pH at a fairly consistent level. Different buffers can be used for agarose electrophoresis depending on the application and the size of the DNA electrophoresed.

Agarose gel electrophoresis buffers are most frequently made using TAE buffer (also known as Tris Acetate EDTA). TAE delivers the finest resolution for bigger DNA while having the lowest buffering capacity of the buffers. TAE also needs longer time and a lower voltage. For tiny DNA fragments, TBE buffer (Tris/Borate/EDTA) is frequently utilized (i.e., less than 500bp). Although sodium borate buffer, often known as

SB buffer, is a novel buffer, fragments bigger than 5 kb cannot be resolved with it. SB has advantages in its low conductivity, allowing higher voltages (up to 35 V/cm). This could allow a shorter analysis time for routine electrophoresis. Two types of buffers are used in the process of agarose electrophoresis.

1. **Electrophoresis Buffer:** This type of buffer is used to bathe the gel placed on horizontal tank. Usually Tris-ace-tate-EDTA (TAE) or Tris-borate- EDTA (TBE) is taken as electrophoresis buffer.
2. **Loading Buffer:** This contains a dense medium (e.g., glycerol) to allow the sample to "fall" into the sample wells, and one or two tracking dyes, which migrate in the gel and allow visual monitoring of the extent of electrophoresis.

(b) **Dye:** This is a tracking agent that aims at visualizing the separated nucleic acid after the process of electrophoresis. In the agarose gel electrophoresis Ethidium bromide is used as a dye. Ethidium bromide is a fluorescent dye that binds to DNA and intercalates between the stacked bases.

When irradiated with UV light of a wavelength of 302 nm, ethidium bromide will emit fluorescence light of a wavelength of 590 nm (orange). After the process of electrophoresis, the gel is observed under the beam of UV light produced by the trans- illuminator. The dye is added to the gel during its preparation only.

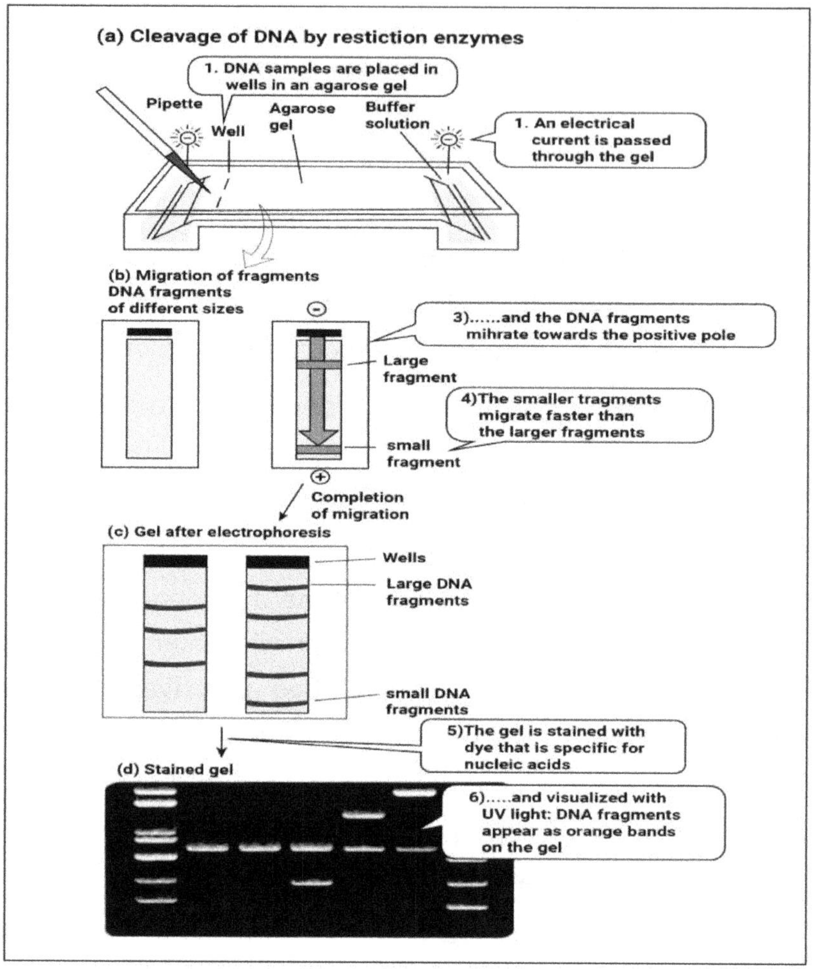

Figure 15.5: Gel Electrophoresis.

3. Procedure:

The agarose powder is first combined with the electrophoresis buffer to the necessary concentration, and then cooked completely in the microwave. The necessary concentration of agarose powder and electrophoresis buffer is first combined, and the mixture is then heated in a microwave until completely melted. Ethidium bromide is typically added to the gel at this point (final concentration: 0.5 mg/ml) to aid in the visualization of DNA following electrophoresis.

The solution is poured into a casting tray that contains a sample comb after being cooled to roughly 60°C and allowed to set up at room temperature. The comb is removed when the gel has hardened, being careful not to shred the wells' bottoms. Samples containing DNA mixed with loading buffer are then pipetted into the sample wells of the electrophoresis chamber while the lid and power leads are secured to the device. A current is then delivered to the gel while it is still in its plastic tray.

Bubbles coming off the electrodes should demonstrate that current is moving. DNA will go in the direction of the positive electrode, which is often red in colour. When sufficient movement has taken place, DNA fragments are stained with ethidium bromide to make them visible. This fluorescent pigment intercalates itself between DNA and RNA bases. However, the gel can also be stained after electrophoresis by soaking in a diluted solution of ethidium bromide. It is frequently incorporated into the gel such that colouring occurs during electrophoresis.

The gel is set up on an ultraviolet trans-illuminator to see DNA or RNA. Be mindful that DNA will disperse with time within the gel, thus an examination or photo should be taken right once after the electrophoresis has finished.

4. Application of Agarose Gel Electrophoresis:

a. Separation of restriction enzyme digested DNA including genomic DNA, prior to Southern Blot transfer. It is often used for separating RNA prior to Northern transfer.

b. Analysis of PCR products after polymerase chain reaction to assess for target DNA amplification.

c. Allowing estimation of the size of DNA molecules using a DNA marker or ladder which contains DNA fragments of various known sizes.

d. Allows the rough estimation of DNA quantity and quality.

e. Quantity is assessed using lambda DNA ladder which contains specific amounts of DNA in different bands.

f. Quality of DNA is assessed by observing the absence of streaking or fragments (or contaminating DNA bands).

g. Other techniques rely on agarose gel electrophoresis for DNA separation including DNA fingerprinting.

Advantages and Disadvantages of Agarose Gel Electrophoresis:

The gel's pourability and lack of denaturement of the samples are benefits. Additionally, samples can be retrieved.

The drawbacks include the possibility of gels melting during electrophoresis, the possibility of running out of buffer, and the potential for unexpected genetic material behaviour.

SDS-Page:

5. Introduction:

Proteins are typically separated according to size using polyacrylamide gel electrophoresis with sodium dodecyl sulphate (SDS). One of the most effective methods for separating proteins based on their molecular weight is this one.

6. Principle:

Sodium Dodecyl Sulfate (SDS), an anionic detergent used in this method, denatures polypeptides into their constituent polypeptide subunits and imparts a uniformly negative charge along each one. SDS also completes another crucial duty.

It compels polypeptides to stretch out into similar charge-to-mass ratios. As a result, the impacts of shape variations are eliminated by SDS treatment, leaving only the chain length, which represents their molecular mass, to determine the rate of protein migration during electrophoresis.

We acquire distinct bands of proteins ordered in a decreasing order of their molecular mass from the cathode to the anode when these denatured polypeptides are loaded at the cathode end of an electrophoretic tank with polyacrylamide gel (as the supporting media). The size of the gel's pores and the intensity of the electric field both affect how quickly things move. The vertical gel apparatus is typically employed in SDS-PAGE. Although it is used to separate proteins on a routine basis, SDS-PAGE can also be used to separate DNA and RNA molecules.

6. Instrumentation:

A. Physical Apparatus:

This includes the physical body of the experimental set-up. It is of following two types:

a. **Electrophoretic Apparatus:** Vertical horizontal tank with electrodes, gel cassettes, Teflon spacers, clips, pipette or syringe, comb, acrylic cover

b. **Power Supply:** A power supply of 100-200 volts is needed. This is ideal for running and transferring protein resolving gels.

c. **Staining Box:** These are trays in which the gels are stained and made up of clear plastics. These are resistant to most organic dyes, silver and other stains.

B. Chemical Components:

This includes the following:

(a) **Supporting Media:** SDS-PAGE The supporting medium is acrylamide. When acrylamide dissolves in water, it turns into a white, crystalline powder that then goes through a polymerization step to create a structure resembling a net known as polyacrylamide. Acrylamide subunits combine to produce the polymer ($CF_2CHCONH_2$) known as polyacrylamide, which is easily cross- linked.

This kind of electrophoresis uses a discontinuous gel system, meaning that there are physically stacked two separate gel systems in the electrophoretic tank. These are as follows:

I. Resolving Gel: This is also known as flowing gel or separating. About 2/3 of the length of the gel plate is taken up by the separating gel, which is made up of 5-10% acrylamide. This gel's sieving ability is impacted by the many, smaller-diameter holes that are created once the polyacrylamide is cross- linked.

Gel Electrophoresis

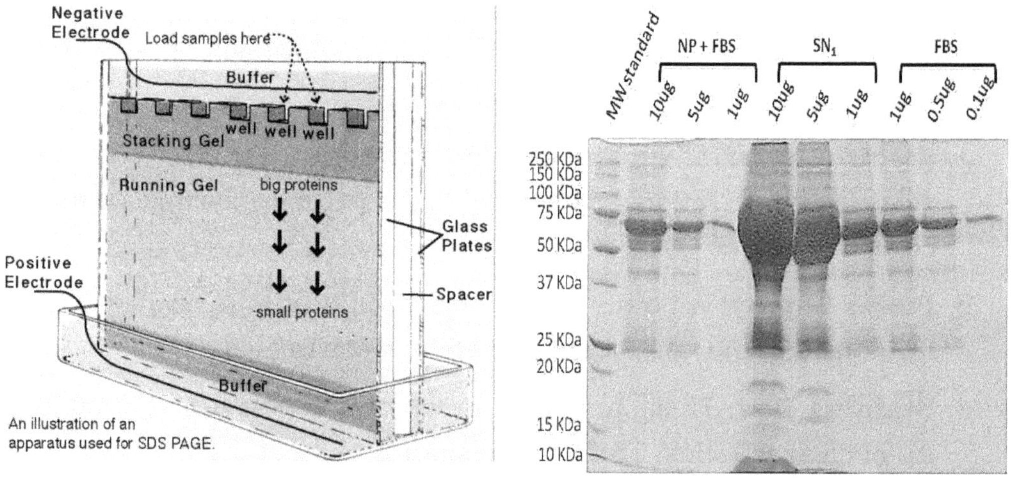

Figure 15.6: Sodium Dodecyl Sulphate (SDS) Polyacrylamide Gel Electrophoresis.

II. Stacking Gel: Resolving gel is put on top of stacking gel, and the well is created by inserting a gel comb. It is the top gel layer and makes up one-third of the gel plate. Depending on the size of the protein that one wants to detect or probe in the sample, the amount of acrylamide is selected.

The proportion that should be applied should increase as the known weight decreases. In stacking gel, acrylamide typically makes about 2-5%. It is very porous and does not behave as a molecular sieve.

(b) Buffer: SDS-PAGE employs two different kinds of buffers. Amine buffers are present in the bottom reservoir (which contains the flowing gel). HCl is used to modify it. The top reservoir (which contains stacking gel) also contains amine buffers, but the pH there is somewhat higher and it is changed using glycine rather than HCl.

(c) Dissociating Agent: The most popular dissociating agent for separating native proteins into separate polypeptides is SDS. When SDS is added to a protein mixture and it is heated to 100 °C, the detergent wraps around the polypeptide backbone. A constant weight ratio of 1.4 g/g of polypeptide is used in its binding to polypeptides. When compared to the negative charges contributed by SDS during this process, the inherent charges of polypeptides become insignificant. As a result, following treatment, polypeptides take on a rod- like shape and have a consistent charge density with the same net negative charge per unit length.

(d) Stains: The stains are used to see the bands of separated proteins after the process of electrophoresis. Coomassie Brilliant Blue R-250 (CBB) is the most popular protein stain. It is an anionic dye, which binds with proteins non-specifically.

Proteins in the gel are fixed by acetic acid and simultaneously stained. The excess dye incorporated in the gel can be removed by de-staining with the same solution but without the dye. The proteins are detected as blue bands on a clear background.

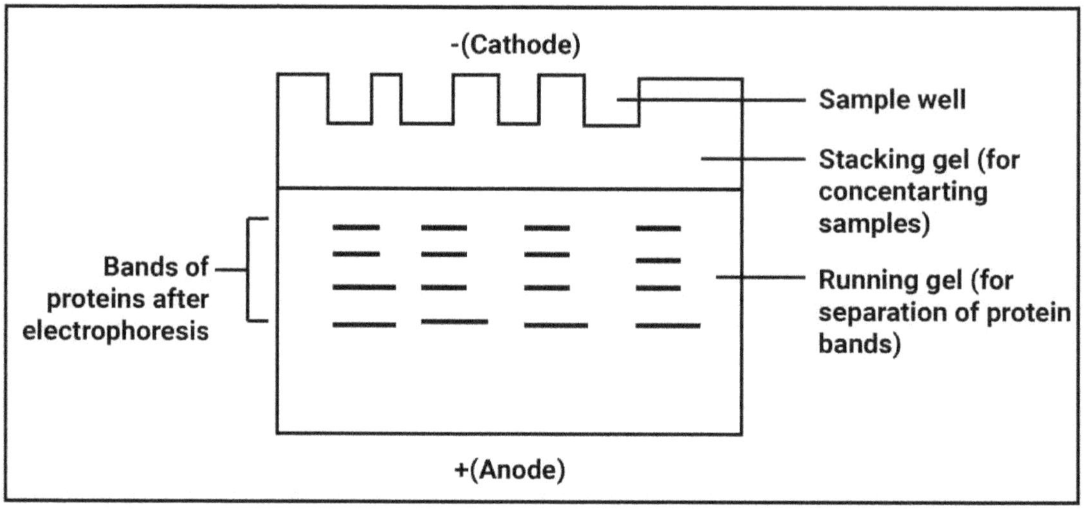

Figure 15.7: Instrumentation of SDS-PAGE.

6. Procedure:

The solution of proteins to be analysed is first mixed with SDS, an anionic detergent, an anionic detergent which denatures secondary structure. Besides addition of SDS, proteins may optionally be boiled in the presence of a reducing agent, such as Di-Thio-Threitol (DTT) or 2- mercaptoethanol, which further denatures the proteins by reducing disulfide linkages, thus overcoming some forms of tertiary protein folding, and breaking up quaternary protein structure (Oligomeric subunits).

This is known as reducing SDS-PAGE and is most commonly used. Non-reducing SDS- PAGE (no boiling and no reducing agent) may be used when native structure is important in further analysis (e.g., enzyme activity, shown by the use of zymograms). The denatured proteins are subsequently loaded into the wells of stacking gel flooded with stacking buffer. This end is connected with the cathode of power supply. Then an electric current is applied across the gel, causing negatively charged proteins to migrate across the gel towards anode. After crossing the stacking gel, denatured proteins enter the running gel which has its own buffer system (running buffer).

Depending on their size, each protein will move differently through the gel matrix: short proteins will more easily fit through the pores in the gel, while larger ones will have more difficulty.

After the separation is over the gel is gently taken out and transferred to the staining box and treated with the staining dye, e.g., CBB R-250. Excess of stains are removed by de-staining using acetic acid solution. The bands appear to be blue stained which are then analysed according to the need of the experiment.

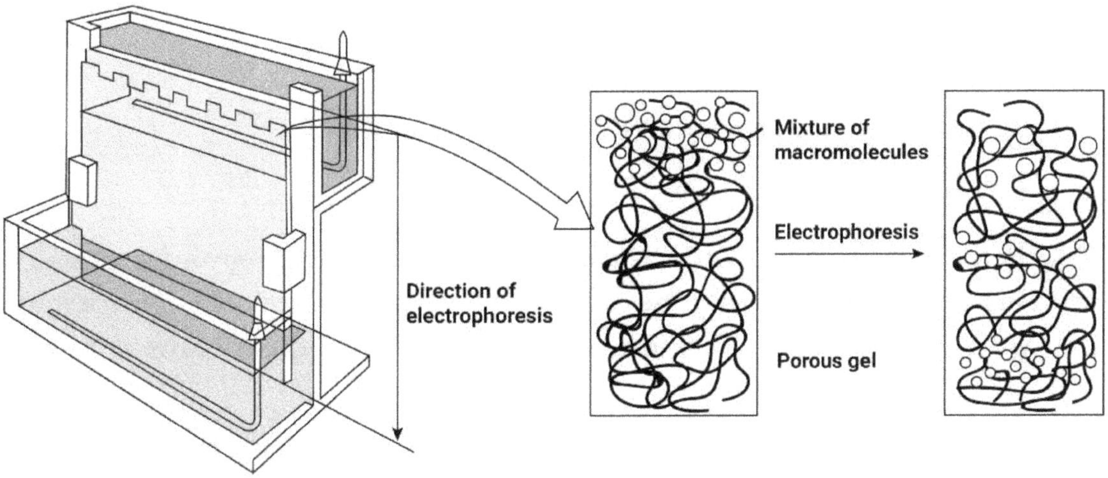

(a) Gel electrophoresis apparatus (b) Sieving action of polyacrylamide gel

Figure 15.8: Gel Electrophoresis Apparatus.

7. Application: SDS-PAGE has many applications. It is mostly used for following purposes:

(i) Establishing protein size

(ii) Protein identification

(iii) Determining sample purity

(iv) Identifying disulfide bonds

(v) Quantifying proteins

(vi) Blotting applications

8. Advantages of SDS-PAGE:

SDS-PAGE has following advantages:

(i) Mobility of the molecules is high and separation is rapid.

(ii) All the proteins are negatively charged; therefore, all migrate towards anode.

(iii) The proteins treated with SDS fixed dyes are better than the native proteins.

(iv) SDS solubilizes all proteins, including very hydrophobic and even denatured proteins.

15.5 PULSE FIELD GEL ELECTROPHORESIS (PFGE)

1. Principle

SDS is the most widely used dissociating agent for dividing native proteins into distinct polypeptides. The detergent wraps around the polypeptide backbone when SDS is added to a protein mixture and the mixture is heated to 100°C.

In order to bind to polypeptides, it uses a constant weight ratio of 1.4 g/g of polypeptide. The intrinsic charges of polypeptides become negligible in comparison to the negative charges added by SDS throughout this process. Due to this, polypeptides exhibit a rod-like structure and a constant charge density with the same net negative charge per unit length after treatment. This forces the large DNA molecules in the gel to relax upon removal of the first and elongate to align with the new field.

2. Procedure

1. Bacterial cells from an agar plate are taken.
2. They are mixed with melted agarose and poured into a plug mold.
3. The bacterial cells are broken open with biochemicals, or lysed, so that the DNA is free in the agarose plugs.

4. DNA gelatin plug is loaded into a gel, and places it in an electric field that separates DNA fragments according to their size.
5. The gel is stained, so that DNA can be seen under ultraviolet (UV) light. A digital camera takes a photograph of the gel and stores the picture in the computer.

A DNA fingerprint with a particular pattern is created by the DNA pieces. Each lane on the agarose gel in the picture reflects a unique DNA fingerprint or pattern. Because PFGE can separate very large fragments to create a fingerprint by continuously altering the direction of the electric field, it differs from traditional DNA electrophoresis.

The public health laboratory uses a tool called Bio Numeric to examine the DNA Finger print once it has been made. After analysis, the laboratory uploads its pattern to the national database, where database managers from Pulse Net Central will check the pattern to see if it is the origin of an epidemic or a component of an on-going one.

3. Advantages of PFGE

(i) High concordance with epidemiological relatedness.

(ii) Can be applied as a universal generic sub typing method for many different bacteria with only the choice of the restriction enzyme and electrophoresis conditions optimized for each species.

(iii) Stable and reproducible DNA restriction patterns.

(iv) More discriminating than methods such as ribo typing or multi-locus sequence typing for many bacteria.

4. Limitations of PFGE

1. Time consuming
2. Does not discriminate between ALL unrelated isolates
3. DNA restriction patterns can vary slightly between technicians

4. Cannot optimize separation in every part of the gel at the same time
5. Bands of same size may not come from the same part of the chromosome
6. Change in one restriction site can result in more than one band change
7. "Relatedness" should be used as a guide, not as a true phylogenetic measure
8. Some strains cannot be typed by PFGE
9. Does not differentiate isolates to the same degree that can be achieved by whole genome sequencing (WGS)

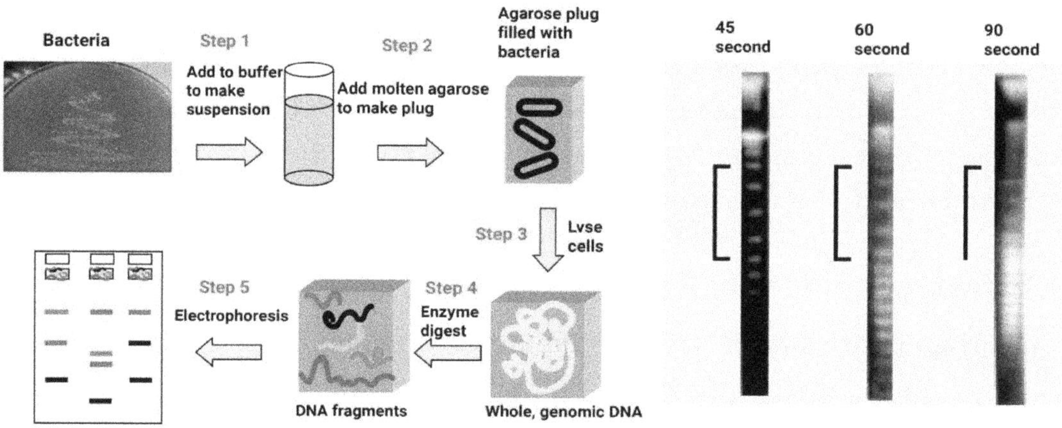

Figure 15.9: Pulse Field Gel Electrophoresis.

Two-Dimensional Electrophoresis:

This is a very sensitive technique to purify a mixture of polypeptides. It is carried out in two dimensions:

(i) **1st Dimension Separation:** Here, we perform a procedure known as isoelectric focusing. Any protein's entire positive and negative charges make up its net charge. The proteins' prosthetic groups and ionizable acidic and basic side chains control these charges.

A polypeptide's isoelectric point (pi) is the pH level at which it has no net charge. At this moment, the polypeptides in the gel are unable to migrate and form bands. To determine a protein's isoelectric point (pi), a method known as isoelectric focusing is utilized (Figure 10).

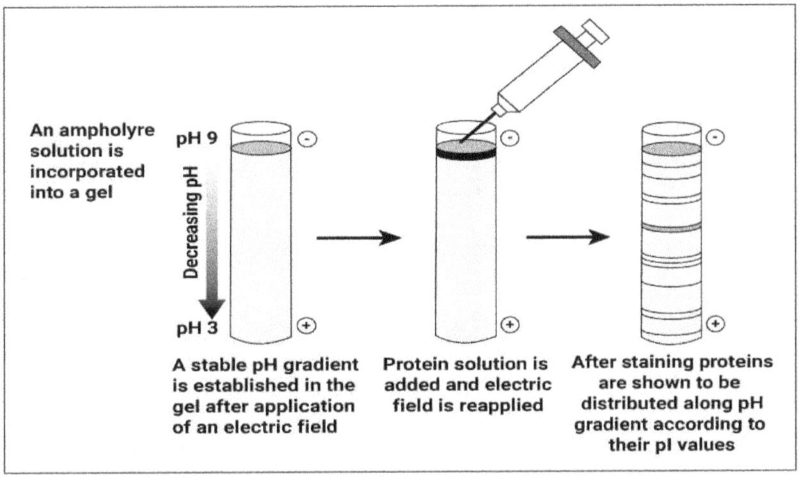

Isotectric focussing is the 1st dimension separation in two-dimensional electrophoresis (Source : Biochemistry - Lehninger et al.)

Figure 15.10: 1st Dimension Separation in Two-dimensional.

Electrophoresis Iso electric Focusing

By allowing a mixture of low molecular weight organic acids and bases known as ampholytes to distribute themselves in an electric field created over the gel, a pH gradient is established. Each protein migrates when a protein combination is administered until it reaches the pH that corresponds to its pi. As a result, proteins with various isoelectric points are distributed in the gel in various ways.

(ii) **2nd Dimension Separation:** Isoelectric focusing is followed by SDS-PAGE as discussed above. In this process the proteins will move from cathode to anode in the decreasing order of their molecular mass (Mr).

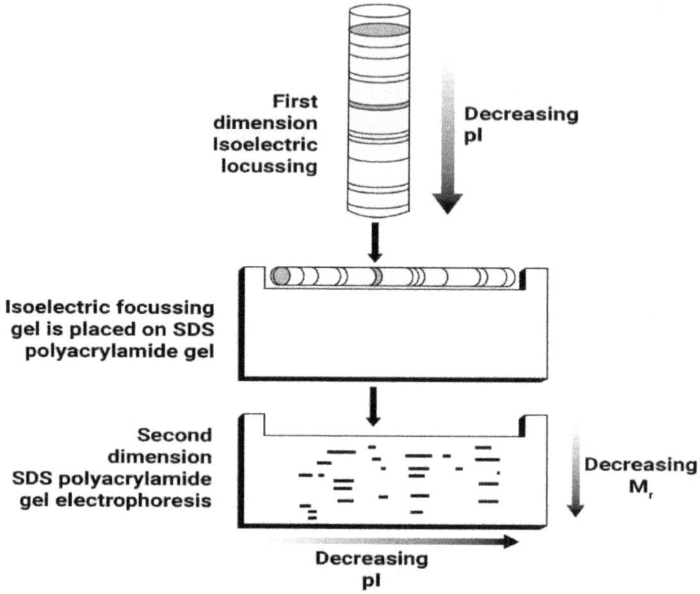

Figure 15.11: Isoelectric Focusing is followed by SDS-Page.

15.6 CELLULOSE ACETATE ELECTROPHORESIS

1. Introduction

It is an adaptation of paper electrophoresis, which Kohn created in 1958. Instead of using standard chromatography paper in this sort of electrophoresis, bacteriological acetate membrane filters are used.

2. Procedure

i. As previously mentioned, entire blood is used to make hemolysate (in K_2EDTA).

ii. To prepare the electrophoresis tank, fill it with roughly 900 ml of TEB buffer. Wicks were then cut from Grade No. 3 chromatography paper and positioned along the tank's 22 cm- long bridges.

iii. The cellulose acetate membranes are cut in 40xl00 mm each and soaked (shiny side down) in TEB buffer for 5 minutes. Five strips are plotted and placed on the electrophoresis tanks.

iv. Voltage current is applied at 250 V for 5 minutes to the membranes to equilibrate the membranes with the buffer.

v. The current is cut off, and a capillary tube is used to apply 8–10 l of haemolysate (10 g/l) to each membrane at the cathodal end.

vi. After that, each strip receives a steady current of 2 mA at a voltage of 250–300 V.

vii. Until there is a clear region between the bands, the electrophoresis is conducted for around 45 to an hour.

viii. The separated HbA2 on the cellulose acetate membrane is then sliced and placed in a tube containing 4 ml of distilled water, while the HbA is placed in a tube containing 16 ml of distilled water. The current is then switched off. Depending on how much of a haemoglobin variation is present, it is split individually into either 4 or 16 ml of distilled water. It should be noted that a blank is made from the same run by cutting a clear cellulose acetate strip that has been submerged in 4ml distilled water.

ix. The tubes are then placed on a roller mixer for 30 minutes for the haemoglobin elution.

x. The strips are removed and the tubes are then centrifuged for 10 minutes at 3.000 rpm.

xi. The absorbance of each haemoglobin is read at 413 nm against the blank on a spectrophotometer.

3. Advantage

(i) The strips of cellulose acetate are commonly used as barriers in the free movement of big molecules because they are chemically pure and free of lignin and hemicelluloses.

(ii) Cellulose acetate strips are ideal for polysaccharide electrophoresis because they contains less glucose.

(iii) Because cellulose acetate is not hydrophilic, it maintains relatively little buffer, aiding in a quicker and better resolution.

(iv) Applications: It is particularly utilized in clinical research to separate blood's glycoproteins, lipoproteins, and haemoglobin. E. Capillary electrophoresis:

The samples are separated using capillarity in a small-bore tube according to their size to charge ratio. Comparatively speaking to more established separation methods like agarose gel electrophoresis or SDS-PAGE, capillary electrophoresis (CE) is a relatively recent technology.

It has several really alluring characteristics that both make it competitive and a solid option. The capacity to distinguish between charged and non-charged molecules is one of CE's key benefits over other separation methods. In CE, the electrolyte solution (background electrolyte) that is contained in a small fused-silica capillary is employed to separate analyte ions.

The capillary's ends are inserted into vials with electrolyte solutions at both the intake and outflow, along with electrodes that are linked to a high voltage source. By exerting pressure (hydrodynamic injection) or voltage (electro kinetic injection), the sample solution is injected into the capillary as a tiny plug.

Zones of analyte arise owing to various electrophoretic mobilities of ionic species when high voltage (5–30 kV) is applied across the capillary and move towards the outlet side. In fact, when their charge/size ratios alter, various ions may be distinguished. The separated analyte bands are detected immediately through the capillary wall before they reach the capillary's end.

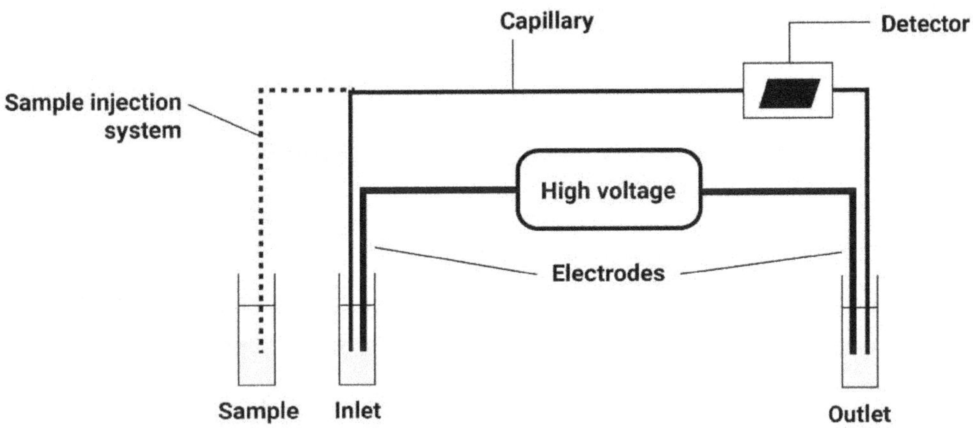

Figure 15.12: Typical Capillary Electrophoresis Instrumentation.

4. Advantages:

(a) High separation efficiency

(b) Short analysis time

(c) Low sample and electrolyte consumption

(d) Low waste generation

(e) Ease of operation

(f) Disadvantages:

Due to small diameter of the capillary tube, heat is dissipated that causes increased diffusion. Due to this the resolution is not always proper.

5. Applications:

CE is used in the following analysis of food, pharmaceutical products and environmental pollutants.

15.7 MOVING-BOUNDARY ELECTROPHORESIS

1. Introduction

A method for electrophoretically separating chemical compounds in a free solution is known as moving-boundary electrophoresis (MBE; sometimes known as free-boundary electrophoresis).

Arne Tiselius created moving-boundary electrophoresis in 1930. For his work on the separation of colloids using electrophoresis—the movement of charged particles through a stationary liquid under the influence of an electric field—Tiselius won the 1948 Nobel Prize in chemistry.

2. Apparatus

The moving-boundary electrophoresis device has electrodes submerged at the ends of a U-shaped cell that is filled with buffer solution. Any combination of charged elements, such as a protein mixture, might be the sample used. Depending on their charges, the compounds will migrate to the anode or cathode when voltage is applied. Schlieren optics are used at both ends of the solution in the cell to measure the change in refractive index at the border of the separated compounds.

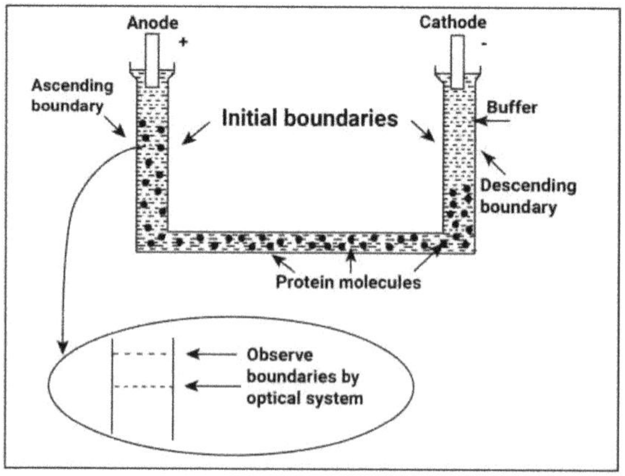

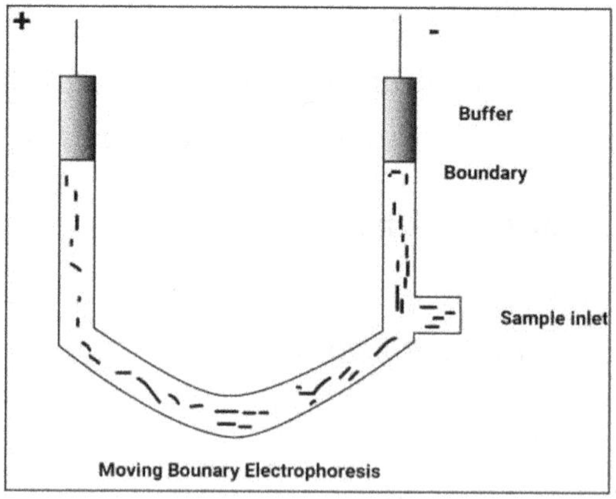

Figure 15.13: Moving-boundary electrophoresis Apparatus.

3. Method

This technique conducts the electrophoresis in solution without the use of a supporting medium. The buffer dissolves the sample, and the molecules travel to the appropriate counter charge electrodes. Platinum electrodes are affixed to the ends of both arms of a U- shaped tube, which is used for moving boundary electrophoresis. Refractometers are located at either end of the tube to track changes in the buffer's refractive index brought on by the presence of molecules during electrophoresis. The device is linked to an external power source once the sample is put into the U tube's center. As molecules travel through the refractometer and go to the opposing electrode, a change may be observed. Samples can be removed from the equipment along with the buffer as the desired molecule passes.

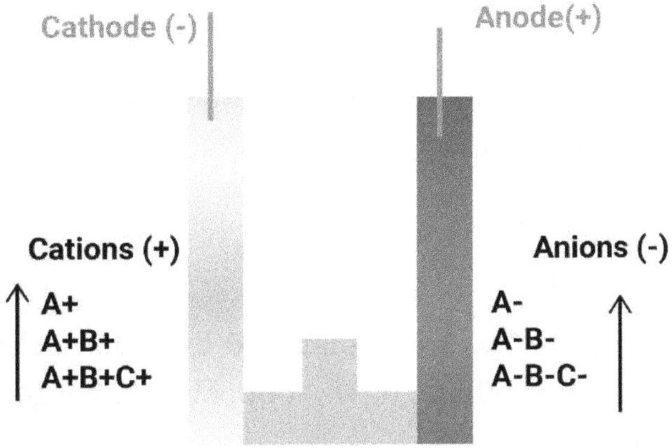

Figure 15.14: Movement of the charged particle in a moving boundary electrophoresis.

4. Applications

(i) DNA sequencing

(ii) Medical research

(iii) Protein research

(iv) Agricultural testing

(v) Separation of organic acids, alkaloids, amino acids, glycosides, alcohols

(vi) In food analysis

(vii) It is employed in biochemical and clinical field ex. Analysis of blood, haemoglobin

(viii) In the analysis of terpenoids, steroids and antibiotics

15.8 ZONE ELECTROPHORESIS

Any electrophoretic method that separates components into zones or bands in a buffer and stabilises them on solid, porous, or any other support medium, such as filter paper, agar gel, or polyacrylamide gel.

Types of Zone electrophoresis

In this technique the charged particles are separated into different zones or bands. This is of two types as: -

1. Paper electrophoresis$
2. Gel Electrophoresis$

The Whatman filter paper No. 1 is moistened by a buffer and linked at both ends to two electrodes that have opposing charges in the paper electrophoresis procedure.

The sample is then attached to one end and allowed to undergo component separation under electric gradients. The paper is dried and dyed to create coloured bands after separation.

By contrasting these coloured bands with the standard, it is possible to determine the sample's nature. Paper electrophoresis can separate five bands of proteins from a blood sample. Similar to paper electrophoresis, gel electrophoresis uses an agarose or SDS gel as the carrier medium (sodium dodecyl sulfate). Because molecules move slowly and the separation area is bigger by thickness, it is more effective than paper-based separation.

An electric field is provided to the sample, which may cause molecules to separate. These molecules can be identified by staining and comparing the bands they create to those of reference samples. The technique is more efficient than paper, and for instance, 15 protein bands may be extracted from a serum sample.

Note: $These electrophoresis techniques have been discussed in the chapter in detail.

CHAPTER 16 RADIO IMMUNO ASSAY (RIA)

16.1 INTRODUCTION

As the name suggests, the radio immune assay (RIA) is an immunological assay that examines any antigen or antibody in the patient's serum to identify the condition. One of the most accurate & sensitive immunological test techniques is this one. Radioimmunoassay is a method of detecting the antigen-antibody complex that uses radioisotopes rather than enzymes as labels to be coupled with antigens or antibodies (RIA). An in vitro test known as a radioimmunoassay (RIA) uses extremely high sensitivity to detect the presence of an antigen. Solomon Berson and Rosalyn Yalow of the Veterans Administration Hospital in New York originally devised RIA in 1960 for the detection of endogenous plasma insulin. The range of sensitivity is 0.0006-0.006 g/ml of antibody.

The foundation of traditional RIA techniques is the idea of competitive binding. In this approach, radiolabeled antigen and unlabeled antigen compete for binding to particular antibodies. As a result, the amount of radiolabeled antigen that is free from antibody binding when mixes of radiolabeled and unlabeled antigen are incubated with the matching antibody is precisely proportional to the amount of unlabeled antigen in the mixture.

16.2 COMPONENTS OF RADIOIMMUNOASSAY

Antibody: it is a protein that is produced by the body in response to an invading (foreign) substance. Antibodies are produced as part of the body's immune response to protect itself.

Antigen: it is substance that the body is trying to "flight off" by mounting an immune response. Example- the drug is the antigen that binds to the antibody.

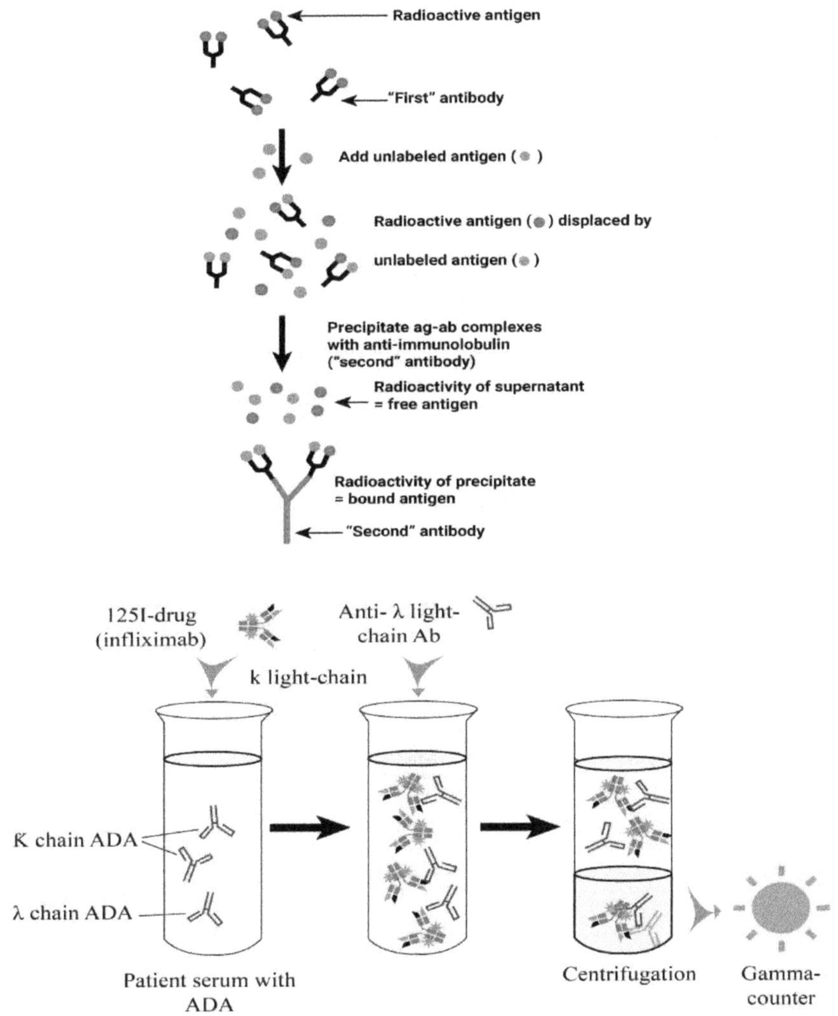

Figure 16.1: Process in radio immuno assay technique.

Immunogen: it is a substance that elicits immune response. Example- drug-protein conjugate.

Analyte: it is anything measured by a laboratory test. In immunoassay utilize one or more selected antibodies to detect analyte of interest. The analytes being measured may be:

1. That are naturally present in the body (such as thyroid harmone)
2. The body produces but are not typically present (such as cancer antigen)
3. Do not naturally occur in the body (such as an abused drug)

16.3 STRUCTURE OF ANTIBODIES

The B lymphocytes creates antibodies. They are immunoglobulin supergene family glycoproteins that the body produces in reaction to an outside stimulus. Immunoglobulin G is the most popular (IgG). Proteins called antibodies are made up of two primary structural and functional sections that differ from one antibody to another in order accommodate various antigens.

The antigen (Ag) binding site found in the Fab region differs amongst various antibodies.

The Fc region is a consistent structural area found in all antibody subclasses.

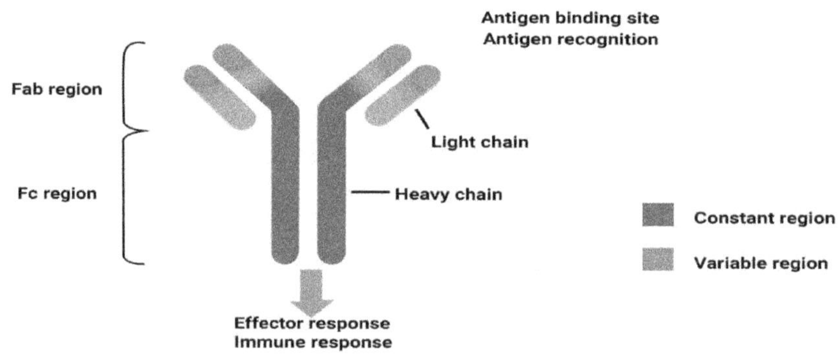

Figure 16.2: Structure of Antibodies.

16.4 PRINCIPLE OF RADIOIMMUNOASSAY

It involves combination of three principles.

1. An immune reaction i.e. antigen, antibody binding.
2. A competitive binding or competitive displacement reaction. (It gives specificity)
3. Measurement of radio emission. (It gives sensitivity)

16.5 IMMUNE REACTION

The body develops specialized antibodies against the antigen when a foreign biological material enters the bloodstream *via* a non-oral route because it identifies the specific chemistry on the substance's surface as an antigen, neutralizing the effects and protecting the body. It is an immunological response since the body's immune system produces the antibodies. Here, chemical impact causes the antibodies or antigens to attach and migrate.

This differs from the electrophoresis concept, in which proteins are sorted based on charge.

Competitive Binding or Competitive Displacement Reaction

When there are two antigens that may bind to the same antibody, this phenomenon occurs when the antigen with the higher concentration attaches widely while the limited antibody displaces the other. So, in this experiment, high affinity antibody is permitted to attach to radiolabelled antigen. After then, unlabelled antigens in the patient serum begin attaching to the antibody and replacing the tagged antigen.

Measurement of Radio Emission

Following incubation, washings are carried out to get rid of any unbound antigens. The antigen antibody complex is then radio emitted, and the gamma rays produced by the radio labelled antigen are measured. The target antigen is radioactively tagged and attached to its particular antibodies (a limited and known amount of the specific antibody has to be added). To start a competitive reaction between the labelled antigens from the preparation and the unlabelled antigens from the serum-sample with the particular antibodies, a sample, such blood serum, is added. A specific amount of tagged antigen will be released throughout the competition for the antibodies. The proportion of labelled to unlabelled antigen determines how much is required. The quantity of antigen in the patient's serum may then be determined by creating a binding curve. Accordingly, more unlabelled antigen attaches to the antibody as its concentration rises, dislodging the tagged form. The bound antigens are then separated from the unbound ones, and the radioactivity of the free antigens remaining in the supernatant is measured.

Antigen-antibody complexes are precipitated either by the addition of chemicals that encourage the precipitation of antigen-antibody complexes or by cross-linking with a different antibody. The amount of radiolabelled antigen that the antibody precipitated with may be calculated by counting radioactivity in the precipitates. Antigen concentrations in patient samples are estimated using a standard curve created by comparing the fraction of antibody- bound radiolabelled antigen against known quantities of a standardised unlabelled antigen.

16.6 MATHEMATICAL EXPRESSION OF PRINCIPLE OF RIA

The added antigen will be distributed between a bound (B) and a free fraction (F). This distribution is governed by the association constant (K_A) of the antibody

$$\text{Ab} + \text{Ag} \longrightarrow \text{AgAb}$$

$$K = \frac{[\text{Ab} + \text{Ag}]}{[\text{AbAg}]}$$

A high affinity antibody was the first step in this process, which then involved the competitive binding of radio-labelled and unlabelled antigens.

The tagged antigen is combined at a concentration that completely saturates the antibody's antigen-binding regions. More labelled antigen will replace unlabelled antigen at the binding site as the concentration of unlabelled antigen rises.

The amount of antigen contained in the sample is determined by measuring the reduction in the amount of radio labelled antigen bound particular antibody in the presence of the test samples.

As the amount of unlabelled antigen in the sample rises, the amount of labelled antigen that is bound to the antibody decreases under typical conditions.

16.7 REAGENTS USED IN RADIO IMMUNE ASSAY

1. A tracer i.e. labelled ligand
2. A binder (antibody) which is the specific antiserum
3. A separation system to separate the 'bound and 'free' phases.
4. A standard (highly pure form)
5. A free human antiserum
6. The radioisotopes which are used β-emitters- ^{3}H, ^{14}C, λ-emitters- ^{125}I

16.8 STEPS FOLLOWED IN RIA

1. Preparation and Characterization of Antigen

The antigen, whose concentration is to be measured, should be available in pure form to be used as calibrator. Also, it is required to be used to create antibodies, which are used in the assay process, to form complexes.

2. Radio Labelling of Antigen

This is also called as tagging where the antigen is tagged with radioactive elements like 125I or 14C or 3H, to be detected using gamma counter or scintillation counter.

3. Preparation of Specific Antibody

Injecting the antigen into mice, rabbits, or guinea pigs results in the production of specific antibodies, which are then collected and purified. When some substances, like morphine or steroids that are not antigenic are coupled with albumin, they become antigenic and cause the formation of antibodies in the serum.

4. Development of the assay methodology
5. Validation of method using parameters like sensitivity, specificity, precision, recovery, linearity and dilution Detailed procedure in RIA

The test is commonly conducted in 96-well plates containing wells, where the inner surface of each well has been coated with antibodies. All of these wells receive radioactive antigen, which combines with antibodies to create a complex. Multiple wells are added with the calibrator (an unlabelled antigen with a known concentration). Additionally, a sample of unknown concentration of antigen is introduced to one of the wells. Due to the restricted number of antibody binding sites, there is competition between labelled and unlabelled antigen. Precipitation, chromatography, gel filtering, and other processes are used to separate radio-labelled antigen bound to antibody from unbound radio-labelled antigen. As a result, radio-labelled antigen is driven out of the antibody complex by unlabelled antigen. The plates are taken out and cleaned after the incubation period. This eliminates unbound and free antigen. The radioactivity of the well plates is then determined using a gamma or scintillation counter. Less radioactivity is present in the complex when the concentration of free antigen is higher. It is possible to determine the antigen concentration from the radioactivity vs. concentration graph.

16.9 ADVANTAGES OF RADIO IMMUNE ASSAY (RIA)

1. Radio immune assay is very sensitive technique which is used to measure the concentrations of antigen without the need of use a bioassay. It can measure one trillionth of a gram of material per millilitre of blood.

2. It is structurally specific as antigen: antibody reactions are highly specific.
3. It is indirect method of analysis
4. It is a saturation analysis as active reagent added in smaller quantity than that of analyte.

16.10 DISADVANTAGE OF RADIO IMMUNE ASSAY

1. Prolonged reaction time as a consequence highly diluted reagent is used.
2. Radioactive iodine used in it is not cheap reagent
3. Possible health hazards due to handling of radioisotopes
4. All the agents must be added precisely
5. Limited assay range
6. Lack of direct relationship between analyte concentration and signal response
7. Difficulty of automation
8. Lengthy counting time

16.11 USES OF RADIO IMMUNO ASSAY (RIA)

1. The test can be used to determine very small quantities (e.g. nanogram) of antigens and antibodies in the serum.
2. The test is used for quantitation of hormones, drugs, HBsAg, and other viral antigens.
3. Analyse nanomolar and picomolar concentrations of hormones in biological fluids.

16.12 LIMITATION OF THE RADIO IMMUNO ASSAY (RIA)

The cost of equipment and reagents

1. Short shelf-life of radio labelled compounds
2. The problems associated with the disposal of radioactive waste.

CHAPTER 17 ELISA

17.1 INTRODUCTION

The fundamental enzyme-linked immunosorbent assay (ELISA), also known as the enzyme immunoassay (EIA), differs from other antibody-based assays in that it can produce quantitative results and separates specific and non-specific interactions through serial binding to a solid surface, typically a polystyrene multi well plate.

The amount of analyte present in the initial sample is indicated by the colour of the end product produced by the ELISA technique.

ELISAs are a highly popular option for the assessment of many research and diagnostic targets since they are quick and straightforward to perform and are created to quickly handle a large number of samples in parallel. Figure 1 illustrates an example ELISA result.

ELISAs were first developed in the early 1970s as a replacement for radio immunoassays.

They remain in wide use in their original format and in expanded formats with modifications that allow for multiple analytes per well, highly sensitive readouts, and direct cell-based output.

17.2 PROCEDURE

An antigen or an antibody is adsorbed to a well of an ELISA plate during the coating step of an ELISA procedure. According to the straightforward schematic picture below, coating is followed by blocking and detecting stages.

Between each ELISA stage, numerous washes are conducted in order to eliminate unbound components because the assay relies on surface binding for separation. In order to prevent the dilution of the solutions added in the following step, it is crucial that surplus liquid be eliminated throughout this operation. For greatest consistency specialized plate washers are used.

ELISAs are capable of measuring protein concentrations in diverse samples like blood, but they may also be highly complicated due to several additional stages. The whole process' most complicated and variable stage is detection, where the signal can be amplified by using numerous layers of antibodies.

17.3 TYPES OF ELISA

The immobilization of a sample's antigen to the well walls of a microtiter plate is the first step in an ELISA investigation. Direct adsorption to the plate's surface or the use of a "capture antibody" can accomplish this. The capture antibody, which is often employed in an ELISA type known as "sandwich ELISA," must be specific to the target antigen. A detection antibody is then added after immobilisation, and it binds to the adsorbed antigen to create an antigen- antibody complex. The detection antibody either offers a binding site for a secondary antibody that has been labelled, or it is directly conjugated to an enzyme, such as horseradish peroxidase (HRP). Generally speaking, ELISAs may be divided into four primary categories: direct, indirect, sandwich, and competitive ELISAs.

Direct ELISA

The direct ELISA setup is shown in Figure 2, where an antigen is immobilised in the well of an ELISA plate. An antibody that is directly conjugated to an enzyme, such as HRP, may then detect the antigen.

Figure 17.1: Direct ELISA.

Because there are fewer processes involved, direct ELISA detection is substantially quicker than other ELISA procedures. Since fewer components and procedures are required, the test is also less prone to mistake; for example, there is no requirement for a secondary antibody that can cause cross-reactions. However, there are significant drawbacks to this approach. Since the immobilisation of the antigen is not specific, compared to indirect ELISA, more background noise may be seen (see below). This is mostly due to the target protein and all other proteins in the sample binding to the plate. Since a unique conjugated primary antibody is required for each target protein, direct ELISA is less adaptable. As there is no secondary antibody utilized, there is no signal amplification, reducing the sensitivity of the experiment. Last but not least, the direct ELISA method is often utilized when the immune response to an antigen needs to be analyzed.

Advantages	Disadvantages
Faster than other ELISA – the technique has fewer steps	Antigen immobilization is not specific- may cause higher background noise than indirect ELISA. Mainly because all proteins in the sample, including the target protein, will bind to the plate
Less prone to error – as less reagents and fewer steps are required	Less flexible - each target protein needs a specific conjugated primary antibody No signal amplification-reduces assay sensitivity

Indirect ELISA

The indirect ELISA method setup is easily understood after looking at Figure 4; antigen is adsorbed to a well of an ELISA plate. It takes two steps to detect something. The particular antigen is first bound by an unlabelled primary antibody. The primary antibody's host species is then used as the target of an enzyme-conjugated secondary antibody.

Since more than one labelled secondary antibody can bind the main antibody, the indirect ELISA approach has higher sensitivity. It is also more cost-effective than direct ELISA since fewer labelled antibodies are required. Since many primary antibodies can be used with a single secondary antibody that has been labelled, indirect ELISA offers more versatility. One of its drawbacks is the potential for secondary antibodies to cross-react with the adsorbed antigen, which might enhance background noise. Additionally, since the secondary antibody needs to be incubated for an extra step, indirect ELISA experiments take longer to complete than direct ELISAs. The best method for figuring the total antibody concentration in samples is indirect ELISA.

Advantages	Disadvantages
High sensitivity - more than one labelled secondary antibody can bind the primary antibody	Possibility of background noise-secondary antibody may be cross- reactive
Economical - fewer labelled antibodies are needed	Longer procedure than direct ELISA technique - additional incubation step for secondary antibody needed
Greater flexibility - different primary antibodies can be used with a single labelled secondary antibody	

Sandwich ELISA

As seen in Figure 4, matching antibody pairs (capture and detection antibodies) are necessary for sandwich ELISAs. Therefore, each antibody has a distinct and non- overlapping epitope or portion of the antigen that it is specific for. To obtain correct findings, it is crucial to test matching antibody pairs precisely in sandwich ELISA to make sure they recognise various epitopes. As suggested by its name, the capture antibody binds the antigen, which may subsequently be detected using either a direct ELISA or an indirect ELISA setup.

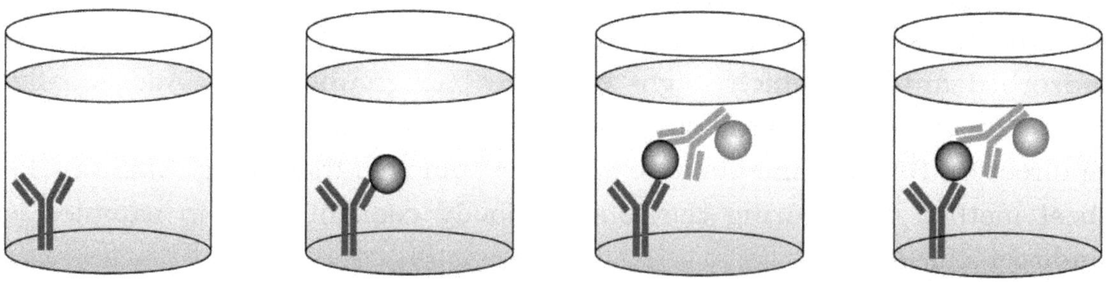

Figure 17.2: Overview of Direct Sandwich ELISA.

The well of an ELISA plate must first be coated with a capture antibody before beginning the sandwich ELISA method. A detection antibody is next added, and finally the analyte or sample. A direct sandwich ELISA is what is known when the detecting antibody is enzyme conjugated. A supplementary enzyme-conjugated detection antibody is needed if the utilized detection antibody is unlabelled. This is a sandwich ELISA test that is indirect. Sandwich ELISAs have a high sensitivity that makes them superior to direct or indirect ELISAs by a factor of 2 to 5. Sandwich ELISA also provides great specificity since it uses two antibodies to find the antigen. Since both direct and indirect approaches may be applied, it provides versatility. The benefits are not without drawbacks, though. Since it's critical to minimise cross-reactivity between the capture and detection antibodies, antibody optimization must be developed in the absence of a tested or standardised ELISA kit or antibody pair. Since the antigen does not need to be purified before the test but still provides excellent sensitivity and specificity, sandwich ELISAs are particularly well suited for the investigation of complicated samples (e.g. measuring cytokine levels in an immune response).

Advantages	Disadvantages
High sensitivity- 2-5 times more sensitive than direct or indirect	Antibody optimization can be difficult – cross – reactivity may occur between the capture and detection antibodies. Needs a standardized ELISA kit or tested antibody pair.
ELISA - High specificity – two antibodies are involved in capture and detection	
Flexibility - both direct and indirect detection can be used	

Competition/Inhibition ELISA

Among all ELISA methods, the competition/inhibition ELISA, commonly referred to as a blocking ELISA, is arguably the most complicated. Each of the aforementioned test methods, however, may be modified for a competitive format. By identifying interference in an anticipated signal output, the competitive/inhibition ELISA is primarily used to determine the quantity of an antigen or antibody in a sample. In essence, a reference and a little quantity of tagged antigen or antibody or sample antigen or antibody compete for binding. The output signal is lower the greater the sample antigen concentration, showing that the output signal and sample antigen concentration is negatively correlated.

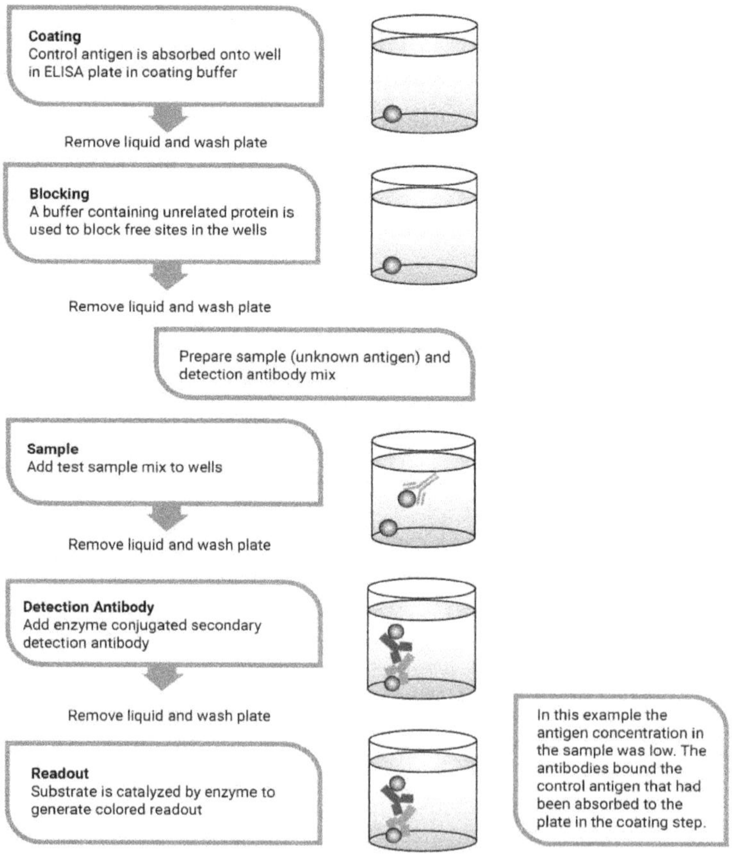

Figure 17.3: Competition ELISA.

Figure 5 depicts an illustration of a competition ELISA to test for antigen based on the direct detection technique.

In this illustration, a multiwell plate is coated with a recognised antigen. After the usual blocking and washing procedures, samples containing an unidentified antigen are introduced. The application of a labelled detection antibody is followed by the use of pertinent substrates, such as 3,3',5,5'-Tetramethylbenzidine (TMB) for detection. A considerable drop in signal output will be seen if the sample contains a lot of antigen. In contrast, there won't be much of a change in the predicted signal output if the sample contains relatively little antigen. There would be a decrease in signal output in the scenario depicted in Figure 5 example.

Advantages	**Disadvantages**
Main advantage - no sample processing is required and crude or impure samples can be used	Same limitations as base ELISA- as each ELISA technique can be adapted to a competitive format
More robust - less sensitive to sample dilution and sample matrix effects than the sandwich ELISA	
More consistent - less variability between duplicate samples and assays	
Maximum flexibility - it can be based on direct, indirect or sandwich ELISA	

17.4 ELISA DETECTION OPTIONS - DIRECT & INDIRECT

By their very nature, ELISAs rely on an enzymatic label to generate a detectable signal that is closely tied to the interaction of an antibody with an antigen. For ELISAs, a limited number of distinct enzyme types and enzyme substrates are commonly utilized. There are several ways to incorporate the enzyme step into the procedure. A fluorescent plate reader or spectrophotometer is used to measure the final assay signal (depending upon the substrate chosen).

The many ways the terms direct and indirect are used in ELISA nomenclature is one feature that frequently causes misunderstanding. We will adhere to the use of these terms as they apply to the detection portion of the assay as indicated below:

Direct ELISA Detection

The most typical ELISA detection method uses alkaline phosphatase (AP) or HRP to directly identify antibodies. A spectrophotometer reads the colorimetric output that is commonly produced by HRP and AP substrates. Additionally, fluorescently-labelled antibodies may be used for detection; in this case, the test is typically referred to as a fluorescence-linked immunosorbent assay (FLISA).

Indirect ELISA Detection

Biotin and antibodies are joined, and then an enzyme step with streptavidin is added. Alternately, unlabelled primary antibodies may be used in conjunction with enzyme- coupled or biotinylated secondary antibodies. Detection requires a third step if the secondary antibody has been biotinylated. In this instance, a suitable substrate is used after treatment with the streptavidin- enzyme combination.

17.5 BIOLUMINESCENCE ASSAY

1. Introduction

A unique kind of chemiluminescence called bioluminescence is present in living things. The process is classified as an enzyme-catalyzed one, with natural evolution providing the high photon emission efficiency. The photon-emitting substrates are luciferins, and the enzymes are known as luciferases. Because bioluminescent chemistries have developed from several different sources, they contain a wide variety of unique molecular structures. Only three of the several natural forms—firefly luciferase, Renilla luciferase, and aequorin—have been extensively employed in HTS.

2. Procedure for Bioluminescence Assay

The monomeric 61 kDa firefly (Photinus pyralis) luciferase is not functionally dependent on posttranslational modifications. It works by first forming luciferyl-AMP, an intermediate that is attached to the enzyme, by combining beetle luciferin with ATP. In a high-energy state, this intermediate interacts with O2 to form oxyluciferin, another bound intermediate. With a spectral maximum of 560 nm, the following energy shift to the ground state produces yellow green light. Luminferase from the marine pansy,

Renilla A 36-kDa monomeric enzyme called Renilla reni form is catalyses the oxidation of coelenterazine to coelenteramide and blue light with a 480 nm spectral maximum. It has mostly been employed as a co-reporter with firefly luciferase. For HTS, it is used in a dual luciferase format to provide an internal control for identifying aber, rant sample data, or to multiplex with firefly luciferase to simultaneously monitor two distinct cellular pathways. Aequorin, a jellyfish toxin almost entirely for measuring intracellular calcium levels, aequorea victoria is a calcium-sensitive photo protein. In the presence of molecule oxygen, apoaequorin and its cofactor coelenterazine combine to generate active aequorin. Aequorin undergoes a conformational shift in response to the binding of a calcium ion, which causes the oxidation of coelanterazine and the emission of a blue light flash. For HTS of G- protein-coupled receptor (GPCR) modulators, the aequorin test has been modified since receptor activity is frequently associated with intracellular calcium mobilisation. For GPCR assays, a cyclic adenosine monophosphate (cAMP) response element (CRE) located upstream of a luciferase gene is used to measure the activity of a receptor connected to Gs protein. When the receptor is activated, intracellular cAMP levels rise, which in turn triggers protein kinase A, which phosphorylates the CRE binding protein. When phosphorylated CRE binding protein binds to the CRE sequence, the rate at which the luciferase gene is transcribed rises, increasing the amount of luciferase in the cells. Response elements for nuclear factor of activated T cells (NFAT), activator protein 1, and serum response element can also be used to track other GPCRs. The luciferase reporter can be positioned downstream of a promoter including a hormone response element or several repetitions of a Gal4 binding region and a mammalian promoter for nuclear receptor experiments. Luciferase gene expression is triggered by nuclear receptor binding at the promoter. Without compromising the quality of the results, luciferase reporter assays designed for HTS offer quick and easy measures of cellular physiology. There are various applications for bioluminescence in the natural world, and it is present in a wide range of creatures, including bacteria, protozoa, fungus, moulds, jellies, insects, squid, fish, worms, crustaceans, and more. They employ it for a range of functions, including warning, communication, attracting and catching prey, defence, camouflage, lighting, and more. The power of bioluminescence is starting to be used by humans. It is used in genetic research to tag genes of interest, in medicine to detect diseases like Alzheimer's or cancer, in dentistry to assess the risk of tooth decay, in warfare to locate and track ships in the water, in the development of Nano materials, in the study of pathogens that are resistant to drugs, in understanding the ecology of the ocean by observing the distribution of bioluminescent organisms, and in the evaluation of toxicity and in developing screening assays; and more. A few specific uses are listed below.

3. Uses of Bioluminescence

Today, humans are finding more and more ways to make use of bioluminescence. Here are just a few:

- **Tourism:** Bioluminescence in the oceans has been observed for centuries (see Darwin's account of milky seas in the History tab). Today, tourists flock to areas such as Puerto Rico's Vieques Island to witness the magic. In 2005, a glowing area roughly the size of Connecticut was first observed from space in the Indian Ocean.

- **Bioluminescent imaging – or BLI** – allows for non-invasive imaging of biological processes in living animals. Among other uses, this makes it possible to study the processes of various diseases and of treatments for those diseases. It can also be used to locate tumors.
- **Bioluminescent Resonance Energy Transfer, or BRET,** is used to map neuronal circuits in order to understand brain function.
- **Quorum sensing**. Studies on bioluminescence in bacteria in sea water led to the discovery of what is known as quorum sensing. J. W. Hastings and E. P. Greenberg reported in the Journal of Bacteriology in May 1999 that at low cell densities, the luciferase gene was not transcribed, but luminescent genes do activate at high cell densities when the light emitted is bright enough to serve a purpose. It is now accepted that cell-cell communication in bacteria is common.
- **Tools** have been developed that use bioluminescence in many ways. Since adenosine tri phosphate (ATP), an energy storing molecule found in all living cells, is required for emission of light, the amount of light is directly proportional to the amount of ATP. Measurements of ATP can therefore detect contamination far more quickly and accurately than traditional culturing. An example of a tool that does this is the Bio Scan made by GE; there was one on display in the exhibit. This small instrument measures bacteria in water simply and almost immediately.

CHAPTER 18 X-RAY CRYSTALLOGRAPHY

18.1 HISTORY

Although traditionally praised for their beauty and regularity, crystals were not properly studied until the 17th century. The hexagonal symmetry of snowflake crystals, according to Johannes Kepler's theory in "A New Year's Gift of Hexagonal Snow" (1611), results from the regular packing of spherical water particles. The first experimental studies of crystal symmetry were conducted by the Danish scientist Nicolas Steno in 1669. Steno demonstrated that all examples of a certain form of crystal had the same angles between the faces, and René Just Haüy revealed in 1784 that each face of a crystal can be represented by straightforward stacking patterns of identical-sized and-shaped blocks. Hence, William Hallowes Miller in 1839 was able to give each face a unique label of three small integers, the Miller indices which remain in use today for identifying crystal faces.

18.2 X-RAY DIFFRACTION

X-rays may be thought of as waves of electromagnetic radiation, much like crystals are regular arrangements of atoms. X-ray rays are largely reflected off of atoms by their electrons. An X-ray impacting an electron causes secondary spherical waves to radiate from the electron, much as an ocean wave striking a lighthouse causes subsequent circular waves to emerge from the lighthouse. Elastic scattering is the term used to describe this phenomenon, and the electron (or lighthouse) is the scatterer. A regular array of spherical waves results from a regular array of scatterers. Even though these waves interfere destructively in most directions, Bragg's law states that they add constructively in the following few directions:

$$2d \sin \theta = n\lambda$$

Here d is the spacing between diffracting planes, θ is the incident angle, n is any integer, and λ is the wavelength of the beam. These specific directions appear as spots on the diffraction pattern called reflections. Thus, X-ray diffraction results from an electromagnetic wave (the X ray) impinging on a regular array of scatterers (the repeating arrangement of atoms within the crystal). X-rays are used to produce the diffraction pattern because their wavelength λ is typically the same order of magnitude (1–100 angstroms) as the spacing d between planes in the crystal.

18.3 PRODUCTION OF X-RAYS

German researcher Wilhelm Rontgen unintentionally discovered X-rays in 1895. Rontgen received the inaugural Nobel Prize in 1901. The study of crystal structure, the analysis of materials, the radiography of metals, and the study of medical sciences have all benefited greatly from the use of this extremely penetrating electromagnetic radiation. Some of the Nobel Prize winners who have made contributions to this discipline include Laue, Henry and Lawrence Bragg, Barkla, and Siegbahn. In addition to the discovery of new elements, some of the side effects of these research included -ray and electron spectroscopy. An electromagnetic spectrum includes X-rays.

Rontgen found that the radiations known as x-rays provide precise pictures of the interior bones when they are transmitted through arms, hands, or any other portion of the body. Every time an individual has an x-ray taken, an x-ray sensitive film is applied to one side of the body before the x-rays are fired through the subject. The bones are thick and absorb more x-rays than the skin, which is translucent. This explains why the skin is invisible in the x-ray but the shadow of the bones is left on the film. The electromagnetic spectrum's many wavelengths are displayed in the image below.

High potential was used to accelerate and cause the impingement of electrons from a hot element on the target (anode). Parallel plates collimate the resulting X-rays before they strike a crystal (LiF, quartz, diamond, etc.). As the inter-atomic distance is of the same order as the wavelength of X-rays diffraction is produced and they are detected by counters or photographic plates. This procedure is shown in figure 18.1.

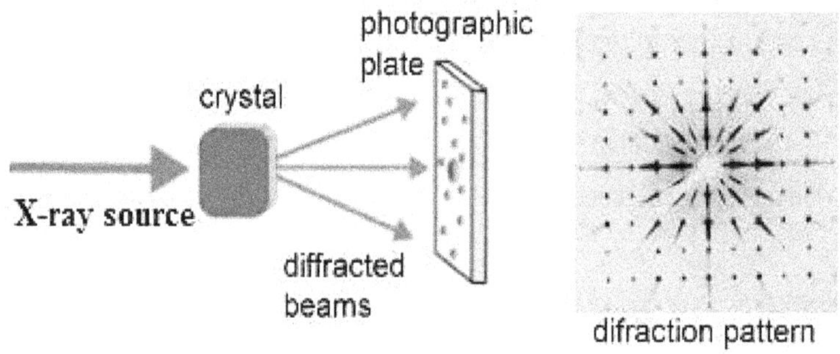

Figure 18.1: X-ray Production.

An accelerating voltage of generally 50 kV is used in an X-ray tube to accelerate the electrons that are released from the cathode towards the metal target anode. Atoms in the metal target are affected by the high energy electrons. The electromagnetic interaction can occasionally cause an electron to stray when it is extremely close to a target's nucleus. The electron undergoes significant energy loss during this procedure, known as bremsstrahlung (braking radiation), which results in the emission of an X-ray photon. The energy of the released photon might range from zero to the maximal energy of the incident electron.

Another effect of the high energy electron is the displacement of an electron near the nucleus in a metal atom. This vacancy is filled by an electron further out from the nucleus. The well-defined difference in binding energy, characteristic of the material, is emitted as a monoenergetic photon. When detected this X-ray photon gives rise to a characteristic X- ray line in the energy spectrum

Properties

Hard X-rays are short wavelength, powerful, deeply penetrating, and extremely damaging X- rays. The x-rays utilised for medical treatment are referred to as soft x-rays since they are less invasive and have longer wavelengths. X-rays are two-sided. We now go through these radiations' varied characteristics:

- They pass through materials more or less unchanged
- They cannot be refracted
- Electric and magnetic fields do not have any effect on these rays
- These radiations ionize the surrounding air by discharging electrified bodies
- They have short wavelength varying between 0.1 A° to 1 A°.
- They are produced when a metal anode is bombarded by very high energy electrons.
- They do not require any medium for propagation
- X-rays cannot be focused on a single point
- These radiations cannot be heard or smelt
- They travel in a straight line in free space
- They cause photoelectric emission.
- Intensity of X–rays depend on number of electrons hitting the target.
- Cut off wavelength or minimum wavelength, where v (in volts) is the p.d. applied to the tube $\lambda min = 12400/VA°$.
- Continuous spectrum appears due to retardation of electrons.

X-ray diffraction methods are frequently used to determine the atomic structure of crystalline substances. Electron and neutron diffraction can also provide complementary structural data. Because the resolution (or smallest object separation distance) to which any radiation can yield useful information is approximately equal to the wavelength of the radiation and because the average distance between adjacent atoms in solids is approximately 10-10m (1), all radiation used must have wavelengths in the range of 0.1 to 10. We don't try to gaze directly at atoms since there isn't a practical method to focus X-rays with lenses or enlarge pictures. Instead, we focus on how X-ray interference is affected when it is dispersed by the atoms that make up a crystal lattice. This is comparable to investigating the interference pattern created when visible light is shone on an optical diffraction grating to determine its structure. (The visible spectrum of light has a wavelength between 0.4 and 0.8 m, and the spacing between the lines on a grating is around 0.5 to 1 μm.) While in a crystal, the atoms (or, more precisely, the electrons around the atom) scatter the incident radiation, the ruled lines in an optical grating serve as scattering centres.

18.4 METHODS OF X-RAY DIFFRACTION

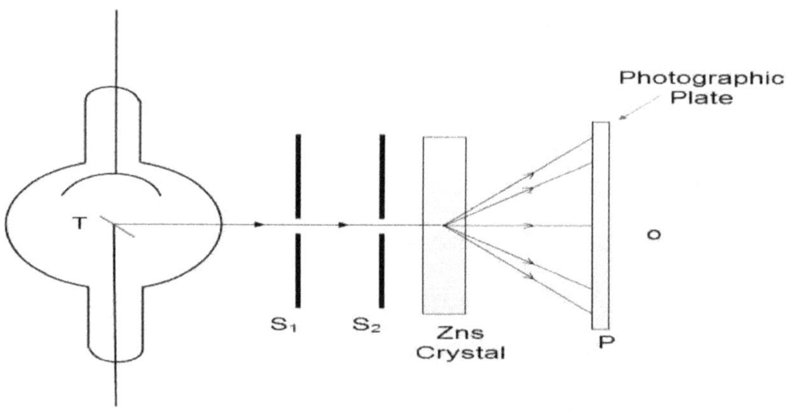

Figure 18.2: X-Ray Diffraction.

Only when the distance between the ruled lines on the grating is of the order of the wavelength of the employed light can the diffraction effects be seen. In the diffraction of a light beam, the grating element for a typical grating is of the order of 10-6 m. On the piece of glass, a transmission diffraction grating contains around 6000 lines per centimetre. Since the slit between two lines has a width on the order of a light wavelength, it is used to analyse the diffraction of common light. The X-ray wavelength is about 1/1000th the wavelength of the grating used for visible light in the visible spectrum. We have suggested that crystals can be used for the diffraction of X-rays. In a crystal grating, the atoms arranged in a regular pattern correspond to the grating lines and the distance between two atoms to the grating element. T is a source of X- rays which gives X-ray beam of a continuous range of wavelengths. A narrow beam of X-rays from the X-ray tube is collimated by two slits S_1 and S_2 and is passed through a zinc sulphide crystal and allowed the emerging beam to fall on a photographic plate as shown in the figure. After an exposure of several hours and on developing the plate, many faints but regularly arranged spots around the central bright spot were observed on the plates as shown in the figure 18.2.

From this experiment, it can be concluded that: -

1. The atoms of a crystal are arranged in a regular three-dimensional lattice.
2. X-rays are electromagnetic waves.

18.5 BRAGG'S LAW

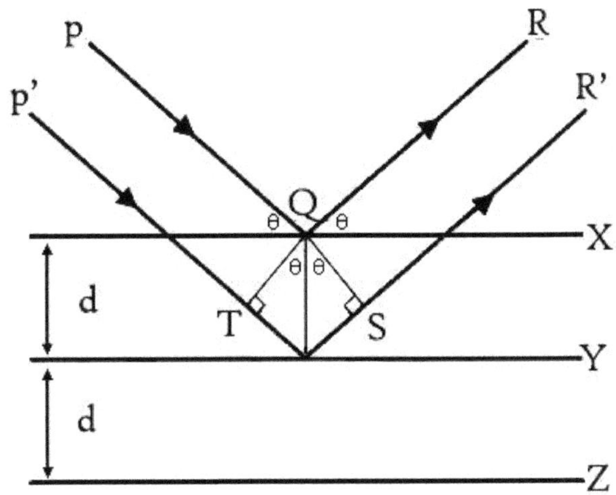

Figure 18.3: Bragg's Law.

Diffraction

Consider a set of parallel atomic planes separated by a distance d. A narrow monochromatic X-ray beam of wavelength λ is allowed to fall on the crystal lattice at a glancing angle θ and after reflection from the planes X and Y goes along QR and Q'R' respectively. Since X-rays are much more penetrating than ordinary light, there is only partial reflection at each plane. The complete absorption takes place only after penetrating several layers. Consider two parallel rays PQR and P'Q'R' in the beams, which are reflected by two atoms Q and Q'. Q' is vertically below Q. the ray P'Q'R' has a longer path than the ray PQR. To calculate the path difference, drop QT and QS perpendicular to P'Q' and Q'R' respectively.

Then, path difference from the right-angled triangle QTQ' and QSQ',

We have ∴ Path difference = TQ′ + Q′S = dsinθ + dsin θ = 2dsinθ

Then, path difference=TQ′+Q′S From the right-angled triangle QTQ' and QSQ',

We have ∴ Path difference = dsinθ + dsinθ = 2dsinθ

Since for maximum intensity, the path difference between two reflected rays should be integral multiple of λ,

Hence, 2dsinθ = nλ2dsin θ = nλ where n = 1, 2, 3,....

This equation is known as Bragg's law or Bragg's equation. The integer n gives the order of the scattered beam. For example, for first order reflection n = 1. If θ1 is the corresponding glancing angle, then from Bragg's equation 2dsinθ1 = λ2dsin θ1 = λ similarly, for second order reflection n= 2. If θ_2 is the corresponding glancing angle, then 2dsinθ2 = 2λ.

18.6 SOURCE OF X-RAY

Coolidge Tube

The high vacuum and the use of a heated filament as an electron source are the defining characteristics of the Coolidge tube. In contrast to cold cathode gas discharge tubes, the tube contains so little gas that it is not necessary for the creation of x-rays.

The Coolidge tube works in the manner described below. The cathode filament emits electrons as it warms up. The amount of electron emission increases as the filament heats up. These electrons are driven in the direction of the positively charged anode, where they collide with the anode, change course, and release a continuous range of x-rays known as bremsstrahlung. The maximum energy of the x-rays is the same as the kinetic energy of the electrons striking the anode. In addition to the x-rays produced at the focal spot of the anode, some undesirable x-rays (stray radiation) are produced by electrons striking other tube components.

The key advantages of the Coolidge tube are its stability, and the fact that the intensity and energy of the x-rays can be controlled independently. Increasing the current to the cathode increases its temperature. This increases the number of electrons emitted by the cathode, and as a result, the intensity of the x-rays. Increasing the high voltage potential difference between the anode and the cathode increases the velocity of the electrons striking the anode, and this increases the energy of the emitted x-rays. Decreasing the current or the high voltage would have the opposite effects. The high degree of control over the tube output meant that the early radiologists could do with one Coolidge tube what before had required a stable of finicky cold cathode tubes. As a bonus, the Coolidge tube could function almost indefinitely unless broken or badly abused.

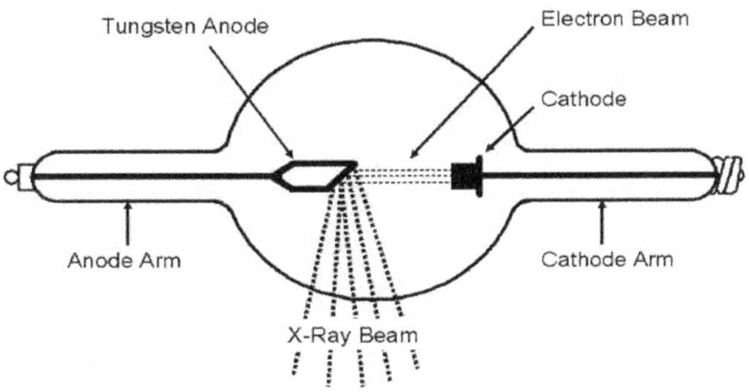

Figure 18.4: Coolidge Tube.

Synchroton Radiation

The radiation that results from the acceleration of charged particles along a curved route or orbit is known as chromotron radiation. Traditionally, electromagnetic radiation is produced by charged particles as they speed in a straight line or travel along a curved route. This radiation is known by a variety of names depending on the situation. For instance, it is referred to as "brehmsstrahlung" radiation when it happens when an electron impacts a solid metal target in an x-ray tube.

The radiation is known as synchrotron radiation, especially when it is used in conjunction with circular particle accelerators like synchrotrons, where charged particles are accelerated to extremely high speeds. This energy is radiated and is inversely proportional to the square of the path's radius and the fourth power of the particle speed. It becomes the constraint on the particle acceleration's ultimate energy in electron synchrotrons like the LEP at CERN. It may be identified and utilised as a tool to assist in the analysis of the scattering event's by products in various situations, such as the detector arrays in accelerators.

The classical formula for the radiated power from an accelerated electron is

$$P = \frac{2Ke^2}{3c^3}a^2$$

18.7 RADIOISOTOPES

An atomic species is defined by two whole numbers: the number of protons in the nucleus (known as Z, or atomic number) and the total number of protons plus neutrons (known as Z, or mass number).

The atoms of an element that have the same number of protons and, therefore, the same chemical properties, but different numbers of neutrons and, subsequently, varying numbers of neutrons, are known as isotopes. Isotopes can be radioactive, unstable, or both. In the latter, their nuclei have a unique characteristic: they produce ionising radiation in an effort to find a more stable structure.

Atomic Number and Mass Number

The chemical element to which an atom belongs is determined by its atomic number. Therefore, all atoms with one proton in their nuclei are hydrogen atoms, regardless of how many neutrons they possess. These eight-proton atoms are all oxygen atoms, etc.

The mass number is the whole number that is closest to the mass (expressed in atomic mass units) of the atom in question. Thus, all the atoms with A = 2 have a mass of approximately 2 mass units; atoms with A = 235 have a mass of approximately 235 atomic mass units.

Annotation: ${}^{A}_{Z}A$ (where X is the atom's element)

Radioisotope

Due to the equilibrium between neutrons and protons in their atomic nuclei, these are radioactive isotopes, and when their unstable atomic nucleus transforms into a more stable form, it emits energy and particles. A Geiger counter or photographic film can be used to measure the energy released during the shift in form. Each radioisotope has a distinctive half-life or disintegration period. Alpha (helium nuclei), beta (electron or positrons), or gamma (electromagnetic energy) rays are the three main types of energy that can be released.

Several unstable and artificial radioactive isotopes have medical uses. For instance, a technetium isotope (${}^{99m}Tc$) may be used to identify blocked blood vessels. Various natural radioactive isotopes are used to determine chronologies, such as the archaeological kind (${}^{14}C$).

18.8 ROTATING CRYSTAL TECHNIQUE

A single crystal is positioned with its axis normal to a monochromatic x-ray beam in the rotating crystal method. It is surrounded by a cylindric film, and the crystal is turned around the selected axis.

Sets of lattice planes will eventually produce the proper Bragg angle for the monochromatic incident beam as the crystal spins, at that point a diffracted beam will be created.

The surfaces of hypothetical cones are where the reflected beams are found. The diffraction spots appear as horizontal lines on a flattened film.

The chief use of the rotating crystal method is in the determination of unknown crystal structures.

The Laue Method

The Laue method is mainly used to determine the orientation of large single crystals. White radiation is reflected from, or transmitted through, a fixed crystal.

The arrays of spots created by the diffracted beams are located along the film's curves. For each set of planes in the crystal, the Bragg angle remains constant. For the values of d and involved, each set of planes selects and diffracts the specific wavelength from the white light that meets the Bragg law. As a result, each curve represents a distinct wavelength. Any curve's spots are reflections from planes in a particular zone. Laue reflections from the same zone's planes are all located on the top of a hypothetical cone, whose axis is the zone axis.

- **Experimental**

The orientation of massive single crystals is mostly ascertained using the Laue method. A fixed crystal either reflects white energy or transmits it through it.

The back-reflection Laue method and the transmission Laue method are two useful variations of the Laue method. You can study these below:

The locations of the dots can be used to establish the crystal's orientation. Using certain charts, each place can be indexed, or assigned to a specific plane. For back-reflection patterns, the Greninger chart is utilised, and for transmission patterns, the Leonhardt chart.

The size and shape of the spots can also be employed in the Laue procedure to determine the crystallinity of a sample. The dots deform and blur if the crystal has been bent or twisted in any way.

- **Back-reflection Method**

The film is positioned between the crystal and the x-ray source in the back-reflection technique. A record is made of the beams that are refracted backward.

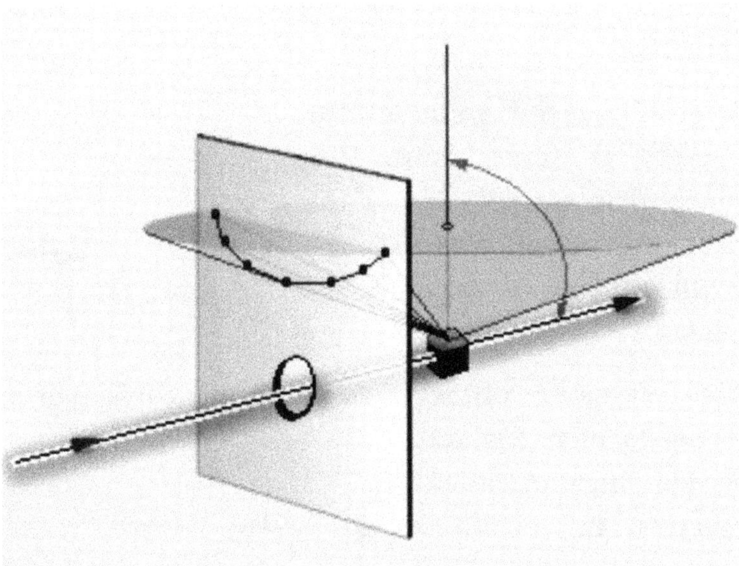

The transmitted beam establishes the perimeter of one side of the cone of Laue reflections. The film crosses the cone, and the spots caused by diffraction typically lie on a hyperbola.

Transmission Laue

When using the transmission Laue method, a film is positioned behind the crystal to capture the rays that are transmitted through it. The transmitted beam outlines one side of the cone of Laue reflections. When the film crosses the cone, the diffraction spots typically fall on an ellipse.

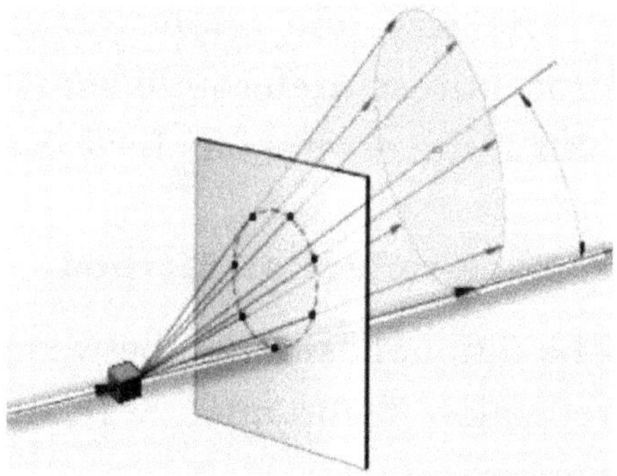

The Powder Method

Accurately determining the value of the lattice parameters is done using the powder approach. The magnitudes of the unit vectors a, b, and c, which specify the unit cell for the crystal, are known as lattice parameters.

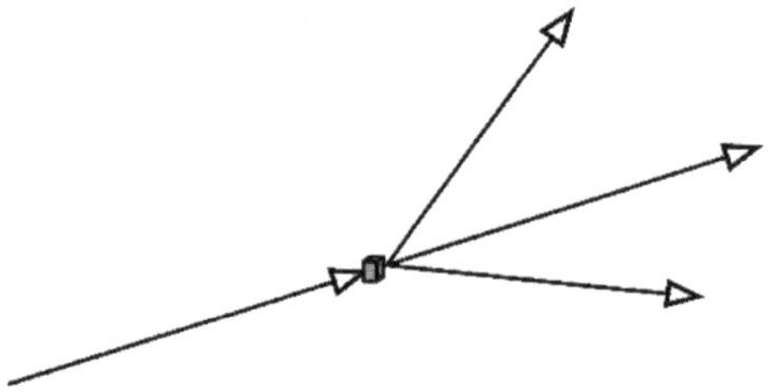

The diffracted beams are observed to lie on the surface of many cones if the sample consists of a few tens of randomly oriented single crystals. The cones could appear in both forward and reverse orientations.

The diffracted beams create continuous cones, as demonstrated by a sample made up of several hundred crystals (also known as a powdered sample).

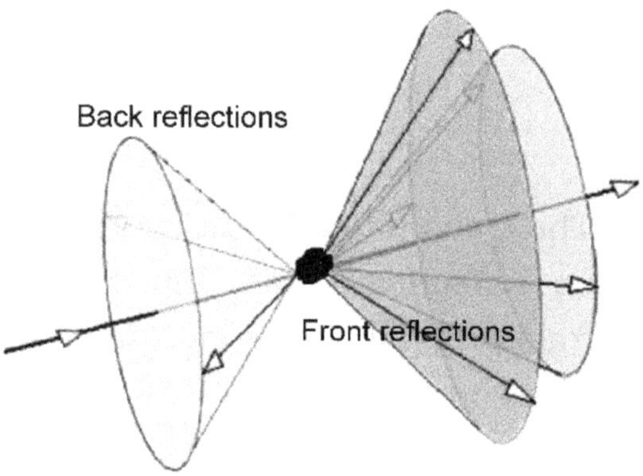

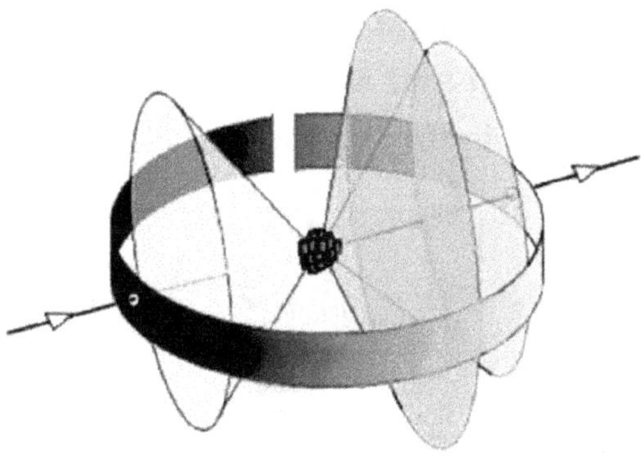

The diffraction pattern is captured on a circle of film as displayed. Diffraction lines are produced when each cone intersects the film. On the film, the lines appear as arcs.

By chance, there will always be one or more crystals in each plane of crystals that are oriented correctly to provide the proper Bragg angle and meet the Bragg's equation. Diffraction is thus possible on any crystal plane. A lot of tiny spots, each from a different crystal, make up each diffraction line. Each point appears to be a continuous line because of how little it is. The diffraction lines seem spotted if the crystal is not ground precisely enough. The Debye Scherrer camera shown here achieves this configuration practically.

- **Debye Scherrer camera:**

A little amount of material that has been powdered is enclosed inside a tiny capillary tube constructed of glass that doesn't diffract x-rays. The sample is loaded into the Debye Scherrer camera and precisely positioned so that it is in the centre of the device. X-rays are introduced into the camera by a collimator.

According to Bragg's law, the powder causes the x-rays to diffract, resulting in cones of diffracted beams. In the cylindrical camera, a strip of photographic film is crossed by these cones, creating a distinctive pattern of arcs on the film.

- **Powder Diffraction film**

The diffraction lines and the holes for the incident and transmitted beams are visible on the film after it has been taken out of the camera, flattened, and processed.

The highest angle back-reflected arcs are doubled because the x-ray beams Ka and Kb always have two arcs. This makes it obvious which hole in the film is for the incident beam and which is for the transmitted beam.

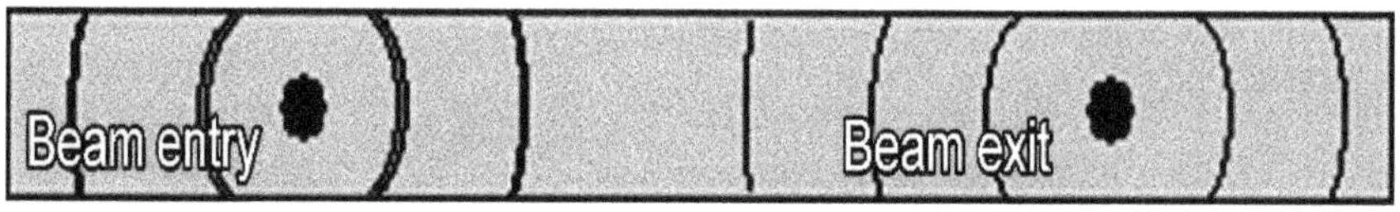

Experimental Procedure for Powder diffraction

In this procedure we consider the powder patterns from a sample crystal. The sample is known to have a cubic structure, but we don't know which one.

We remove the film strip from the Debye camera after exposure, then develop and fix it. From the strip of film, we make measurements of the position of each diffraction line. From the results it is possible to associate the sample with a particular type of cubic structure and also to determine a value for its lattice parameter.

- When the film is laid flat, S_1 can be measured. This is the distance along the film, from a diffraction line, to the centre of the hole for the transmitted direct beam.
- For back reflections, i.e. where 2θ > 90θ you can measure S_2 as the distance from the beam entry point.

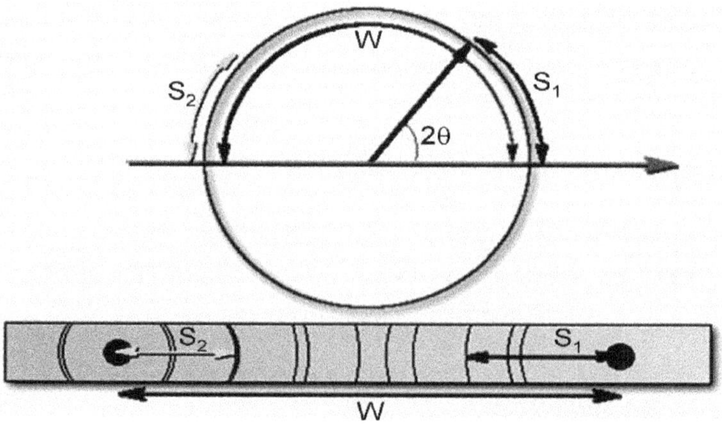

- The distance $S1$ corresponds to a diffraction angle of 2θ. The angle between the diffracted and the transmitted beams is always 2θ. We know that the distance between the holes in the film, W, corresponds to a diffraction angle of θ = θ. So, we can find θ from:

$$\theta = \frac{\pi S_1}{2W}$$

or

$$\theta = \frac{\pi}{2}\left(1 - \frac{S_2}{W}\right)$$

Bragg's Law:

$n\lambda = 2d\sin\theta$ and the equation for interlunar spacing, d, for cubic crystals is given by:

$$d_{kkl} = \frac{a}{\sqrt{h^2 + k^2 + l^2}}$$

Where a is the lattice parameter

- From the measurements of each arc we can now generate a table of S_1, θ and $\sin^2\theta$.
- If all the diffraction lines are considered, then the experimental values of $\sin^2\theta$ should form a pattern related to the values of h, k and l for the structure.
- We now multiply the values of $\sin^2\theta$ by some constant value to give nearly integer values for all the $h^2+k^2+l^2$ values. Integer values are then assigned.

18.9 PHARMACEUTICAL APPLICATIONS OF X-RAY DIFFRACTION

- **Phase analysis and polymorph screening**

The distinctive diffraction patterns of different phases or polymorphs can be used by XRPD to discriminate between them. The search to develop and analyse all available polymorphs of a given therapeutic molecule has grown to be a field that attracts great work because the choice of polymorph might be essential in connection to qualities like solubility, bioavailability, and stability. The search for every polymorph of a target molecule is an essential step toward patent protection since a novel crystalline form of an API could be patented as a new pharmaceutical product.

- **Crystallinity Determination**

XRPD has been successfully used to determine percent crystallinity, which is the volume concentration of, for example, amorphous filler to a crystalline active matrix inside a drug's dosage form. Percent Crystallinity can affect both the processing behaviour and the pharmacological activity of a medication.

- **R&D Applications**

The most basic, yet critical, use of XRPD is in the identification or fingerprinting of crystalline phases, with various crystal structures producing unique powder diffraction patterns. This method of qualitative assessment of materials has several uses, including quality control and polymorph screening.

- **Crystallography and Crystal Structure Determination**

Although a general powder diffraction pattern can be used to detect a material's crystal structure, in most situations identifying the lattice type and unit cell size is sufficient (indexing). This type of investigation is very beneficial for identifying alternate forms or polymorphs of approved medications whose patents are about to expire. In addition, information such as displacement parameters, coordinates of atoms inside the unit cell, site occupancy, and preferred orientation may be retrieved using this approach.

- **Compatibility Studies**

Because XRPD is non-destructive, it is a good technique for systematic drug-excipient compatibility tests in Preformulation. To achieve consistent release and bioavailability and to avoid unanticipated formulation stability concerns in later phases of formulation development, careful excipient selection and systematic study of drug-excipient interaction are required.

- **Manufacturing and Production**

Because XRPD can identify and quantify polymorphism contamination, the amount of crystallographic alterations, and the active component in the final dosage form, it may be used to monitor and enhance manufacturing efficiency and cost. The morphological characteristics evaluated by X-ray diffraction can be directly connected to the final medication performance once the active component of a pharmaceutical product is in its final dose form.

- **Control of Ingredients**

The crystal shape of active substances or excipients can be monitored using XRPD. This is significant because any change in the morphology of fillers or the crystalline form of active components in the final product caused by the manufacturing process might affect the bioavailability of a medicine. The X' Celerator (PAN alytical) has significantly decreased the lower limit of detection for minority phases, down to 0.05% in some instances.

- **Stability Studies**

In situ powder diffraction investigations performed as a function of temperature and/or relative humidity can give a direct way of assessing a pharmaceutical compound's stability and the occurrence of hydration/ dehydration processes. Non-ambient diffraction investigations of this type can be carried out at any step of the drug development process.

- **Process Control**

The potential of XRPD to estimate structural characteristics, together with its non-destructive analytical capability, makes it suitable in a wide range of applications. One such use is the use of XRPD to determine the best range of tableting pressure. This enables producers to monitor an API's crystallographic structure to verify that the completed tablet meets the desired dissolving rate.

- **Batch/dosage uniformity**

XRPD is useful for checking batch/dosage homogeneity because it allows materials to be evaluated directly under the settings in which they are employed in specific applications. In situ analysis of the exact percentages of each active component in the final dosage form of a medicine, as well as the amount of any amorphous or crystalline packing substances utilised, is achievable. Even tiny quantities of crystalline aerosol medication given by a pressured metered dosage inhaler may be identified and quantified using XRPD.

There have been several innovations in lipid analysis using mass spectrometry. The most widely used lipidomics techniques use triple quadrupole analyzers and electrospray ionisation (ESI) sources. It is feasible to ascertain the lipid structure's molecular weight, elemental makeup, branching location, and kind of substituents using mass spectrometry.

Analysis of Proteins and Peptides

The study of all proteins presents in a biological system, including those that have undergone co- and post-translational modifications as well as alternatively spliced versions, is known as proteomics. Today, mass spectrometry is a critical tool in practically all proteomics investigations. It makes it possible to precisely determine both the sequences and molecular masses of peptides. *De novo* sequencing, post-translational modification identification, and protein identification are all very much possible with the use of this knowledge.

Analysis of Oligonucleotides

Oligonucleotides (RNA or DNA) are nucleotide linear polymers. These are made up of a phosphate group, a ribose sugar, and a nitrogenous base. The covalent modifications that occur naturally on tRNA and rRNA as well as artificial ones brought on by interactions with foreign substances can both occur on oligonucleotides. These modifications may be found using mass spectrometry, which can also be used to determine their structure and location within the oligonucleotide. It not only enables oligonucleotide molecular weight determination but also, either directly or indirectly, oligonucleotide sequence determination.

CHAPTER 19 POTENTIOMETRY

19.1 PRINCIPLE OF POTENTIOMETRY

The principle involved in the Potentiometry is when the pair of electrodes is placed in the sample solution it shows the potential difference by the addition of titrant or by the change in the concentration of ions.

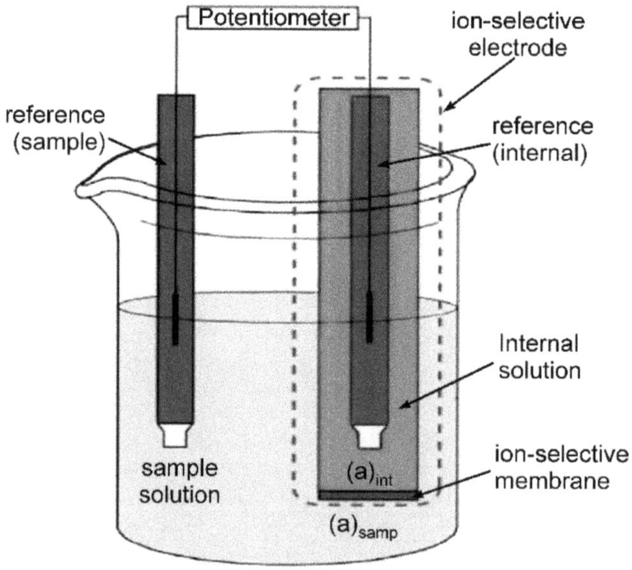

The reference electrode is the electrodes which contains of its own potential value and it is stable when dipped into sample solution. The salt bridge is used to prevent the interference of the analyte solution with that of the reference solution. Here analyte solution is the solution whose potential is to be measured. The indicator electrode is the electrode which responds to change in the potential of analyte solution.

The electromotive force of the complete cell is given by the following equation-

$$E_{cell} = E_{reference} + E_{indicator} + E_{junction}$$

Where $E_{reference}$ is electromotive force of reference electrode. $E_{indicator}$ is electromotive force of indicator electrode. $E_{junction}$ is electromotive force of junction electrode.

Theory

The main theory involved in the Potentiometry is, when the known potential electrode is immersed in the sample solution then the potential is given by Nernst equation:

$$E = E^0 + (0.592/n) \log c$$

Where E is the potential of the solution and E^0 is the standard electrode potential; n is the valency of ions; c is the concentration of sample solution; 0.592 is the value obtained from the RT/F; where R is the gas constant and T is the temperature in kelvin; F is the faradeys constant

19.2 POTENTIOMETRY TITRATION

Potentiometric titration is a technique similar to direct titration of a redox reaction. It is a useful means of characterizing an acid. No indicator is used; instead the potential is measured across the analyte, typically an electrolyte solution. To do this, two electrodes are used, an indicator electrode (the glass electrode and metal ion indicator electrode) and a reference electrode. Reference electrodes generally used are hydrogen electrodes, calomel electrodes, and silver chloride electrodes. The indicator electrode forms an electro chemical half-cell with the interested ions in the test solution. The reference electrode forms the other half cell.

Principle:

The principle involved in the Potentiometry is when the pair of electrodes is placed in the sample solution; it shows the potential difference by the addition of the titrant or by the change in the concentration of the ions.

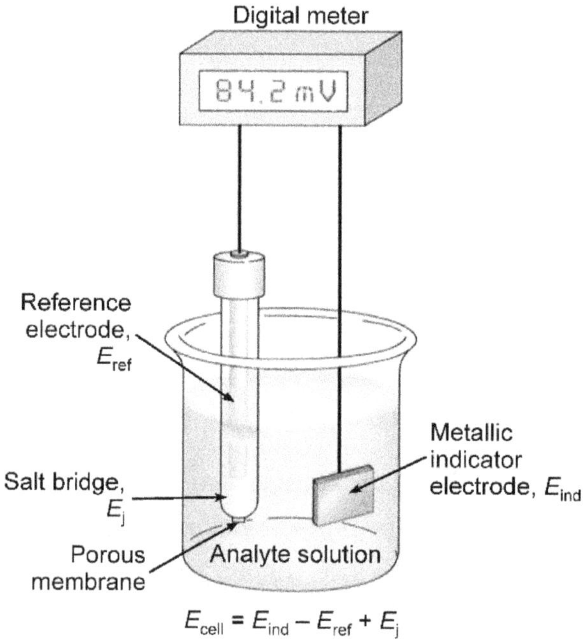

Figure 19.1: Electrochemical Cell/Potentiometric Titration.

The accurate, precise and effective potentiometric measurements can be made with the help of the following two types of electrodes namely:

Reference Electrodes

(a) Standard Hydrogen Electrode,

(b) Saturated Calomel Electrode, and

(c) Silver-Silver Chloride Electrode.

Indicator Electrodes

(a) Metal Indicator Electrode, and

(b) Membrane Indicator Electrode

Standard Hydrogen Electrode (SHE)

The standard hydrogen electrode (SHE), is considered to be the universally accepted reference electrode. The metal electrode has a small piece of platinum foil with finely divided platinum, usually termed as platinum black because of its dark look. The coated foil is immersed in an acidic medium having concentration of 0.1N, and through which H2 gas is bubbled. The Pt- black-foil possesses a relatively large-surface-area thereby allowing it to absorb an appreciable amount of H2 gas, ultimately bringing it into direct contact with the surrounding H+ ions at the electrode surface.

Silver-Silver Chloride Electrode

Silver-Silver chloride electrode which comprises of a Silver wire coated with Silver chloride and is duly placed in a 1M KCl solution saturated with AgCl.

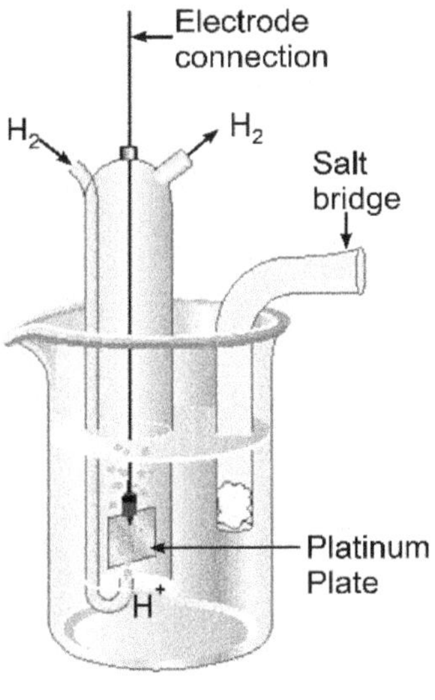

Figure 19.2: Standard Hydrogen Electrode.

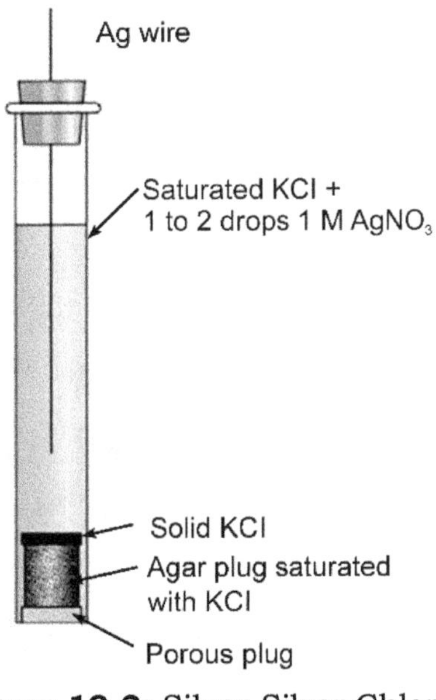

Figure 19.3: Silver-Silver Chloride Electrode.

Saturated Calomel Electrode

It essentially consists of a platinum wire immersed in a slurry made up of pure mercury, solid mercurous chloride Hg2Cl2 (commonly known as calomel), and aqueous saturated solution of KCl, packed in the inner-tube having a small hole. The outer-tube contains a saturated solution of KCl having a porous ceramic fiber at its lower end. It serves as a salt-bridge which allows the entire set- up immersed directly into the solution to be measured. The porous ceramic fiber permits electrical contact between one side of the salt-bridge and the solution under the examination and serves as a barrier between the said two solutions. The small opening at the top end of the salt-bridge tube serves as a fill-hole through which either KCl solution may be filled or replaced as and when required.

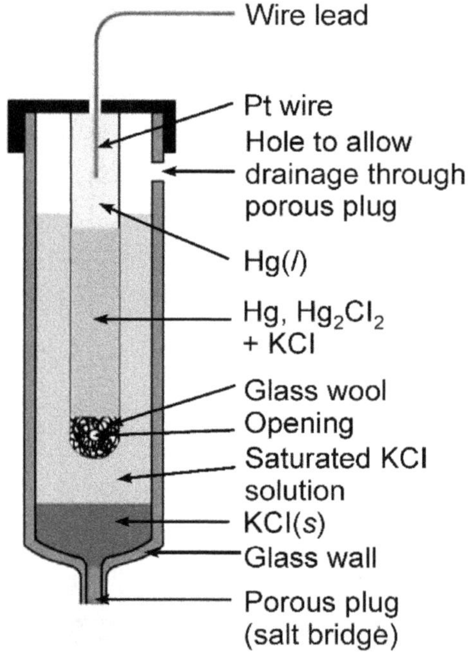

Figure 19.4: Standard Calomel Electrode.

Metal Indicator Electrodes

These develop electric potential in response to redox reaction on the metal surface. Platinum or Au are used as metal indicator electrodes. These are mainly classified into three types of electrodes used in the Potentiometry. They are as follows:

- **First Kind Electrodes:** They are composed of the metal rod immersed in its metal solution. These electrodes respond to the ionic activity of the electrode.

  Ex: silver electrode dipped in the silver nitrate solution. copper electrode dipped in the copper sulphate solution.

- **Second Kind Electrode:** These are composed of the metal wires coated with the salt precipitates. These electrodes respond to the changes in the ionic activity through the formation of the complex.

  Ex: Ag/ AgCl/ KCl Hg/ Hg_2Cl_2/ KCl

- **Third kind electrodes:** These electrodes are also known as inert electrodes and redox electrodes. They are composed of inert metal electrode immersed in the redox solution.

  Ex: Pt-H_2 electrode

Membrane Indicator Electrodes (or Ion-Selective Electrodes)

The underlying principle of this type of electrode is that the potential developed due to an unequal charge generated at the opposing surfaces of a 'special' membrane. The resulting charge at each surface of the membrane is controlled and monitored by the exact position of an equilibrium involving analyte ions, which in turn, depends upon the concentration of those ions present in the solution.

These are classified further into the following four kinds, namely:

(i) Glass membrane electrodes,

(ii) Polymer (liquid) membrane electrodes,

(iii) Crystalline membrane electrodes, and

(iv) Gas-sensing electrodes

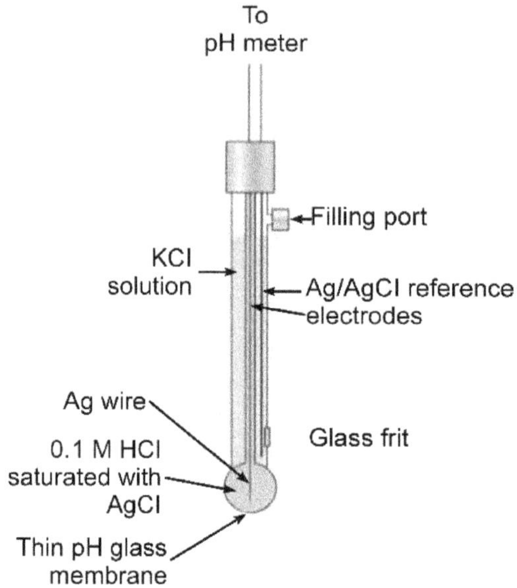

Figure 19.5: Glass Electrode.

19.3 GENERAL METHOD FOR POTENTIOMETRY

- Switch on the instrument.
- Connect the saturated calomel electrode to the positive terminal or socket and the glass electrode to the negative.
- Adjust the meter to zero and subsequent readings are to be taken with the stirrer motor running.
- Rinse the beaker and electrodes thoroughly with water, then with the solution to be titrated and place a measured volume in the beaker. Add sufficient water to cover the bulb of the glass electrode adequately.
- Switch on the stirrer and measure the pH of the solution.
- Add about 2ml of titrant, allow sufficient time to mix and measure the pH of the solution.

- Add further quantities of titrant and as the end point is approached reduce to 0.1ml increments and measure the corresponding values of the pH.
- Obtain further readings of pH for about 5ml beyond the equivalence point.
- Switch the meter to standby and turn off the stirrer. Wash the beaker and electrodes thoroughly with the distilled water.
- Plot a graph of pH (vs) titrant added. Read off the equivalence point from the graph and calculate any required data from this value.

Ion Selective Electrode

Ion Selective Electrode Principle

Ion Selective Electrode (ISE) is an electrochemical sensor that works based on the principle of a galvanic cell. It converts the activity or concentration of a specific ion presents in a solution into electrical potential.

A typical assembly of an ion selective electrode is given above the picture. It is very useful in environmental chemistry for the analysis of dissolved carbon dioxide from water samples.

Ion selective electrode can be used for the potentiometric determination of several anions (fluoride, chloride, bromide, iodide ion) and cations (sodium, potassium, calcium ion). The electrode can alsobe used for endpoint detection in potentiometric titration.

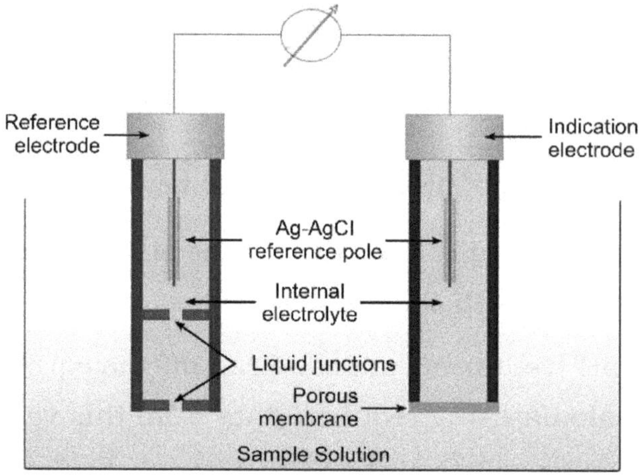

In biochemistry, ion selective electrodes are used for the determination of enzymes and substances which interact with enzymes.

How do Ion Selective Electrodes Work?

Potentiometric ion-selective electrode (ISE) is one of the most important groups of chemical sensors. The working process of potentiometric ion selective electrodes is based on the principle of a galvanic cell. It contains a reference electrode, ion-selective membrane, and voltmeter.

The transport of ions from high concentration to low concentration through the selective membrane creates a potential difference. It can be measured with respect to a standard reference electrode having a constant electrode potential. Under equilibrium conditions, the measured potential (E) can be expressed by the Nernst equation.

$$E_{cell} = E^0 + (0.059/n) \log_M a^{n+} \text{ at } 25^0 \text{ C.}$$

Where n is the charge of the analyte io $_{Mn}$ n, a $^{+}$ is the activity of the sample solution, and E^0 is asymmetric potential. It is developed across the membrane due to internal strain. It is the characteristic constant of each ion selective electrode.

To determine the value of E^0, the electrode is dipped into a solution of known pH value and coupled with a secondary reference electrode such as a calomel electrode.

Ion Selective Electrode Types

The essential part of an ISE is the ion-selective membrane which is commonly placed between the sample and inner solutions that contain an analyte ion. The membrane used in ISE may be a glass, a crystalline solid, or a liquid. Ion selective electrodes are mainly four types according to the nature of membrane material. These are,

- Glass electrodes
- Crystalline electrodes
- Ion exchange electrodes
- Enzyme electrodes

Glass Electrodes

A glass electrode is a type of ISE where a thin bulb shape glass membrane is used as a sensing material. It is sensitive to hydrogen ions in the solution. When a thin glass membrane separates two electrolytes, a potential is developed across the membrane.

A carbon dioxide sensitive electrode is a pH-sensitive glass electrode. It is very useful in environmental chemistry for the analysis of dissolved carbon dioxide in water samples.

The glass electrode has good selectivity for silver (Ag^+), sodium (Na^+), and hydrogen (H^+) ions.

While chalcogenide glass has good selectivity for double-charged metal ions like cadmium (Cd^{2+}) and lead (Pb^{2+}) ions.

Crystalline Electrodes

Crystalline or solid-state membrane electrodes contain an insoluble inorganic salt. Crystalline electrodes have good selectivity. The ions which can introduce themselves into the crystal structure can interfere with the electrode response. An ion-exchange process leads to the formation of potential at the membrane of crystalline electrodes.

Mono- or polycrystalline of a single substance such as $AgCl/Ag_2S$ can be used to determine the activity or concentration of chloride ions.

Single crystal LaF_3 is widely used to determine the activity of fluoride ions. To improve the conductivity, the crystal is usually doped with europium. It was described by Martin and Frant in the year of 1960.

Ion-exchange Electrodes

Ion exchange electrodes are based on the membrane which is electrically conductive. An ion- exchange membrane is a type of organic polymer or ion exchange resin that transports specific dissolved ions from the solution and blocks other ions or neutral molecules.

Important examples of ion-exchange membranes are proton-exchange membranes and anion exchange membranes.

- Proton-exchange membranes are used to transport H^+ ions.
- Anion exchange membranes are used in certain alkaline fuel cells to transport OH^- ions from dissolved solution.

Potassium-selective electrode is a great example of liquid membrane ion exchange electrode where valinomycin uses as an exchanger. It has high selectivity against other alkaline metal cations and ammonium cations. The sensing membrane is based on a polyvinyl chloride matrix. It can be used for several months in clinical analysis.

Enzyme Electrodes

Enzyme electrodes are based on the principles where enzymes can interact with substrates in biological processes. It was first developed by Clark and Lyons.

An amygdalin-sensitive electrode can be made by retaining β-glucosides in a gel layer coupled to a cyanide-sensitive membrane electrode. Glucose and urea can be measured by enzyme electrodes. It is beneficial for diabetic patients.

In clinical application, enzymes play a critical role in the metabolic activities of all living organisms. Therefore, enzyme electrodes are broadly applied in biotechnology and clinical analysis.

Application of Ion Selective Electrode

The application of ion selective electrodes (ISEs) has been well-established in many fields such as clinical, biological, water, air, oceanographic, pharmaceutical research, and analytical determinations.

The application of fluoride, chloride, ammonium, sodium, potassium, and calcium ion selective electrodes are given below.

Fluoride Ion Selective Electrode

A fluoride ISE is a type of ion selective electrode which used to measure the concentration of the fluoride ion in aqueous solutions quickly, simply, accurately, and economically. It is a useful test procedure for the measurement of fluoride in drinking water, bone, cement, fish protein, glass, phosphate-mineral, and toothpaste.

Chloride Ion Selective Electrode

The chloride ion selective electrode is used for a rapid, simple, and reliable analysis of chloride ions in biological materials, food products, soils, and wastewater. It is used mainly for the determination of the salinity of water and chloride ions from blood serum, urine, fish, plant tissues, milk, beef extract, nutrient broth, and orange, tomato, and grapefruit juices.

Ammonium Ion Selective Electrode

The ammonium ion-selective electrode can be used to replace the distillation and titration procedure. It can be used to measure the concentration of ammonium (NH_4^+) ion in aqueous samples. After the conversion of nitrogen to an ammonium ion, the ammonia concentration is determined with the ammonium electrode.

Ammonium ISE is used mainly to measure levels of ammonium ions present in fertilizers.

Sodium Ion Selective Electrode

The sodium ion-selective electrode is designed to detect sodium ions (Na^+) from aqueous solutions. It contains a solid-state PVC polymer matrix membrane. It is suitable for various laboratory applications.

Detection of sodium from blood, food, and soil is very important for modern people. Sodium is one of the essential constituents in the blood and extracellular fluid.

Sodium with potassium maintains various biological functions such as osmotic pressures and moisture inside and outside the cell. They also operate functions of nerves, heart, muscles, etc.

Excessive sodium level in the human body causes high blood pressure or hypertension. Therefore, controlling sodium levels in our body is very important for modern people.

Potassium Ion Selective Electrode

A potassium ISE is an example ion selective electrode used for measurements of potassium ion concentration in an aqueous solution. Highly selective potassium ion exchangers and robust polymeric membranes are used widely in biochemical and biophysical research. In advanced analytical chemistry, these types of membranes can be used to measure the potassium activity in plasma or whole blood.

Calcium Ion Selective Electrode

A calcium ion selective electrode is a membrane-based electrode which used to measure Ca^{2+} ion concentration or activity in an aqueous solution. It is very useful in determining the hardness of the water.

Calcium ISE is also used to determine calcium ions in beer, soil, feedstuffs, flour, minerals, milk, seawater, serum and biological fluids, sugar, pulping liquor, and wine.

A recent development is the use of liquid ion selective membranes in ion selective electrodes. These liquid ion exchange membranes are non-volatile, water-immiscible chelates or coordination complexes.

Fluoride (F^-), chloride (Cl^-), bromide (Br^-), iodide (I^-), cadmium (Cd^{2+}), copper (Cu^{2+}), lead (Pb^{2+}), nitrate (NO_3^-), potassium (K^+), silver (Ag^+), sodium (Na^+), ammonia (NH_3), and several enzymes ion selective electrode are most common, reliable and commercially available electrodes used in the various analysis.

CHAPTER 20 THERMAL TECHNIQUES

DIFFERENTIAL SCANNING CALORIMETRY (DSC)

20.1 INTRODUCTION

Differential Scanning Calorimetry (DSC) is one of the thermal analysis techniques. In case of DSC, differences in heat flow between a specimen and reference are measured against the temperature or time while the specimen is continuously heated under controlled conditions. Function of calorimeter is to measure the heat content which comes in and out of the sample. Throughout the experiment both reference and sample are maintained at nearly constant temperature. Usually for DSC analysis temperature program for sample holder is designed in such a way that its temperature increases linearly with time. For DSC analysis only, few mg materials are required. It is the most used thermal technique due to its speed, availability and simplicity. DSC technique is used for quantitative analysis. These measurements give both quantitative as well as qualitative information regarding the physical and chemical changes which involves endothermic and exothermic processes or variations in heat capacity of the sample.

20.2 PRINCIPLE

To maintain the sample and reference at equal temperature during the physical transformations of the sample (like phase transitions), either more or lesser amount of heat is required to be applied on it then that required for the reference sample or an empty sample pan. This heat required depends on the nature of the transformation process, that is, whether it is exothermic or endothermic. For instance, at a constant heating rate, when a solid sample changes to liquid, more heat is required to be applied to the sample for increasing its temperature. This happens because heat is absorbed by the sample while it changes state from solid to liquid. However, if there is exothermic process in the sample (for instance, crystallization), less amount of heat is needed to increase the temperature of the sample.

Thus, by calculating the heat flow differences between the reference and sample, DSC technique can determine the amount of heat released or absorbed during a transition process.

Types of DSC

Various types of DSC are:

1. **Power Compensated DSC:** In case of power compensated DSC, both reference and sample are heated separately under different furnace. Difference of temperature between reference and sample is maintained at zero i.e. both are at the same temperature and the difference of energy between reference and sample is recorded as a function of sample temperature. Two independent heating unit are employed for power compensation DSC. To rapidly heat, cool or maintaining equilibrium, small heating unit is required. The heating unit needs to be integrated with a relatively larger temperature-controlled heat sink. For continuously monitoring the temperature of the material in reference and sample holders, platinum resistance thermometer is used. The increasing the temperature, suitable power is applied to the reference and sample heaters. This power required to maintain equal temperature of reference and sample is recorded by the power compensated DSC as a function of temperature. Power compensated DSC has lower sensitivities than the heat flux DSC, however power compensated DSC are faster than their heat flux counterparts. Thus, power compensated DSC are often used in studying kinetics wherein very fast equilibrium to a

desired temperature is reached. These instruments also have higher resolution than the heat flux DSC. The calibration constant in power compensated DSC, which converts peak area into joules, is an electrical conversion factor. Basic diagram of power compensated DSC is shown in Figure 1.

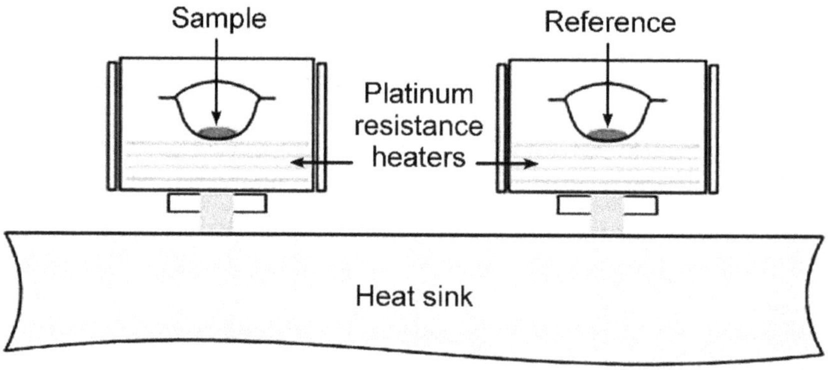

Figure 20.1: Schematics of a Typical Power Compensated DSC Equipment.

2. **Heat Compensated DSC:** Here, both the reference and sample are heated under the same furnace. The difference between the temperatures of the reference and sample is recorded and converted into a power difference and plotted against time or temperature. The main cell assembly of DSC is enclosed within a heated silver block cylinder, from which heat is transmitted onto the specimen by a constantan disc connected to the cylinder. The reference and sample pan are kept on two raised platforms in the system. The underside of both the platforms is connected to the constantan disc via connecting wires and chromel (alloy of nickel and chromium) disks, thereby forming a thermocouple which is used to measure the temperature difference between the two platforms. In addition to this, the individual temperatures of the two platforms can be measured by the junction of alumel wires linking the platforms to the chromel disks. Another separate thermocouple is integrated with the silver block which acts as a temperature controller for programmed heating cycles. Inert gas can be introduced within the cell at constant flow rate of

~40nm/min. Unlike the power compensated DSC, the calibration constant (which converts peak area into joule) in heta flux DSC is a thermal factor.

Total heat flow dH/dt in heat flux DSC is:

$$dH/dt = Cp\ dT/dt + f\ (T,t)$$

Where, H is enthalpy in J/mol f (T,t) is kinetic response of the specimen in J/mol Cp = specific heat capacity in $JK^{-1}mol^{-1}$.

Therefore, total heat flow is equal to the sum of the two terms; where one term is related to the kinetic response and the other is related to the heat capacity. Figure 2 shows heat compensated DSC.

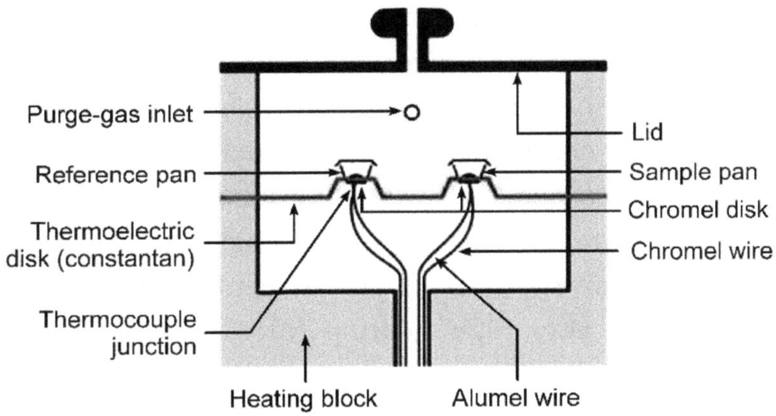

Figure 20.2: Heat compensated DSC.

3. **Modulated DSC:** In case of modulated DSC, the cell and heating arrangement are analogous to those used in heat flux DSC. This is a relatively recent technique and was proposed in 1993. A separation of overlapping events in the DSC scans is the main advantage of this technique. In modulated DSC, a linear heating ramp usually is overlapped with a sinusoidal function described by an amplitude and frequency to create a sine wave shaped temperature which varies with time.

Fourier transformation can be used to break the DSC signal in two parts: reversible and reflecting events, as:

$T = T_0 = bt + B \sin(wt)$ $dq/dt = C [b + Bw \cos(wt)] + f(t,T) + K \sin(wt)$ here, T represents the temperature, t is time, C is specific heat, f (t,T) is the average underling kinetic function obtained by subtracting the effect of sine wave modulation, and w is frequency [b+Bw cos (wt)]= is the calculated quantity dT/dt or Curve reversing. K= kinetic response amplitude of the sine wave modulation.

MDSC technique is a valued extension of conventional DSC. Applications of this DSC includes study of the energy of relaxation and precise determination of glass transition temperature.

- **Hyper DSC**: New type of power compensating DSC gives high resolution for melting analysis and detection of glass transition temperature (Tg) in medications or crystallisation of metals. This DSC can perform accurate measurements of heat flow with very high linear controlled rates (till 500 K/min) mainly during cooling, i.e., at relatively higher rates than conventional power compensated DSC which works below 10 K per minute. These devices benefit by avoiding unwanted transformation like solid– solid transformation, offer greater sensitivity at higher rates, etc. Hyper DSC is extensively used in pharmaceutical industries at varying temperatures where very high heating rates are required to eliminate various undesirable reactions etc.

4. **Pressure DSC:** This technique is used to characterize samples at specific environment conditions upto 10MPa as a function of time or temperature. It is often employed in evaluation of catalysts, studying pressure sensitive reactions, and resolution of overlapping transitions. Instrumentation. Figure 3 shows the block diagram of DSC instrument.

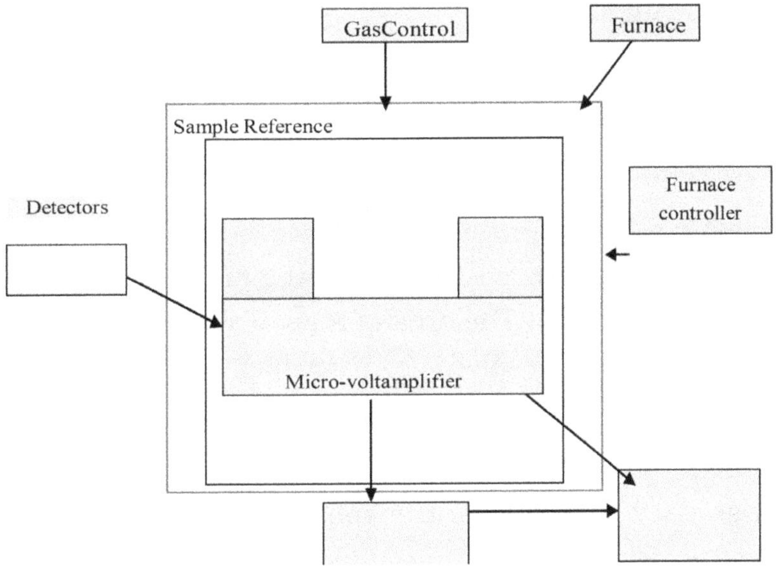

Figure 20.3: Block Diagram of DSC.

1. **Detector:** In case of detector thermocouple is used to measure the temperature change while the sample heated under controlled environment. For the case of low temperature copper- constantan or cromel alumel thermocouple is used and for the case of corrosive atmosphere or high temperature pt/13%rh thermocouple is used.
2. **Sample Container:** Sample container is designed in such a a way that it can be used under high pressure and thermal environment. For high temperature case platinum or ceramic is used for sample holder and for low temperature case aluminium is used.
3. **Reference Material:** Generally, reference material is made up of calcined alumina Al_2O_3 or carborundum, silicon carbide.
4. **Temperature Controller:** Temperature controller is used to maintain the temperature of the reference and sample at the desired value.
5. **Furnace:** One block of furnace is required in case of heat compensated DSC and two blocks of furnace is required in case of power compensated DSC.

20.3 DSC THERMOGRAM

DSC curve is employed to determine the enthalpy of transitions by integrating the peak area for given transitions. The transition enthalpy is found as follows:

$$\Delta H = KA$$

here, **K** is the calorimetric constant **A** is the area under the peak and **ΔH** is the enthalpy of transition. The area of a peak scales directly with the heat absorbed (endothermic) or evolved (exothermic) during a reaction, and the peak's height varies directly with the reaction rate. Transitions involve glass transition temperature, melting temperature, crystallization temperature.

DSC curve also used to calculate the specific heat capacity of the material using equation:

Specific heat capacity (Cp) = Absolute value of heat flow/Heating rate Where Absolute value of heat flow = Heat supplied per unit time

And Heating rate = Temperature increase per unit time Therefore $Cp = q/t / \Delta T/t$ $Cp = q/\Delta T$.

Let's consider the case of polymer, initially on heating it absorbs heat and curve look like flat after absorbing certain amount of heat its temperature starts to rise and its heat capacity increase on further heating plot will go downward and polymer reach to its glass transition (second order as there is no latent heat involved) temperature with further increase it comes to its crystallization (first order latent heat involve) temperature and give off certain amount of heat and reaches to the state of ordered arrangement on further heating it absorbs heat and reaches to its melting (first order) temperature. Figure 4 shows DSC curve.

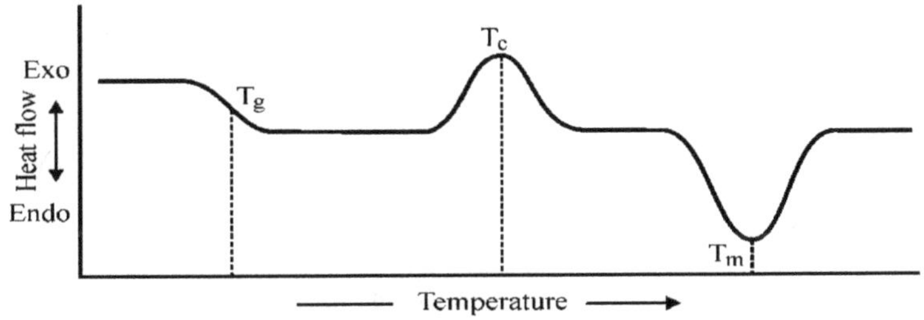

Figure 20.4: DSC Curve of Polymer.

20.4 FACTORS AFFECTING DSC CURVE

1. **Instrumental Factors:** These include parameters such as – Furnace heating rate, furnace atmosphere, recording speed, geometry of sample holders, location of sensors, sensitivity of the recording system and material of the sample container.
2. **Sample Characteristics:** Parameters including type and weight of sample, particle size, solubility of evolved gases in the sample, heat of reaction and thermal conductivity.

20.5 APPLICATIONS OF DSC

DSC can be used in studying heat of melting, crystallization, percentage of crytallinity, heat capacities, thermal stabilities, purities, oxidative stabilities, food science, drug analysis, and liquid crystals.

20.6 THERMOGRAVIMETRIC ANALYSIS (TGA)

- Thermogravimetric analysis or thermal gravimetric analysis (TGA) is a method of thermal analysis in which the mass of a sample is measured over time as the temperature changes.
- This measurement phenomena, provides information about physical such as phase transitions, absorption and desorption as well as chemical phenomena including chemisorptions, thermal decomposition, and solid-gas reactions (e.g., oxidation or reduction)

20.7 TYPES OF THERMOGRAVIMETRY

There are three types of thermogravimetry:

1. **Isothermal or static thermogravimetry**: In this technique the sample weight is recorded as function of time at constant temperature.
2. **Quasistatic thermogravimetry:** In this technique the sample is heated to constant weight at each of series of increasing temperatures.
3. **Dynamic thermogravimetry:** In this technique the sample is heated in an environment whose temperature is changing in a predetermined manner generally at linear rate. This type is generally used.

20.8 PRINCIPLE OF THERMO GRAVIMETRY

- In thermo-gravimetric analysis, the sample is heated in a given environment (air, N_2, CO^2, He, Ar, etc.) at controlled rate. The change in the weight of the substance is recorded as a function of temperature or time.
- The temperature is increased at a constant rate for a known initial weight of the substance and the changes in weights are recorded as a function of temperature at different time interval.
- This plot of weight change against temperature is called thermo-gravimetric curve or thermo-gram, this is the basic principle of TGA.
- The instrument used for themo-gravimetry is a programmed precision balance for rise in temperature known as Thermo-balance.
- Results are displayed by a plot of mass change versus temperature or time and are known as Thermogravimetric curves or TG curves.

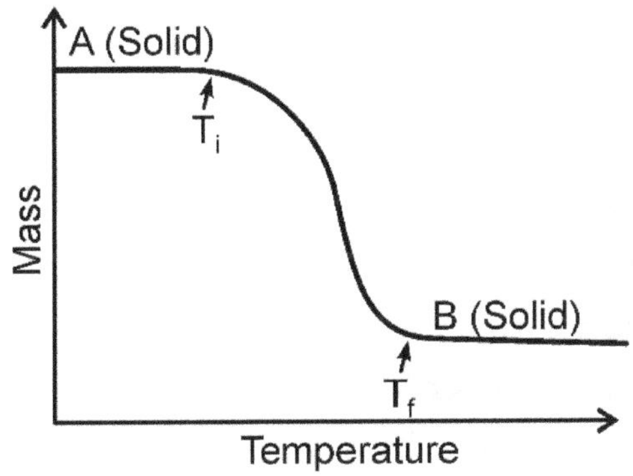

20.9 TGA CURVE

- TG curves are normally plotted with the mass change (D_m) in percentage on the y-axis and temperature (T) or time (t) on the x-axis.
- There are two temperatures in the reaction, Ti(procedural decomposition temp.) and Tf (final temp.) representing the lowest temperature at which the onset of a mass change is seen and the lowest temperature at which the process has been completed respectively.
- The reaction temperature and interval (Tf-Ti) depend on the experimental condition; therefore, they do not have any fixed value.

TGA curve of $AgNO_3$:

Example: TGA Curve for $AgNO_3$

- The horizontal portion of the curve indicates that, there is no change in weight (AB & CD) and the portion BC indicates that there is weight change.
- The weight of the substance ($AgNO_3$) remains constant upto a temperature of 473°C indicating that $AgNO_3$ is thermally stable upto a temperature of 473°C. The figure indicates the TGA curve for $AgNO_3$.

$$AgNO3 \rightarrow Ag + NO_2 + O_2$$

- At this temperature it starts losing its weight and this indicates that the decomposition starts at this temperature. It decomposes to NO_2, O_2 and Ag. The loss in weight continues upto 608°C leaving metallic silver as the stable residue. Beyond this temperature the weight of the sample remains constant (CD).

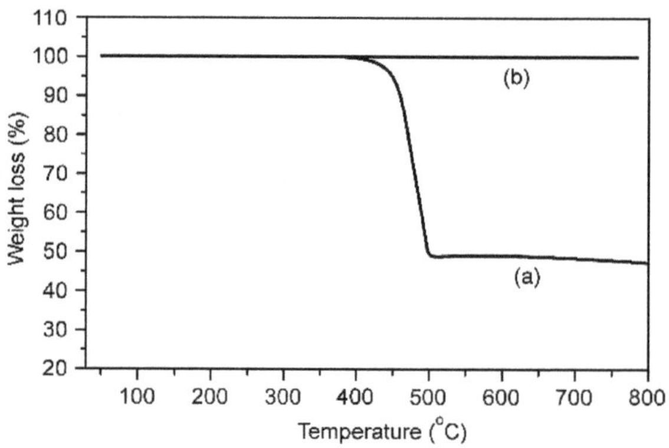

20.10 INSTRUMENTATION OF TGA

Instrumentation/Block diagram of TGA

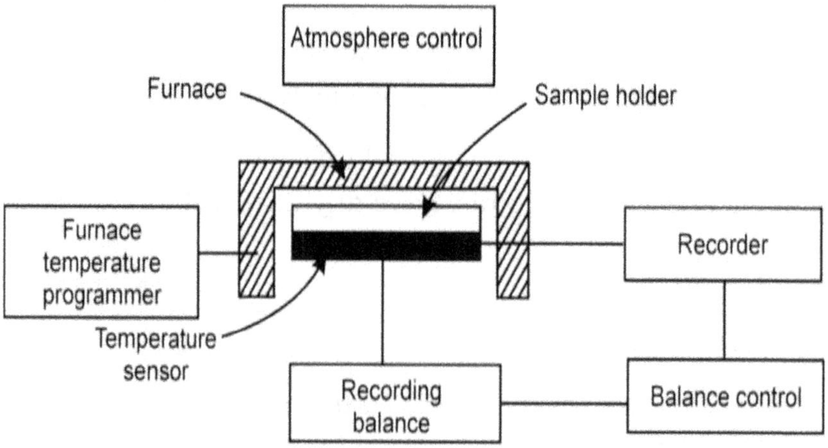

- Recording balance
- Sample holder
- Furnace
- Temperature programmer/ controller (thermocouple)
- Recorder

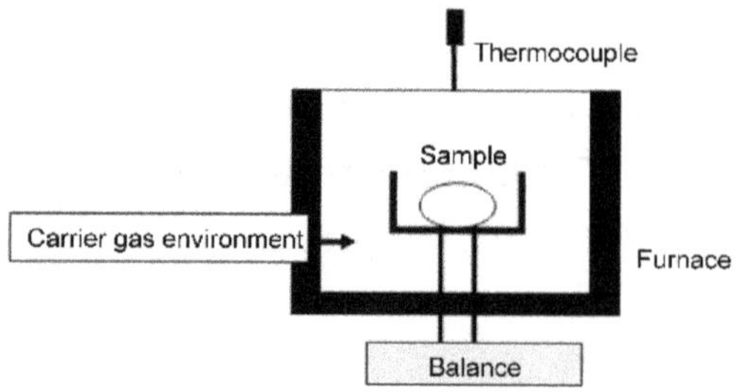

Recording Balance:

A microbalance is used to record a change in mass of sample/substance an ideal microbalance must possess following features:

- It should accurately and reproducibly record the change in mass of sample in ideal ranges of atmospheric conditions and temperatures.
- It should provide electronic signals to record the change in mass using a recorder.
- The electronic signals should provide rapid response to change in mass.
- It should be stable at high ranges, mechanically and electrically.
- Its operation should be user friendly.

After the sample has been placed on microbalance, it is left for 10-15min to stabilize. Recorder balances are of two types:

I. Deflection-type instruments and

II. Null-type instruments

I. Deflection Balances: they are following types-

i. Beam type   ii. Helical type

iii. Cantilevered beam   iv. Torsion wire

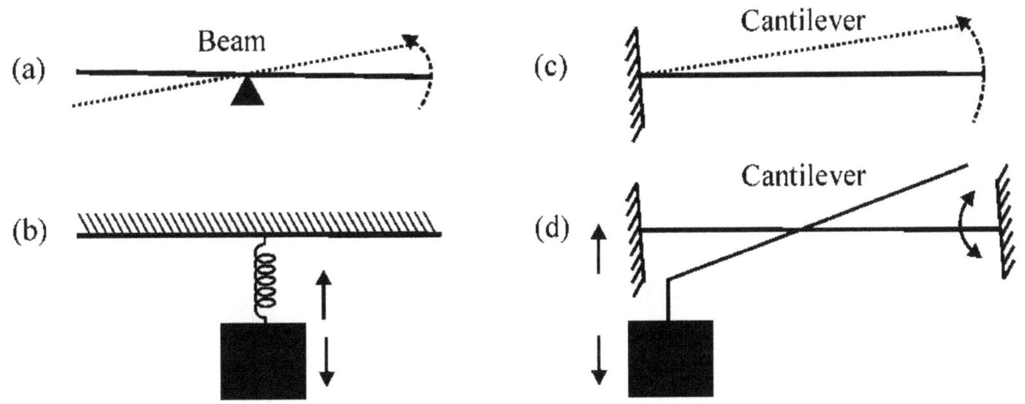

Null point balances: It consist of a sensor which detects the deviation from the null point and restores the balance to its null points by means of restoring force.

Sample Holder

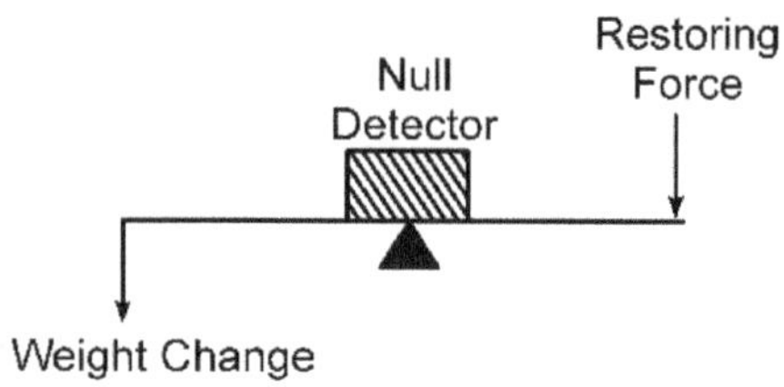

- The sample to be studied is placed in sample holder or crucible. It is attached to the weighing arm of microbalance.
- There are different varieties of crucibles used. Some differ in shape and size while some differ in materials used.
- They are made up from platinum, aluminum, quartz or alumina and some other materials like graphite, stainless steel, glass etc.

Crucible

Crucibles should have temperature at least 100K greater than temperature range of experiment and must transfer heat uniformly to sample. Therefore, the shape, thermal conductivity and thermal mass of crucibles are important which depends on the weight and nature of sample and temperature range.

There are different types of crucibles. They are:

1. Shallow pans (used for volatile substances)
2. Deep crucibles (Industrial scale calcination)
3. Loosely covered crucibles (self-generated atm. Studies)
4. Retort cups (Boiling point studies)

Types of Crucible

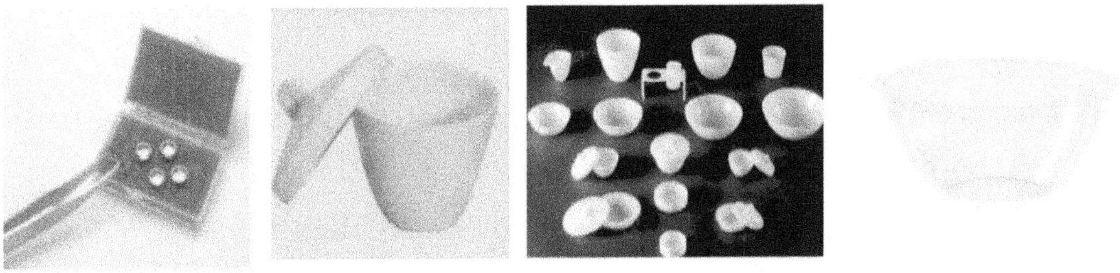

(a) Shallow Pans (b) Deep Crucible (c) Loosely covered crucibles (d) Retort cups

Figure 20.5: Different Types of Sample Holders.

Furnace

- The furnace should be designed in such way that it produces a linear heating range.
- It should have a hot zone which can hold sample and crucible and its temperature corresponds to the temperature of furnace.
- There are different combinations of microbalance and furnace available. The furnace heating coil should be wound in such a way that there is no magnetic interaction between coil and sample or there can cause apparent mass change.

Temperature Programmer/Controller

- Temperature measurement is done in no. of ways thermocouple is the most common technique.
- The position of the temperature measuring device relative to the sample is very important.

The major types are:

A. The thermocouple is placed near the sample container and it has no contact with the sample container. This isn't a good arrangement where low-pressure are employed.

B. The sample is kept inside the sample holder but not in contact with it. This arrangement is better than that of (a) because it responds to small temperature changes.

C. The thermocouple is placed either in contact with sample or with the sample container.

This is the best arrangement of sample temperature detection.

Thermocouple in a Thermo-Balance:

Recorder

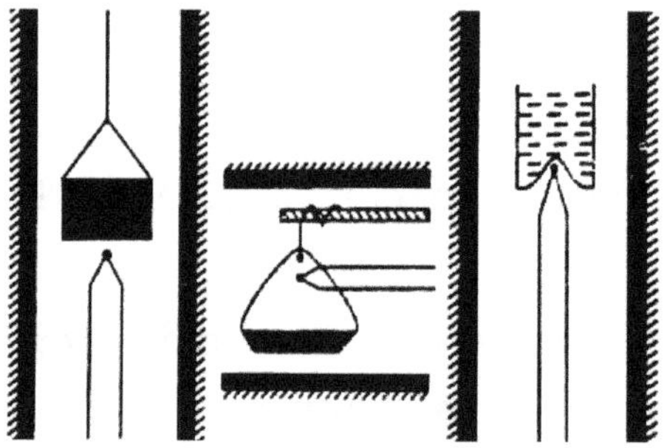

(a) (b) (c)

The recording systems are mainly of 2 types-

1. Time-base potentiometric strip chart recorder.
2. X-Y recorder.

- In some instruments, light beam galvanometer, photographic paper recorders or one recorder with two or more pens are also used.
- In the X-Y recorder, we get curves having plot of weights directly against temperatures.
- However, the percentage mass change against temperature or time would be more useful.

20.11 FACTORS AFFECTING TGA

1. Instrumental factors:

a. Furnace heating rate: The temperature at which the compound (or sample) decompose depends upon the heating rate. When the heating rate is high, the decomposition temperature is also high. A heating rate of 3.5°C per minute is usually recommended for reliable and reproducible TGA.

b. Furnace atmosphere: The atmosphere inside the furnace surrounding the sample has a profound effect on the decomposition temperature of the sample. A pure N_2 gas from a cylinder passed through the furnace which provides an inert atmosphere.

(a) Furnace heating rate

(b) Furnace atmosphere

2. Sample characteristics It includes:

a. Weight of the sample: A small weight of the sample is recommended using a small weight eliminates the existence of temperature gradient throughout the sample.

b. Particle size of the sample: The particle size of the sample should be small and uniform. The use of large particle or crystal may result in apparent, very rapid weight loss during heating.

- Sample holder
- Heat of reaction
- Compactness of sample
- Previous history of the sample

20.12 ADVANTAGES OF TGA

- A relatively small set of data is to be treated
- Continuous recording of weight loss as a function of temperature ensures Equal weightage to examination over the whole range of study.

- As a single sample is analyzed over the whole range of temperature, the variation in the value of the kinetic parameters, if any, will be indicated.

20.13 LIMITATIONS OF TGA

- The Chemical or physical changes which are not accompanied by the change in mass on heating are not indicated in thermo-gravimetric analysis.
- During TGA, Pure fusion reaction, crystalline transition, glass transition, crystallization and solid-state reaction with no volatile product would not be indicated because they provide no change in mass of the specimen.

20.14 APPLICATIONS OF TGA

- From TGA, we can determine the purity and thermal stability of both primary and secondary standard.
- Determination of the composition of complex mixture and decomposition of complex OR composition of complex systems.
- For studying the sublimation behavior of various substances.
- TGA is used to study the kinetics of the reaction rate constant.
- Used in the study of catalyst: The change in the chemical states of the catalyst may be studied by TGA techniques. (Zn-ZnCrO4) Zinc-Zinc chromate is used as the catalyst in the synthesis of methanol.
- Analysis of the dosage form.
- Oxidative stability of materials.
- Estimated lifetime of a product.

DIFFERENTIAL THERMAL ANALYSIS

20.15 INTRODUCTION

- A technique in which the difference in temperature between the sample and a reference material is monitored against time or temperature while the temperature of the sample, in a specified atmosphere, is programmed.
- The sample and the reference are placed symmetrically in the furnace. The furnace is controlled under a temperature program and the temperature of the sample and the reference are changed. During this process, a differential thermocouple is set up to detect the temperature difference between the sample and the reference. Also, the sample temperature is detected from the thermocouple on the sample side.

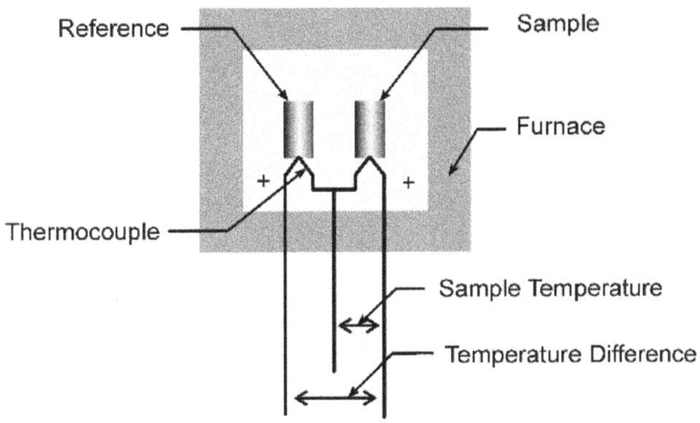

Graph (a): Temperature change of the furnace, the reference and the sample against time.

Graph (b): Change in temperature difference (ΔT) against time detected with the differential thermocouple.

ΔT Signal: DTA signal. Matters that do not change in the measurement temperature range (usually α-alumina) are used as reference.

When the furnace heating begins, the reference and the sample starts heating with a slight delay depending on their respective heat capacity, and eventually heat up in according to the furnace temperature.

ΔT changes until a static state is reached after the heating begins, and after achieving stability, reaches a set amount compliant with the difference in heat capacity between the sample and the reference. The signal at the static state is known as the baseline.

When the temperature rises and melting occurs in the sample, for example, the temperature rise stops as shown in graph (a) and the ΔT increases. When the melting ends, the temperature curve rapidly reverts to the baseline.

At this point, the ΔT signal reaches the peak, as shown in graph (b). From this, we can detect the sample transition temperature and the reaction temperature from the ΔT signal (DTA signal).

In graph (b), the temperature difference due to the sample endothermic change is shown as a negative direction and the temperature difference due to the sample exothermic change is shown as a positive direction.

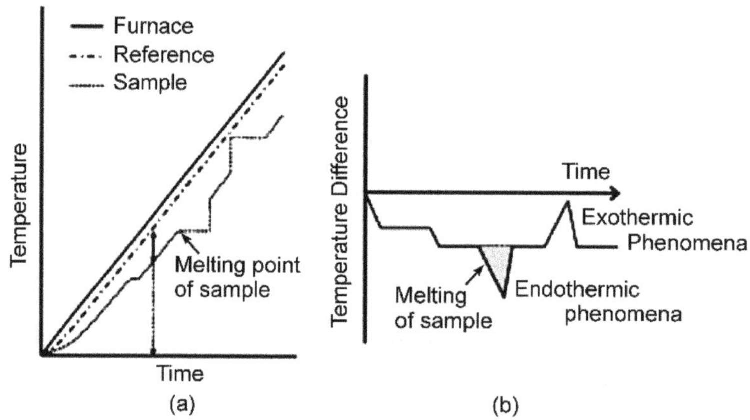

20.16 APPARATUS

The basic components of a DTA apparatus are

- Temperature-controlled furnace containing sample and reference cells
- A pair of matched temperature sensors connected to recording apparatus

- The temperature sensors (usually thermocouples) are in contact with the sample and reference or their containers, and the output is amplified and recorded.

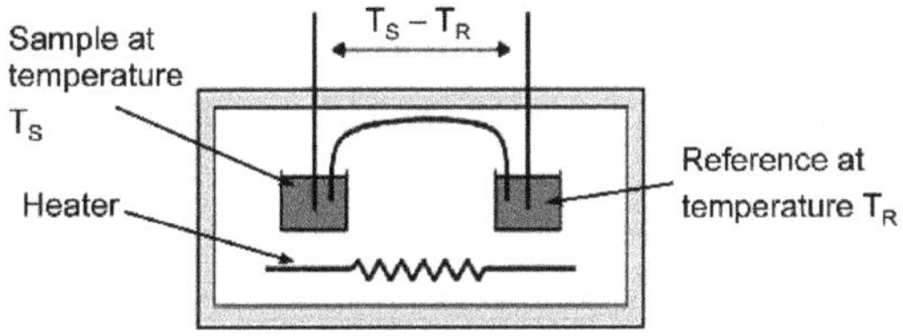

- DTA data may be plotted as a function of sample temperature, reference temperature (as is usually the case), or time.
- In both DTA and DSC, the measurement relies on the occurrence of a temperature difference between a sample and reference (ΔT) as a result of the thermal event in question.

When the sample melts, the rate of temperature increase for the sample will be lower than that of the reference, as the energy imparted by the heating signal will be contributing to the breaking of solid–solid bonds rather than simply the raising of the sample temperature.

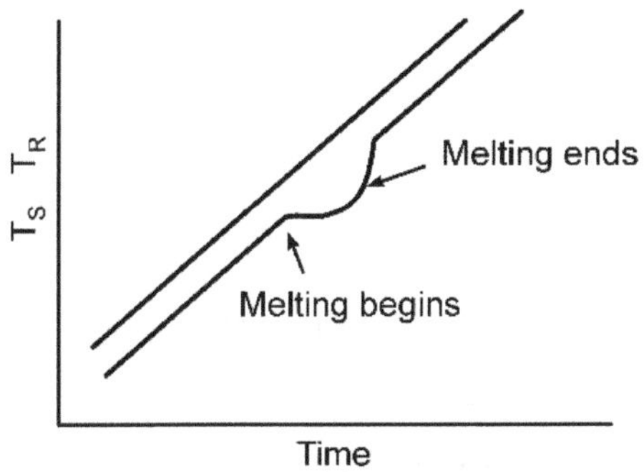

(a)

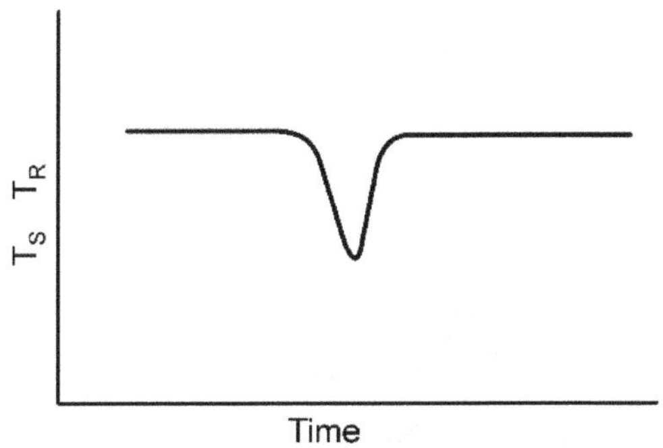

(a)

The heat input into the sample contributes to the melting process rather than the increase in temperature, whereas the heat input into the reference continues to lead to a temperature increase. When melting is complete, the sample returns to the programmed temperature; hence, by examining the difference in temperature between the two pans, a peak is seen, as shown in Figure b.

20.17 INSTRUMENTATION

Composed of five basic components:

(i) Sample holder with built-in thermocouple assembly,

(ii) Flow-control system,

(iii) Furnace assembly,

(iv) Preamplifier and Recorder, and

(v) Furnace Power Programmer and Controller.

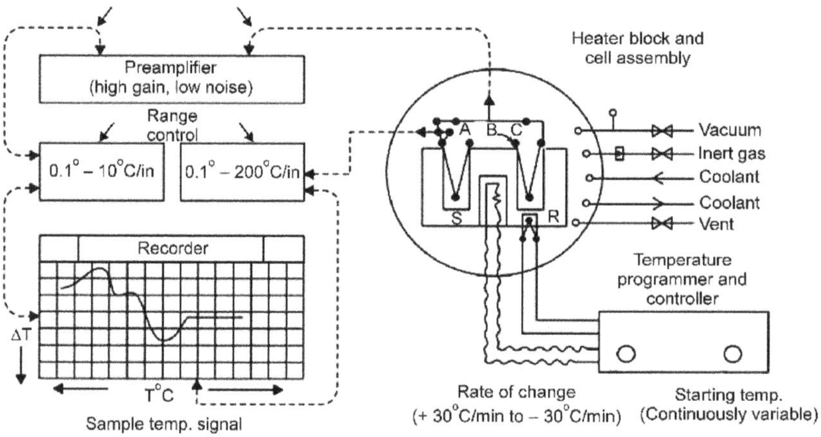

(a) Thermocouples employed are normally unsheathed Platinum Vs Platinum and Sodium Vs 10% Rhodium.

- Two thermocouples measure the difference in temperature between a sample S and an absolutely inert reference substance R, as both are subjected to heating in a ceramic/metal block inside a furnace being operated by a temperature programmer and controller.

(b) The output of the differential thermocouple is amplified adequately through a high gain, low-noise preamplifier and subsequently hooked to the recorder, one axis of which is driven by the block temperature signal and is measured by a third thermocouple.

20.18 WORKING

(i) Insert a very thin thermocouple into a disposable sample tube, 2 mm in diameter and containing 0.1-10 mg of sample

(ii) Another identical tube is either kept empty or filled with reference substance, such as quartz, sand, alumina or alundum powder

(iii) The two tubes are simultaneously inserted into the sample block and heated (or cooled) at a uniform predetermined programmed rate,

(iv) DTA - is a dynamic process so, vital aspects for getting reproducible results are:

- Pre-treatment of the specimen
- Particle size and packing of the specimen
- Dilution of the specimen
- Nature of the inert diluents
- Crystalline substances must be powdered, and sieved through 100-mesh sieve
- For colloidal particles (e.g., clays), micelle-size is very critical, and
- Either to suppress an unwanted reaction (e.g., oxidation), or to explore the study of are action (e.g., gaseous reaction product)-the atmosphere should be controlled adequately.

Differential thermal analysis investigation of calcium acetate monohydrate at a uniform programmed heating rate of 12°C/minute

The chemical reactions involved in the differentiated thermal analysis of calcium acetate monohydrate may be expressed as follows:

Stage I: The endothermal dehydration of calcium acetate monohydrate occurs giving rise to the anhydrous salt. It is easily noticed by an endothermal band on DTA curve between 200°C and 250°C.

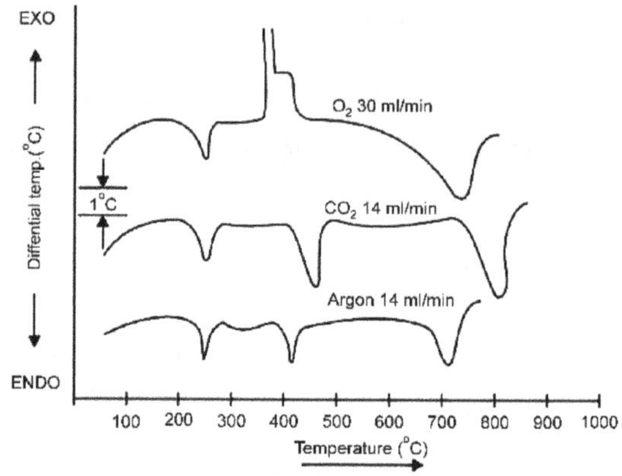

DTA - Investigation of Calcium Acetate Monohydrate, 12°C. min^{-1}

Stage II: The anhydrous salt undergoes endothermal decomposition reaction at 350-400°C resulting into the formation of $CaCO_3$ It has been observed that this decomposition reaction seems to be almost alike in the presence of either CO_2 or Ar.

Stage III: The decomposition of calcium carbonate to calcium oxide, which is a function of the partial pressure of the CO_2 in contact with the sample. The endothermal band for the carbonate decomposition is sharply peaked spread over a relatively narrower temperature range in an atmosphere of CO_2.

$$Ca(CH_3COO)_2.H_2O \xrightleftharpoons[\text{(Stage-I)}]{200-250°C} Ca(CH_3COO)_2 \xrightleftharpoons[\text{(Stage-II)}]{350-400°C} CaCO_3 \xrightleftharpoons[\text{(Stage-III)}]{800-950°C} CaO$$

20.19 DERIVATIVE DIFFERENTIAL THERMAL ANALYSIS

- A method for precise determination in thermograms of slight temperature changes by taking the first derivative of the differential thermal analysis curve (thermogram) which plots time versus differential temperature as measured by a differential thermocouple. Also known as DDTA.

- The temperatures of peaks of bands as well as details often overlooked in DTA curves, such as inflections which appear as peaks in DDTA curves, make this technique useful for characterization of substances as well as for studying reaction kinetics using a duplicate sample as the reference material and maintaining a constant temperature differential in the applied temperatures between both samples.

- The principle of this technique permits automatic recording of the DDTA curve and is the basis for the derivative thermogravimetric curves

20.20 APPLICATIONS

The various important applications of DTA are:

(i) Rapid identification of the compositions of mixed clays,

(ii) Studying the thermal stabilities of inorganic compounds,

(iii) Critically examining in a specific reaction whether a new compound is actually formed or the product is nothing but an un-reacted original substance, and

(iv) DTA offers a wide spectrum of useful investigations related to reaction kinetics, polymerization, solvent retention, phase-transformations, solid-phase reactions and curing or drying properties of a product.

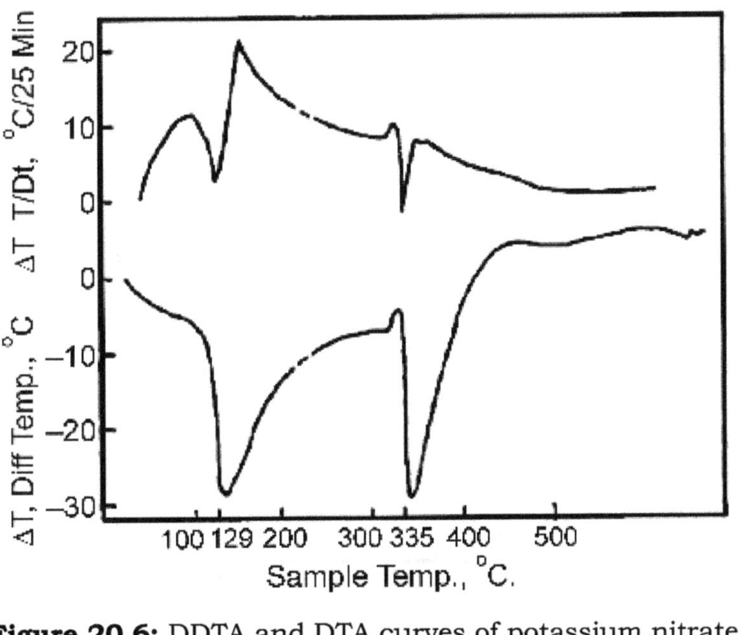

Figure 20.6: DDTA and DTA curves of potassium nitrate.

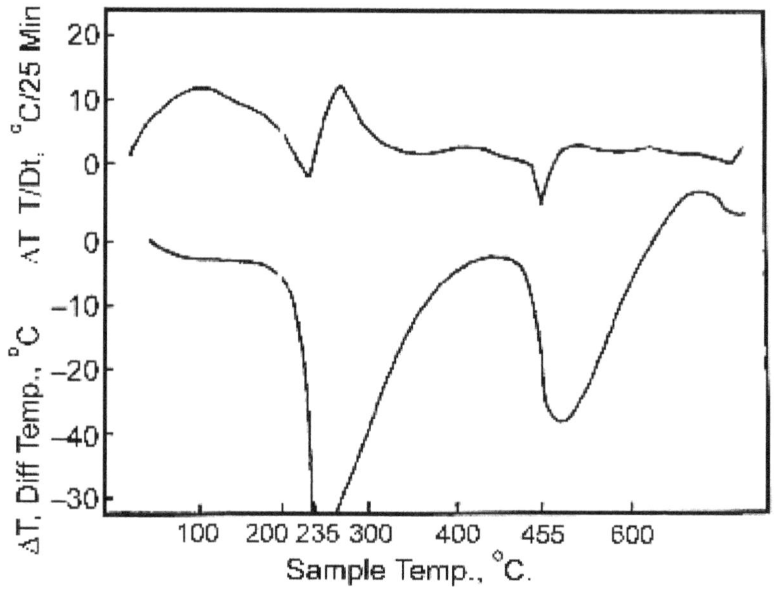

Figure 20.7: DDTA and DTA curves of potassium perchlorate.

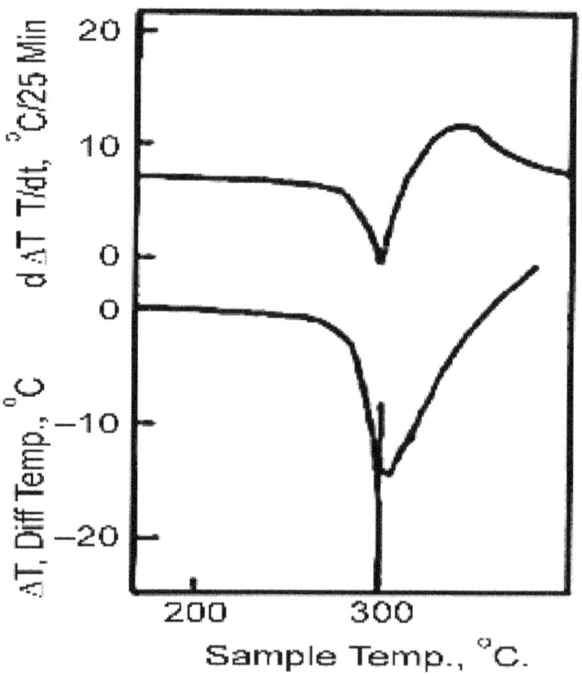

Figure 20.8: DDTA and DTA curves of calcium oxalate monohydrate.

TGA	DTA	DSC
TGA is Thermal Gravimetric Analysis	DTA is Differential Thermal Analysis	DSC is Differential Scanning Calorimetry
The change of the mass of a sample with the change of the temperature is observed and analyzed	The temperature difference developed between a sample and a reference compound is measured at identical heat treatments	The heat flow is measured against the temperature change at a particular time
Used to analyze inorganic materials, metals, polymers, plastics, ceramics, glasses and composite materials	Used to analyze thermal properties of minerals, for the characterization of polymers, and biological materials	Used to analyze proteins, antibodies, etc.
Sample can be used as a solid substance	Sample can be used as a solid substance	Sample is always a liquid

CHAPTER 21

HIGH PERFORMANCE THIN LAYER CHROMATOGRAPHY (HPTLC)

21.1 INTRODUCTION

The chromatographic techniques showed continuous improvement beginning from use of starch as a binder, silicic acid as sorbent, and use of silica as stationary phase in TLC. The TLC exhibited wide applicability in the separation science and gained quick response throughout the world because of its important features like ability to modulate the layer thickness, layer uniformity, binding sites, and controlling pore size, volume, specific surface area and particle size of sorbent. It was commercialized in the form of pre-coated TLC plates and considered as a fast and cost-effective technique for separation purposes. After the establishment of silica coated TLC as an efficient tool for quantitative techniques, effect of small sized silica coatings on Rf values and plate height were observed. The plates with small sized silica (termed as nano-plates) were found advantageous and were called as HPTLC plates. This led to the introduction of high-performance thin layer chromatography (HPTLC).

It is a type of planar (flatbed) chromatography and is sophisticated version of TLC with the enhancements like increased resolution of components, use of higher quality plates and small sized stationary phase. The modern HPTLC technique involves automated sample application and densitometric scanning. It is highly sensitive and is suitable for both the qualitative and quantitative analysis. It is better over other chromatographic techniques as it provides fingerprints for visualization and ability to store data in the form electronic library.

21.2 PRINCIPLE

The principle of HPTLC is same as TLC (i.e. separation by adsorption). In this technique, mobile phase is driven by capillary action and carries various components. Depending on their affinity towards adsorbent, the components exhibit adsorption on the stationary phase. The components with larger efficiency for stationary phase interact with the surface and move slowly in the mobile phase whereas components with lesser affinity for stationary phase move fast. This variation in the movement of components results in the separation of components on the chromatographic plate.

Features	TLC	HPTLC
Handling	Manual	Automated/Instrumental
Layer	Lab made/Pre-coated	Pre-coated
Shape of sample	Circular	Rectangular
Size of sample	Uncontrolled	Controlled
Compatibility with PC/software	Non-Compatible	Compatible
Wavelength Range	Visible Region	UV and Visible Region
Mode of results	Manual operation	Software operated

21.3 ADVANCEMENT OF HPTLC OVER TLC

Although HPTLC works on the same principle as TLC, however, it offers advantages because it is robust, simple, rapid, efficient in quantitative analysis, gives better resolution and limit of detection. Some of the important features of TLC and HPTLC are compared below.

Key features of HPTLC

Some of the important features of HPTLC are given below:

- It produces complex information about the entire sample in the form of visible chromatograms at a glance.
- Simultaneously, sample and standard can be analyzed for better precision and accuracy.
- Various samples can be analyzed and compared simultaneously with the help of images.
- It gives data in the form of visible chromatograms as well as peak data.
- The data can be evaluated either by the image-based software Video scan or by scanning densitometry with TLC Scanner, measuring the absorption and/or fluorescence of the substances on the plate.
- The technique is cost-effective and has low cost for maintenance.
- The sample preparation is simple and different types of samples can be analyzed by the technique.
- Prior treatment of solvents i.e. filtration and degassing is not required.
- The use of harmful solvents is less as compared to other chromatographic techniques.
- The chances of contamination are less because it utilizes fresh stationary and mobile phases for each analysis

21.4 WORKING OF HPTLC

The various steps of HPTLC are discussed below:

1. Selection of HPTLC Chromatographic Layer and Mobile Phase

In HPTLC, plates coated with small sized particles and narrow size distribution is used. Thus, the surface area of plates is smooth. The size of the plates is comparatively small as compared to TLC i.e. (10 10-20 cm) and the development distance is 6 cm. The selection of HPTLC stationary phase is based upon the type of analyte. The most common HPTLC stationary phases are listed below:

S.No.	Types of TLC	Stationary Phase
1.	Normal Phase absorption	Silica gel
2.	Reverse phase TLC	-18, C-8, C-2; Phenyl Chemically modified silica gel, hydrocarbon impregnated silica gel
3.	Chiral	Chiral layers produced C-18 modified silica gel, optically active enantiomerically pure hydroxyproline derivative
4.	Others	Aluminium oxide, magnesium silicate, magnesium Oxide, polyamide, cellulose, keiselguhr, ion exchangers, and polar modified silica gel layers that contain bonded amino, cyano, diol and thio groups

A care must be taken while handling the plates to avoid contamination. The plates should be observed under UV light to know any damage or presence of impurities on the adsorbent. The HPTLC plates should be prewashed to remove the impurities (if any) adsorbed on their surface. However, pre-washing is required to study the reproducibility of results and for quantification purposes. The washing may be done by ascending, dipping or continuous method. The most common solvents used for washing purposes are methanol, chloroform or their mixtures. The plates kept in the open must be activated by placing in an oven at 110-130 C for 30 min. The selection of mobile phase is made on the basis of type of adsorbent, and physical and chemical properties of analyte.

2. Sample Preparation

The samples may be prepared methanol, chloroform: methanol (1:1 v/v), ethyl acetate: methanol (1:1 v/v), chloroform: methanol: ammonia (90:10:1 v/v), methylene chloride: methanol (1:1 v/v) to avoid interference from impurities and water vapours.

3. Application of Sample

The sample is applied with the help of some applicators such as 1) capillary tubes 2) micro-bulb pipettes, 3) micro-syringes, and 4) automated sample applicators. Using these applicators, sample can be applied in the form of spot or band. The concentration range is 0.1-1μg /μL because above this range, separation becomes poor.

In case of applying a sample as a spot, a fixed volume pipette having capillary action is used. It is filled with the sample and touched on the surface of plate, thereby delivering the sample to the stationary layer. If variable volumes are needed, then, a syringe with micrometer control can be used. Proper care must be taken during the application of sample i.e. the spots should be precise in position and layer should not undergo any damage during application. In sample applicators, Camag Nanomat is a mechanized spotting device with fixed volume glass capillaries. These are lowered onto the layer with reproducible contact pressure (Figure 1), which controls the position of the spot. Similarly, Desaga PS 01 Sample Applicator uses microlitre syringes for the application of sample. Another method i.e. sample application as narrow band provides the highest resolution in the separation. In this case, sample is filled in a syringe and vacated with the help of a motor. Both the syringe and plate move linearly to produce a band. Another applicator i.e. Linomat (Figure 2) allows sample application in narrow bands of variable length.

Figure 21.1: Camag Nanomat.

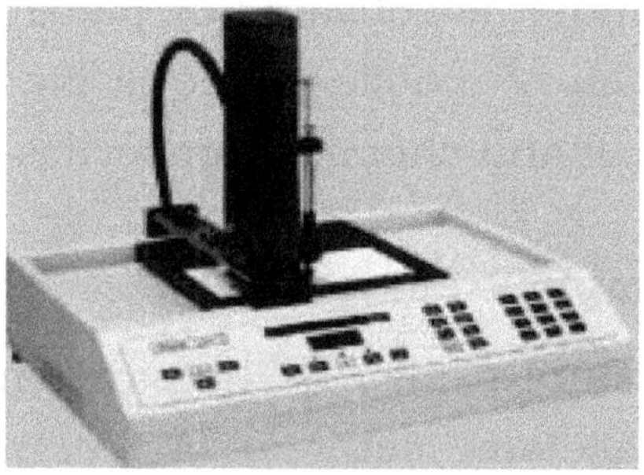

Figure 21.2: Linomat Applicator.

Apart from this, automatic samplers are computer controlled and can apply samples automatically. The samples are picked from the vials and transferred to plate with the help of steel capillary in the form of spots or bands. These devices offer choice to select the sample volume, dispensing speed and application pattern.

4. Chromatograph Development

The chromatogram development is the most important step in the HPTLC procedure. The HPTLC chamber is pre-conditioned with solvent to get uniform vapours of the solvent in the chamber. The chromatograms can be developed in four ways 1) Vertical method, 2) Vario- method, 3) horizontal method and 4) automatic multiple development. The HPTLC plates are generally developed in twin-trough chambers, or horizontal-development chambers. The saturated twin-trough chambers fitted with filter paper offers the best reproducibility and avoids solvent vapor preloading and humidity.

In the cortical method, the lower edge of the plate is immersed in the developing chamber having solvent at the bottom. The solvent ascends in the plate and layer interacts with the vapours in the tank. This method does not provide reproducibility as the development of chromatograms varies with the dimensions of the plate. In the horizontal development, chromatogram is developed by applying the sample parallel to both opposing edges of the plate. The chromatogram is developed from both the sides towards the centre of the plate. Therefore, the number of samples can be doubled. In this method, the volume of solvent required for the development is very less, therefore, it is economical. In automatic development, the development of chromatogram can be controlled by an instrument. In offers the advantage to select various parameters like preconditioning, tank of sandwich configuration, solvent migration distance, etc. prior to the development of chromatogram. In this case, software is used to decide the composition of developing solvent and developing distance. In addition, the volumes are measured with syringes and migration distance can be measured by sensors.

5. Detection of Spots (Scanning) and Documentation

The developed plates can be detected by using UV cabinet or chamber which provides a non-destructive analysis. Alternatively, the spots are analyzed at 254 nm or 366 nm if the compounds are fluorescent. Moreover, fluorescent stationary phases may be used to if the compounds exhibit quenching properties. These days, design of UV cabinets is improved, which allows fixing of digital camera for recording images of the plate. Further, the components may be quantified on the same plates.

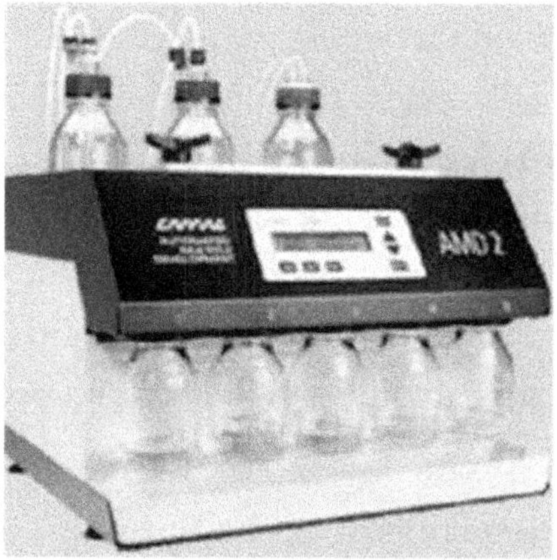

Figure 21.3: Camag automated multiple development chamber.

6. Densitometer Measurements

In densitometery, separation tracks are evaluated with the help of a light beam in the form of a slit with adjustable dimensions. The reflected light is measured by the photosensor and the difference between optical response of blank and the sample zone is correlated with various sample zones. Nowadays, a planar chromatogram is evaluated by video technology.

Application:

- **Forensic Analysis:** A challenge in forensic toxicology is the identification of unknown poisonous substances in intoxication cases. HPTLC offers rapid identification as well as qualitative and quantitative analysis for toxic substances.

- **Herbal Applications:** HPTLC fingerprint technology can be used in the identification of botanical materials that are very complex in nature.
- **Food Industry:** To evaluate nutrients, beverages, vitamins, and pesticides in fruit, vegetables, and other foodstuffs.
- **Pharmaceutical Industry:** Used in post-production quality control. analysis of forced degradation studies, stability testing, and to check the presence of impurities in the drug.
- **Cosmetic Industry:** HPTLC technique can be employed for the detection of UV filters used in the formulation of cosmetic products. The identified filter can be further confirmed using Mass Spectrometer.

21.5 ADVANTAGES

1. It is a flexible, robust, and cost-effective separation techniques employed in the discovery, development, and analysis of new drugs.
2. More than one analyst can work on the system at a time.
3. Shorter developing and analysis time.
4. No prior treatment of solvents like filtration and degassing is required.
5. Fresh stationary and mobile phase are used for each analysis so no interference or contamination comes in the analytical process.
6. It can be used alone or in combination with other techniques like MS, FTIR, and Densitometry.

QUESTION BANK

Seat No.: _____ Enrolment No. _____________

GUJARAT TECHNOLOGICAL UNIVERSITY

B. PHARM- SEMESTER-VII • EXAMINATION – WINTER-2022

Subject Code: **BP701TP** **Date: 22/12/2022**

Subject Name: **Instrumental Methods of Analysis**

Time: **10:30 AM TO 01:30 PM** **Total Marks: 80**

Instructions:

1. **Attempt any five questions.**
2. **Make suitable assumptions wherever necessary.**
3. **Figures to the right indicate full marks.**

Q.1	**(a)**	Explain the principle, working and advantages of FTIR with a labelled diagram.	**06**
	(b)	Discuss about interferences in AAS. Write merits and demerits of AAS over AES	**05**
	(c)	Enlist various detectors used in Gas chromatography. Explain any anyone in detail.	**05**
Q.2	**(a)**	Write a note on Radiation Source, detectors and monochromators used in UV– VIS spectrophotometer	**06**
	(b)	Define: (i) Limit of detection (ii) Accuracy (iii) Precision (iv) Rf value (v) Calibration	**05**
	(c)	Write a brief note on Nephlometry and Turbidimetry with its applications	**05**
Q.3	**(a)**	Write application, advantages and limitations of atomic absorption and atomic emission spectroscopy	**06**
	(b)	Discuss the effect of solvent and pH on the spectral characteristic in UV visible spectroscopy	**05**
	(c)	Define: (i) Retention time (ii)Tailing factor (iii)Capacity factor (iv) Selectivity factor (v) Resolution	**05**
Q.4	**(a)**	Explain Principle and applications of HPLC	**06**
	(b)	Explain terms HETP, Peak asymmetry factor, Retention volume, Resolution	**05**
	(c)	Explain the terms with reference to EMR: Diffraction, Reflection and Refraction	**05**
Q.5	**(a)**	Explain the principle and Instrumentation of affinity chromatography	**06**
	(b)	Discuss various Detectors and Pumps used in HPLC	**05**
	(c)	Draw a well-labelled diagram of Spectrofluorimeter. Write instrumentation advantages, Limitations and application of fluorescence spectroscopy.	**05**
Q.6	**(a)**	Explain instrumentation with a Schematic diagram and applications of HPTLC	**06**
	(b)	What is gas chromatography? Explain different stationary phases used in gas chromatography	**05**
	(c)	Explain in detail the flame and nebulizer burner system in flame photometry	**05**
Q.7	**(a)**	Explain instrumentation with a Schematic diagram and applications of HPTLC	**06**
	(b)	Explain HOOK'S LAW for the prediction of IR frequency. Discuss factors affecting IR frequency.	**05**

	(c)	What is the Pharmacopoeial application of IR spectroscopy, how is it helpful in the identification	05

****

Seat No.: _____ Enrolment No. _____________

GUJARAT TECHNOLOGICAL UNIVERSITY

B. PHARM- SEMESTER-VII • EXAMINATION – WINTER-2021

Subject Code: **BP701TP** **Date: 03/08/2021**
Subject Name: **Instrumental Methods of Analysis**
Time: **10:30 AM TO 01:30 PM** **Total Marks: 80**

Instructions:

1. **Attempt any five questions.**
2. **Make suitable assumptions wherever necessary.**
3. **Figures to the right indicate full marks.**

Q.1	**(a)**	Give brief account on (i) Photomultiplier tube (ii) Auxochromes	**06**
	(b)	State and derive Beer-Lambert's Law	**05**
	(c)	Write a detail note on UV-Spectrophotometry	**05**
Q.2	**(a)**	Describe the factors affecting fluorescence	**06**
	(b)	Explain the terms (i) Quenching (ii) Singlet, doublet and triplet electronic states	**05**
	(c)	Write a detail note on sample handling in IR spectroscopy	**05**
Q.3	**(a)**	Explain the working principle of FTIR spectroscopy. Explain the difference between dispersive IR and FTIR.	**06**
	(b)	Explain with example- Fundamental modes of vibrations in poly atomic molecules	**05**
	(c)	Give a brief account on (i) Golay cell (ii) Bolometer	**05**
Q.4	**(a)**	Write a brief note (i) Applications of atomic absorption spectroscopy in Pharmaceutical science (ii) Nephelometry	**06**
	(b)	Explain the working principle of flame photometer with neat diagram	**05**
	(c)	What are the types of paper chromatography? Give the applications of paper chromatography in pharmaceutical science	**05**
Q.5	**(a)**	Explain the terms (i) HETP (ii) Tailing (iii) Resolution	**06**
	(b)	Explain the basic principle and applications of zone electrophoresis	**05**
	(c)	Discuss about derivatization in gas chromatography	**05**
Q.6	**(a)**	Explain the principle of HPLC. Explain its applications in pharmaceutical science	**06**
	(b)	Differentiate between HPLC and GC	**05**
	(c)	Give brief account on resins used in ion exchange chromatography.	**05**

Q.7	**(a)**	Write short note (i) Flame ionization detector (ii) Gel chromatography	**06**
	(b)	Write a short note on stationary phase and mobile phase used in HPLC	**05**
	(c)	Explain the basic principle of affinity chromatography. Enumerate applications of affinity chromatography.	**05**

*****

Seat No.: _____ Enrolment No. _____________

GUJARAT TECHNOLOGICAL UNIVERSITY

B.Ph. - SEMESTER–VII • EXAMINATION – SUMMER-2022

Subject Code: BP701TP **Date: 01/06/2022**

Subject Name: Instrumental Method of Analysis

Time: 02:30PM TO 05:30PM **Total Marks: 80**

Instructions:

1. **Attempt any five questions.**
2. **Make suitable assumptions wherever necessary.**
3. **Figures to the right indicate full marks.**

Q.1	**(a)**	State and derive Beer-Lambert's Law	**06**
	(b)	Write applications of UV-Spectrophotometry	**05**
	(c)	Describe the factors affecting fluorescence	**05**
Q.2	**(a)**	Explain the terms (i) Auxochromes (ii) Singlet, doublet and triplet electronic states (iii) Quenching	**06**
	(b)	Explain the principle of flame photometry. What are the applications of flame photometry?	**05**
	(c)	Explain the different modes of vibrations in poly atomic molecules	**05**
Q.3	**(a)**	Write a brief note (i) Instrumentation of atomic absorption spectroscopy (ii) Nephelometry	**06**
	(b)	Explain the working principle of Michelson Interferometer. What are the advantages of FTIR?	**05**
	(c)	Give advantages and disadvantages of adsorption chromatography	**05**
Q.4	**(a)**	What are the types of paper chromatography? Give the applications of paper chromatography in pharmaceutical science	**06**
	(b)	Explain Rf value. Describe the working principle of thin layer chromatography	**05**
	(c)	Write a brief note on resins used in ion exchange chromatography	**05**
Q.5	**(a)**	Give a brief account on (i) Capillary electrophoresis (ii) Factors affecting electrophoretic mobility	**06**
	(b)	Explain the basic principle of affinity chromatography. Enumerate its applications	**05**
	(c)	Explain the instrumentation of gel chromatography	**05**
Q. 6	**(a)**	Explain the terms (i) HETP (ii) Tailing (iii) Resolution	**06**
	(b)	Give brief account on columns used in HPLC	**05**
	(c)	Discuss about Derivatisation in gas chromatography	**05**
Q.7	**(a)**	Give brief account on (i) Photomultiplier tube (ii) Applications of HPLC	**06**
	(b)	Describe the sample handling in IR spectroscopy	**05**
	(c)	Draw the schematic diagram of the Flame Ionization Detector. What ate the advantages of gas chromatography?	**05**

****

Seat No.:______ Enrolment No. ______________

GUJARAT TECHNOLOGICAL UNIVERSITY

B.Ph. SEMESTER–VII • EXAMINATION – WINTER-2020

Subject Code: BP701TP **Date:01/01/2021**

Subject Name: Instrumental Method of Analysis

Time: 10:30AM To 12:30PM **Total Marks: 54**

Instructions:

1. **Attempt any THREE questions from Q-1 to Q-6.**
2. **Q.7 is compulsory to attempt.**
3. **Make suitable assumptions wherever necessary.**
4. **Figures to the right indicate full marks.**

Q.1	**(a)** Derive Beer's Law. Give reasons for deviations from Beer's law?	**06**
	(b) Define Chrmphores, auxochromes and Bathochromic shift with example.	**05**
	(c) What is chemical quenching? Give its example.	**05**
Q.2	**(a)** Explain sample handling in IR spectroscopy.	**06**
	(b) Describe Principle and instrumentation of Flame photometry.	**05**
	(c) Describe thermal detectors used in IR spectrophotometry.	**05**
Q.3	**(a)** Describe principle involved in separation in TLC along with stationary Phases used in TLC.	**06**
	(b) Give advantages and disadvantages of Adsorption chromatography	**05**
	(c) What are the modes of development in paper chromatography?	**05**
Q.4	**(a)** Write a note on Gel electrophoresis along with its applications.	**06**
	(b) Give applications of Thin Layer Chromatography.	**05**
	(c) Describe principle and applications of Atomic absorption spectroscopy	**05**
Q.5	**(a)** What is the principle and which carrier gas is suitable for use in a. Katharometer b. Flame ionization detector c. Electron capture detector	**06**
	(b) Differentiate between isocratic and gradient elution technique.	**05**
	(c) Define Retention time, Retention Volume, Resolution and HETP.	**05**
Q. 6	**(a)** What is an Ion exchange resin?	**06**
	(b) Write factors affecting ion exchange chromatography	**05**
	(c) Give application of Gel and affinity chromatography.	**05**
Q.7	**(a)** Which principle is involved in Normal Phase and Reverse Phase chromatography	**06**
	OR	
	(a) What are the different types of vibrations? Explain in detail	**06**
	OR	
	(a) Explain Instrumentation of UV-Visible spectrophotometer	**06**

****

Seat No.: _____ Enrolment No. ____________

GUJARAT TECHNOLOGICAL UNIVERSITY

B. Pharm- SEM-VII• EXAMINATION – WINTER-2021

Subject Code:BP701TP **Date: 24/11/2021**

Subject Name: Instrumental Methods of Analysis

Time: 10:30 AM TO 01:30 PM **Total Marks: 80**

Instructions:

1. **Attempt any five questions.**
2. **Make suitable assumptions wherever necessary.**
3. **Figures to the right indicate full marks.**

Q.1	**(a)**	Explain Principle and applications of HPLC	**06**
	(b)	Discuss various Detectors and Pumps used in HPLC	**05**
	(c)	Define: (i) Retention time (ii)Tailing factor (iii)Capacity factor (iv)Selectivity factor (v)Resolution	**05**
Q.2	**(a)**	Explain instrumentation with Schematic diagram and applications of HPTLC	**06**
	(b)	What is gas chromatography? Explain different stationary phases used in gas chromatography	**05**
	(c)	Enlist various detectors used in Gas chromatography. Explain any one in detail.	**05**
Q.3	**(a)**	Explain the principle and Instrumentation of affinity chromatography	**06**
	(b)	Explain terms HETP, Peak asymmetry factor, Retention volume, Resolution	**05**
	(c)	Write a brief note on Nephlometry and Turbidimetry with its applications	**05**
Q.4	**(a)**	Explain instrumentation with Schematic diagram and applications of HPTLC	**06**
	(b)	Define: (i) Limit of detection (ii) Accuracy (iii) Precision (iv) Rf value (v) Calibration	**05**
	(c)	Explain in detail flame and nebulizer burner system in flame photometry	**05**
Q.5	**(a)**	Write application, advantages and limitation of atomic absorption and atomic emission spectroscopy	**06**
	(b)	Discuss about interferences in AAS. Write merits and demerits of AAS over AES	**05**
	(c)	What is the Pharmacopoeial application of IR spectroscopy, how it helpful in identification	**05**
Q. 6	**(a)**	Explain the principle, working and advantages of FTIR with labeled diagram.	**06**
	(b)	Explain HOOK'S LAW for prediction of IR frequency. Discuss factor affecting IR frequency.	**05**
	(c)	Draw a well labeled diagram of Spectrofluorimeter. Write an instrumentation advantages, Limitation and application of fluorescence spectroscopy	**05**
Q.7	**(a)**	Write a note on Radiation Source, detectors and monochromators used in UV – VIS spectrophotometer	**06**
	(b)	Discuss the effect of solvent and pH on spectral characteristic in UV visible spectroscopy	**05**
	(c)	Explain the terms with reference to EMR: Diffraction, Reflection and Refraction	**05**

****

INSTRUMENTAL METHOD OF ANALYSIS VII SEM
MODEL QUESTIONS

	LONG ESSAYS	2x10=20 Marks
1.	Describe and derive the equation for Beer's–Lambert's law. Add a note on deviations and limitations of beers law. OR Write a note on theory and applications of IR spectrophotometry. Explain different sampling techniques employed in IR spectroscopy.	
2.	Describe in brief the principle, instrumentation and applications of gas chromatography.	
3.	Explain the principle, instrumentation and applications of UV-Visible spectroscopy. OR What are the different vibrational modes of polyatomic molecules upon IR absorption? Write in brief on the various detectors used in IR Spectroscopy.	
4.	Describe the principle, instrumentation and applications of HPLC.	
5.	What are the essential components of a UV-Visible Spectrophotometer? Draw a diagrammatic sketch and explain the functions and working of each unit. OR Explain the theory involved in IR spectroscopy with brief outline of IR spectroscopy instrumentation.	
6.	Explain the instrumentation of HPLC with neat diagram with more emphasis on pumps and detectors used.	
7.	Explain in brief about monochromators and any two detectors used in UV spectroscopy. OR Explain the principle, instrumentation, sampling techniques and applications of IR spectroscopy.	
8.	Describe Gas Chromatograph with a neat labelled diagram. Explain the type of GC columns, carrier gases and detectors used.	
9.	Draw and explain with a neat label diagram of double beam UV spectrophotometer. Explain various spectrophometric titrations with suitable graphs. OR	

Table Contd...

	Explain the construction and working of flame emission spectrometry with neat labeled diagram and discuss the various types of interferences occurred in atomic spectroscopy.
10.	Describe in brief instrumentation of gas chromatography with neat labeled block diagram.
11.	State and derive the equation for Beer – Lambert's law. Give the reasons for deviation from law. OR Discuss the principle, theory of IR spectroscopy and give its applications.
12.	Write elaborately the principle, instrumentation and applications of Gas chromatography.
13.	Discuss in detail about the concept of EMR, energies in organic molecule and electronic transitions in UV-Visible spectroscopy. OR Draw a neat labelled instrumentation layout of IR spectrophotometer and explain the sample handling techniques in IR.
14.	Draw a neat schematic diagram of GC. Explain about columns and detectors used in GC..
15.	Draw a neat labelled diagram of double beam UV-Visible spectrophotometer and explain the working principle of monochromators and any two detectors. OR Describes the principle, working and instrumentation of AAS.
16.	Draw a neat schematic diagram of HPLC. Explain about pumps and detectors used in HPLC.
17.	Define & derive Beer and Lambert's law. Add a note on its deviations and limitations. OR Explain briefly the instrumentation of IR spectroscopy.
18.	Enlist the Detectors and sample injection techniques used in Gas Chromatography & explain in detail each of two.
19.	Explain the working of double beam UV-Visible spectrophotometer with the help of neat labelled diagram. OR Discuss the different sources of radiations & detectors used in IR spectroscopy.
20.	Discuss the different pumps & detectors used in HPLC.

SHORT ESSAYS	7x5=35 Marks
1.	Define and distinguish between fluorescence and phosphorescence. Write the various factors affecting the phenomenon of fluorescence. OR Define Wavelength, Wavenumber, Frequency, Transmittance and Absorptivity?
2.	Explain the instrumentation and working of atomic absorption spectroscopy. OR Define and classify chromatography with suitable examples.
3.	Explain the practical steps involved in TLC for separation of components.
4.	Describe the practical steps involved in paper electrophoresis.
5.	Explain the instrumentation of HPLC with block diagram.
6.	What are ion exchange resins? Classify and explain the ideal properties of ion exchange resins.
7.	Explain the principle and theory of gel chromatography.
8.	Write the statement and derive the equation for Beer 's – Lambert's law. OR Explain in brief the effect of solvent on absorption UV-Visible radiation by the molecules.
9.	Explain the instrumentation and working of flame emission spectrometry. OR Explain the various methods of preparation of TLC plates.
10.	Briefly explain the operational techniques of column chromatography.
11.	Add a note on gel electrophoresis.
12.	Explain the concept of plate theory and rate theory for increasing the efficiency of column in chromatography.
13.	What are ion exchange resins and explain the operational techniques of ion exchange chromatography.
14.	Write the practical steps involved in size exclusion chromatography gel chromatography.
15.	Explain the phenomenon of Fluorescence and Phosphorescence. Write the requirement of molecules to exhibit fluorescence. OR

Table Contd…

	Explain in brief the various types of shifts occur in UV-Visible spectroscopy.
16.	Name the burners used in flame photometry and explain in detail any one. OR Write the advantages of TLC over paper chromatography.
17.	Explain the factors affecting efficiency of column in chromatography.
18.	Define electrophoresis and explain the various factors affecting electrophoresis.
19.	Explain the principle and working of thermal conductivity and flame ionization detectors.
20.	Write the principle, techniques and applications of ion exchange chromatography.
21.	Discuss the principle, instrumentation and applications of affinity chromatography.
22.	Discuss the working principle and construction of specrtofluorimeter. OR Explain the multiple component analysis of drugs by UV spectroscopy.
23.	What are Nephelometry and turbidometry? Write principle involved for the same. OR Enlist and explain the various development techniques in paper chromatography.
24.	Explain the separation techniques involved in column chromatography.
25.	Give an account of gel electrophoresis with representation of neat diagram.
26.	Explain about the various detectors used in HPLC.
27.	Define and classify ion exchange resins and explain the manufacture of cation exchange resin and anion exchange resin.
28.	Explain the principle, theory and applications of gel chromatography.
29.	What is Quenching? Enumerate the various factors which influence quenching effect. OR Define Wavelength, Bathochromic shift, Hypsochromic shift, Hyperchromic effect and Hypochromic effect.
30.	Describe the detectors of an IR spectrometer. OR Write the practical aspects of development techniques in paper chromatography.

Table Contd...

31.	Explain the packing method of adsorbent in column chromatography with their merits and demerits.
32.	What is zone electrophoresis? Explain any one in detail.
33.	Describe the pumps, sample injection techniques and applications of HPLC.
34.	Principle, classification and mechanism of ion exchange process in ion exchange chromatography.
35.	Principle, ligands used and applications of affinity chromatography.
36.	Enumerate and discuss the different factors that affect the intensity of fluorescence. OR Explain the single component and multi component analysis by UV spectrometry.
37.	Explain the principle and applications of Flame photometry with neat labelled diagram? OR What is electrophoresis? Describe paper electrophoresis technique.
38.	Explain the experimental methodology involved in preparing TLC plates. Add a note on detection methods in TLC?
39.	Discuss different methods of preparation and elution techniques of column chromatography.
40.	Mention the detectors used in HPLC and explain in detail any two.
41.	Explain the principle and theory of gel chromatography.
42.	Explain affinity chromatography.
43.	Write a note on effects of solvents (solvatochromic effect) in UV spectroscopy. OR Discuss the factors affecting the fluorescence.
44.	Write the diagram of flame and explain the different regions. OR Define electrophoresis. Discuss the factors affecting the electrophoresis.
45.	Discuss the development and visualization techniques in paper chromatography
46.	Explain the packing, elution and detection techniques involved in column chromatography.
47.	Write the construction and working of any two detectors used in HPLC.

Table Contd...

48.	What is ion exchange chromatography? Give the steps involved in the mechanism of ion exchangers used.
49.	Discuss the principle involved in separations by gel chromatography.
50.	Draw a neat schematic diagram of fluorimeter. Why the light source and detectors are placed perpendicular to each other and two monochromator used in flourimeter. OR Write a note on effects of solvents (solvatochromic effect) in UV spectroscopy.
51.	Explain the construction and working of golay cell and bolometer detectors used in IR Spectroscopy. OR Discuss the development and visualization techniques in paper chromatography.
52.	Explain the experimental methodology involved in paper electrophoresis and its applications.
53.	Discuss the preparation, activation and visualisation of TLC.
54.	Draw a neat schematic diagram of GC. Explain about columns used in GC.
55.	Write a note on affinity chromatography with special emphasis on ligands used.
56.	Write a note on cationic and anionic exchangers.
57.	Explain the construction & working of photomultiplier tube and barrier layer cell. OR Discuss the single component & multi component analysis by UV spectroscopy.
58.	Discuss the principle and various gels used in gel chromatography. OR Discuss the principle & applications of Flame photometry.
59.	What is adsorption and partition column chromatography. Give its advantages and disadvantages.
60.	Discuss the applications of HPLC.
61.	Define and classify Ion Exchange resins. Add a note on factors affecting Ion exchange.
62.	Discuss the different development techniques used in Paper Chromatography.
63.	Explain the principle and techniques involved in Paper Electrophoresis.
64.	Discuss the UV method for analysis of single component and multi component formulations. OR Discuss the principle of fluorescence using Jablonski diagram

Table Contd...

65.	Explain the principle and interferences in Atomic spectroscopy. OR Discuss briefly rate and plate theory.
66.	Write the different methods for preparations of TLC plates.
67.	Define Electrophoresis & discuss the factors affecting Electrophoretic mobility.
68.	Write the principle and mechanism of Ion Exchange Chromatography.
69.	Write the theory & applications of Affinity Chromatography.
70.	Discuss the classification of chromatographic methods based on mechanism of separation.

SHORT ANSWERS	**10x2=20 Marks**
1.	Mention in brief the importance of multi component analysis.
2.	Define chromophore and auxochrome with suitable examples.
3.	Name the fuel gases used in flame emission spectroscopy.
4.	Write the vibrational frequency of alcohol, carboxyl group and amide.
5.	Write the differences between nephelometry and turbidimetry.
6.	What are the elution techniques in column chromatography.
7.	Define R_f and Rm value with their significances.
8.	What is Guard column? Write its significance.
9.	What is the role of ligand in chromatography?
10.	Write the applications of affinity chromatography.
11.	Define Fluorescence and Phosphorescence.
12.	Write the importance of color wheel.
13.	Write the vibrational frequency of alcohol, aldehyde and amide in IR spectrum
14.	Write the block diagram of Nephelometry.
15.	What are different interferences in flame photometry?
16.	Define Rf and Rm value.
17.	What is electrophoresis?

Table Contd...

18.	What is programmed temperature gas chromatography? Write its importance
19.	Give the example for anion and cation exchange resins.
20.	Write the principle of affinity chromatography.
21.	Define and classify filters and monochromators.
22.	Mention the various methods of single component analysis.
23.	Write the vibrational frequency of amide, amine and ketone in IR spectrum.
24.	Write the applications of Atomic Absorption spectroscopy.
25.	Name the radiation sources used in IR spectroscopy.
26.	What is activation of plates? Write its importance.
27.	What is frontal and displacement analysis?
28.	What is derivatization in GC and write its significance.
29.	Mention the factors affecting ion exchange chromatography.
30.	Name the natural and synthetic gels used in gel chromatography.
31.	Define Absorptivity and Transmittance.
32.	What is Quenching? Give example.
33.	What are the events that occur when the compound of a metal to be investigated is aspirated into a flame?
34.	Define a) functional group region b) finger print region.
35.	Write the formula used to calculate number of fundamental vibrations for Linear and Nonlinear molecules.
36.	Write the difference between normal phase and reverse phase chromatography.
37.	Write the difference of silica gel, Silica gel G, silica gel GF.
38.	What is derivatization? Mention the various methods of derivatization in gas chromatography.
39.	Write the difference between gel chromatography and affinity chromatography.
40.	Importance of ligand in affinity chromatography.
41.	What is molar extinction co-efficient?
42.	Enlist the application of fluorimetry in quantitative analysis of drugs.
43.	Write the vibrational frequency of C=O, OH, amine and amide.

Table Contd...

44.	Write the application of nephelometery and turbidometery.
45.	Differences between flame emission and atomic absorption spectroscopy.
46.	What is two-dimensional paper chromatography?
47.	Classify adsorbents and detecting reagents with examples.
48.	What is programmed temperature gas chromatography.
49.	What are the gels used in gel chromatography?
50.	Write the difference between gel chromatography and gel electrophoresis.
51.	Define chromophore and auxochrome.
52.	What are absorption maxima? Write its significance?
53.	Write the wavenumber of OH group and NH2 groups in IR spectrum.
54.	Write the difference between nephelometery and turdidimetery.
55.	How solid samples are handled into IR spectrometers.
56.	What is the difference between Silica gel H, Silica Gel G and Silica gel GF?
57.	Classify detecting reagents in paper chromatography with suitable examples.
58.	What is Guard column? Write its significance.
59.	Mention the various factors affecting ion exchange chromatography.
60.	Write the applications of gel chromatography.
61.	Define the term absorptivity and wave number.
62.	Write the difference between fluorescence and phosphorescence.
63.	What is the functional group for wavemunber 3400 cm^{-1} and 1715 cm^{-1}
64.	Write the difference between nephelometery and turdidimetery.
65.	Define the term retention factor (Rf).
66.	Differentiate between normal phase & reverse phase chromatography.
67.	Write the expansions of Silica gel 60 GF 254.
68.	Explain any one derivatisation technique in GC.
69.	Why the buffers are used in ion exchange chromatography.
70.	What is the principle involved affinity chromatography?

Table Contd...

71.	Define chromophore and lamda max.
72.	Define molar absorptivity.
73.	Explain the various frequency regions for amides and ketones.
74.	Mention the types of interferences in Atomic spectroscopy.
75.	Write the applications of nepheloturbidometry.
76.	What is the difference between isocratic and gradient elution in chromatography?
77.	Define edge effect? Mention the method to prevent.
78.	Mention the importance of guard column in GC?
79.	Name the stationary phase used in gel chromatography.
80.	Enumerate the applications of affinity chromatography.
81.	Define chromophore and auxochrome? Give one example for each.
82.	Solvent effect on UV absorption spectra.
83.	Write the vibrational frequencies of alcohols and amines in IR spectroscopy.
84.	Write the principle involved in nepheloturbidometry.
85.	What is temperature programming in gas chromatography.
86.	Define Rf value? Name the factors that affect Rf value.
87.	What is regeneration of ion exchange resins.
88.	What is affinity chromatography?
89.	Name the molecular vibrations in IR spectroscopy.
90.	What is edge effect? How to minimize it.
91.	Name the spectral shifts that occur in UV region.
92.	What is fingerprint region in IR spectroscopy.
93.	Name the electronic transitions that occur in UV region.
94.	Give any two applications of Nepheloturbidometry
95.	Name the different migration parameters used in planar Chromatography.
96.	Write the principle involved in Gel Chromatography.
97.	Write the properties of ideal Ion exchange resins.

Table Contd...

98.	What is derivatization in Gas Chromatography?
99.	How aldehyde and ketone can be differentiated in IR spectrum.
100.	What is Normal phase & Reverse phase Chromatography?

THE TAMIL NADU DR. M.G.R. MEDICAL UNIVERSITY

[MPHARM 0921] **SEPTEMBER 2021** **Sub. Code: 2941**
(OCTOBER 2020 EXAM SESSION)

M.PHARMACY DEGREE EXAMINATION
SEMESTER-I (PCI New regulations 2016)
PHARMACEUTICAL CHEMISTRY - MPC
PAPER I – MODERN PHARMACEUTICAL ANALYTICAL TECHNIQUES
Q.P. Code : 262941

Time : Three hours **Answer ALL Questions** **Maximum : 75 Marks**

I. Elaborate on: **(2 x 20 = 40)**

1. a) Principle, instrumentation and factors affecting results of thermal gravimetry analysis.
   b) Principle and application of Carbon-13 nuclear magnetic resonance spectroscopy.

2. a) Theory and sample handling in Infrared spectroscopy.
   b) Write a interpretation of Infrared spectrum of the following compounds
      i) 1-Hexane
      ii) 1- butanol

II. Write notes on: **(7 x 5 = 35)**

1. Instrumentation and application of spectroflourimetry.
2. Quantum Numbers and their role in Nuclear Magnetic Resonance spectroscopy.
3. Matrix Assisted Lasser Desorption Ionization (MALDI).
4. Write a note on ultra high performance liquid chromatography.
5. Boundary electrophoresis and isoelectric focusing.
6. Thermal transition in modulated Differential scanning calorimetry.
7. Solvent and solvent effect in ultraviolet spectroscopy.

****

THE TAMIL NADU DR. M.G.R. MEDICAL UNIVERSITY

[MPHARM 0921] SEPTEMBER 2021 Sub. Code: 2931
(OCTOBER 2020 EXAM SESSION)

M.PHARMACY DEGREE EXAMINATION
SEMESTER-I (PCI New regulations 2016)
PHARMACEUTICS - MPH
PAPER I – MODERN PHARMACEUTICAL ANALYTICAL TECHNIQUES
Q.P. Code : 262931

Time : Three hours **Answer ALL Questions** **Maximum : 75 Marks**

I. Elaborate on: **(2 x 20 = 40)**

1. a) Principle, instrumentation and application of AAS.
   b) Principle involved in Ion exchange chromatography.

2. a) Brief outline of principles of FT-NMR and 13C NMR.
   b) Applications of NMR spectroscopy, Chemical shift, Spin-Spin coupling, Coupling constant.

II. Write notes on: **(7 x 5 = 35)**

1. Column Chromatography.
2. Different X-Ray diffraction methods.
3. Capillary electrophoresis.
4. Paper chromatography.
5. Mass fragmentation and its rules.
6. Sampling in IR Spectroscopy.
7. Applications of fluorescence spectrophotometer.

****

THE TAMIL NADU DR. M.G.R. MEDICAL UNIVERSITY

[MPHARM 0921] SEPTEMBER 2021 Sub. Code: 2981
(OCTOBER 2020 EXAM SESSION)

M.PHARMACY DEGREE EXAMINATION
SEMESTER-I (PCI New regulations 2016)
PHARMACOLOGY – MPL
PAPER I – MODERN PHARMACEUTICAL ANALYTICAL TECHNIQUES
Q.P. Code : 262981

Time : Three hours **Answer ALL Questions** **Maximum : 75 Marks**

I. Elaborate on: **(2 x 20 = 40)**

1. a) Discuss about the modes of molecular vibrations and factors affecting vibrational frequencies in IR Spectroscopy.
   b) Write a note on types of ion exchangers and the mechanism involved in ion exchange chromatography.

2. Explain the principle, instrumentation and applications of the HPLC.

II. Write notes on: **(7 x 5 = 35)**

1. Write a note on Bragg's law.
2. Write a note on chemical shift and spin-spin coupling.
3. Describe the principle and applications of isoelectric focusing and zone electrophoresis.
4. Write the instrumentation of atomic absorption spectroscopy.
5. Discuss about the factors affecting chemical shift.
6. Write about the solvent requirement in NMR Spectroscopy.
7. Calculate the concentration in mcg/ml of a solution of tryptophan (molecular weight 204.2) in 0.1M Hydrochloric acid, giving an absorbance at its wavelength maxima, 277nm, of 0.613 in a 4cm cell. The molecular absorptivity at 277 nm is 5432.

****

THE TAMIL NADU DR. M.G.R. MEDICAL UNIVERSITY

[MPHARM 0921] **SEPTEMBER 2021** **Sub. Code: 2951**
(OCTOBER 2020 EXAM SESSION)

M.PHARMACY DEGREE EXAMINATION
SEMESTER-I (PCI New regulations 2016)
PHARMACEUTICAL ANALYSIS - MPA
PAPER I – MODERN PHARMACEUTICAL ANALYTICAL TECHNIQUES
Q.P. Code : 262951

Time : Three hours **Answer ALL Questions** **Maximum : 75 Marks**

I. Elaborate on: **(2 x 20 = 40)**

1. a) Write the instrumentation and solvent requirement in NMR spectroscopy.
   b) Write a detailed note on 13C NMR.
   c) Predict the number of peaks with relative intensity in the spectra of Toluene.

2. a) Write the principle and instrumentation involved in HPLC.
   b) Discuss in detail about the developmental techniques and detection techniques in TLC.

II. Write notes on: **(7 x 5 = 35)**

1. Explain the thermal transitions in DTA curve.
2. Write about the electronic transitions in UV spectroscopy.
3. Explain the sampling techniques in IR Spectroscopy.
4. Explain the theory of fluorescence with Jablonsky diagram.
5. Write a note on types of ion exchangers and the mechanism involved in ion exchange chromatography.
6. Write notes on any two mass analyzers.
7. Explain capillary electrophoresis.

****

Code No:E-12297/PCI

FACULTYOFPHARMACY

M. Pharmacy I Semester(PCI)(Common to all)(Main &Backlog) Examination, May 2023

Subject: Modern Pharmaceutical Analytical Techniques

Time:3Hours **Max.Marks:75**

Note: Answer any Five Questions. All Questions carry Equal marks.

1. a) With a neat labelled diagramex plain UV/Visible instrumentation.
   b) What are the criteia in the solvent selection for UV spectroscopy? Give examples for solvents. What is meant by solvent effect? (9+6)

2. a)Explain the Principle, advantages and instrumentation of FTIR with a neat labelled diagram.
   b) Explain the molecular vibrations in IRspectroscopy. (10+5)

3. a) Explain the principle off luorescence. Add a note on quenching effect
   b) With a diagram explain the instrumentation for AAS. (8+7)

4. a) Explain the principle of proton NMR spectroscopy.
   b) Explainthespin-spincouplinginNMRspectroscopywithsuitableexample.(7+8)

5. a) Explain the principle of mass spectroscopy.
   b) Explain any two mass analysers used in MS in detail. (7+8)

6. a) Explain GC instrumentation with a labeled diagram.
   b) Explain the applications of XRD technique. (9+6)

7. a) Explain the instrumentation & working of HPLC. (8+7)
   b) Explain the factors affecting resolution &Peak symmetry.

8. Define and classify the electro phoretic techniques. Explain the principle and applications of gel electrophoresis. (15)

****

Code No: E-12421/PCI

FACULTY OF PHARMACY

M.Pharmacy I-Semester (PCI) (Common to all) (Backlog) Examination, November-2023

Subject: Modern Pharmaceutical Analytical Techniques

Time: 3 Hours | **Max. Marks: 75**

Note: Answer any Five Questions. All Questions carry Equal marks.

1. a) Explain the electronic transitions with suitable examples
   b) State and explain Beer- Lambert's law. Add a note on the deviations from Beer's law. (6+9)

2. a) Explain the sampling techniques in IR spectroscopy.
   b) What are the applications of IR spectroscopy (9+6)

3. a) What is the principles of flame photometrty? Explain the instrumentation.
   b) What are the factors affecting fluorescence? (9+6)

4. a) Explain chemical shift and the factors affecting chemical shift ?
   b) Draw a schematic NMR spectrum and explain splitting α signal intensity. (10+5)

5. With a neat labelled diagram, explain MS instrumentation. Draw MS spectrum for any two compounds α explain its peaks.

6. a) Classify the ionization techniques in MS. Explain any three methods in detail.
   b) Explain the fragmentation rules in MS. (9+6)

7. a) Explain HPLC instrumentation with a labelled diagram.
   b) Explain the factors affecting resolution & peak symmetry. (8+7)

8. a) Explain the principle and applications of capillary electrophoresis
   b) Classify the types of crystals and add a note on the applications of X-ray diffraction. (8+7)

****

www.ingramcontent.com/pod-product-compliance
Lightning Source LLC
Chambersburg PA
CBHW080930240926
51849CB00003BA/421
* 9 7 8 9 3 4 8 7 3 4 8 1 5 *